MOUNTAINS OF THE WORLD

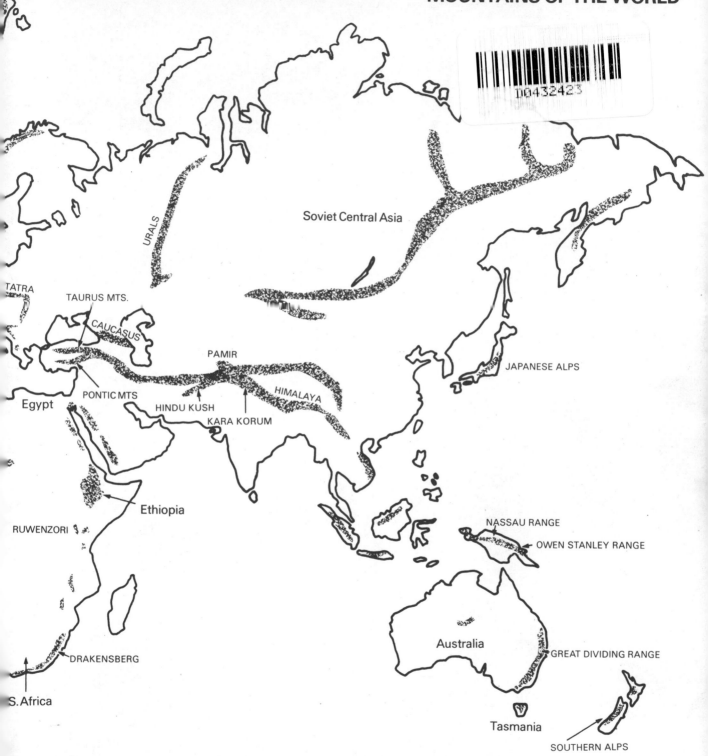

URALS

Soviet Central Asia

TATRA

TAURUS MTS.

CAUCASUS

PAMIR

PONTIC MTS

Egypt

HINDU KUSH

KARA KORUM

HIMALAYA

JAPANESE ALPS

Ethiopia

RUWENZORI

NASSAU RANGE

OWEN STANLEY RANGE

DRAKENSBERG

S. Africa

Australia

GREAT DIVIDING RANGE

Tasmania

SOUTHERN ALPS

MOUNTAINS

MOUNTAINS
John Cleare

To Tom for climbs past and Jocelyn
for hills yet to come

Picture acknowledgements
All the photographs in this book were taken by
John Cleare, apart from those listed below. Grateful
acknowledgement is made to the following for the
use of their material: Glen Denny 101, 108l, 110;
Max Gammon 108r; Ian Howell 198t; Gerald
Lacey 183tl; Hamish McInnes 91r, 136; John
Moore 237bl; Mountain Magazine 241b, 244–5,
(Baxter) 234, 238–9, (Alex Bertulis) 252–3, (Adams
Carter) 249t, (Maurice Conway) 245r, (Leo
Dickinson) 248t, (Frost) 106, (Hamish McInnes)
241t, (Ben Sandelands) 237br, (Ken Wilson) 94br;
Colin Wilson 237t
Diagrams were drawn by Peter Berry

Antipodean material by Chris Baxter

Previous pages: The Chamonix Aiguilles
in the Mont Blanc range

© Macmillan London Limited, 1975

SBN 333 17415 1

Designed by Paul Watkins

First published 1975 by
Macmillan London Limited
London and Basingstoke
Associated companies in New York, Toronto,
Dublin, Melbourne, Johannesburg and Delhi

Filmset by Servis Filmsetting Limited, Manchester

Printed in Great Britain
by Jolly & Barber, Rugby
and by BAS Printers Limited,
Over Wallop, Hampshire

Contents

1 Mountain kaleidoscope

One of my earliest memories is of Bodmin Moor, small but lonely hills in northern Cornwall. My grandmother pointed to a granite tor rising slightly above the swelling distance, dappled with cloud shadow. 'That is Brown Willy', she said. 'The highest mountain in Cornwall.' 'What's a mountain?' I asked. 'In England,' she replied authoritatively, 'a mountain is a hill over a thousand feet high.' Brown Willy happens to be 1377 feet above sea-level. She was wise, my granny; she'd travelled too. She'd walked up Snowdon before the railway came and she'd viewed the Rockies from Lake Louise. And she was not wrong, for a mountain – like beauty – is in the eye of the beholder. Who could deny mountain status to Stac Polly, that clump of sandstone ridges and turrets rising to only 2018 feet above the weird moorland lochs of Assynt in Sutherland, and once described as 'a porcupine in a state of extreme irascibility'? In the more sublime realms of the Himalaya the Nepalese Government, God bless them, have ruled that a permit must be obtained before climbing one of their mountains. Fair enough, it's their country. But it seems that 'mountains' must be over 20,000 feet high, for below that height they become mere 'viewpoints' and can be attempted willy-nilly on the authority of a generally available trekking permit. Needless to say, there are many virgin and obviously difficult 'viewpoints' worthy of very serious attention from experienced mountaineers: but the line must be drawn somewhere!

Mankind has never been indifferent to the mountains which have always marked his horizons. Usually the emotions the high places engendered have been strong – either those of repulsion or of awe. Sometimes the 'incubus hills' were peopled by fearsome beings – trolls, ogres, demons and hobgoblins, and even by the Devil himself; even in recent times local people believed it was He who hurled down the regular rock fall from the Matterhorn. The alpine peasant invented appropriate names for the seemingly malevolent mountains that surrounded him. 'Les Diablerets', 'Aiguilles du Diable' and 'Teufelsberg' are obvious references to the Devil, while 'Mont Maudit' (accursed mountain), 'Monte Disgrazia' (disaster mountain) and 'Eiger' (ogre) are other sinister names. The peasant needed little imagination to see fearful explanations for the everyday phenomena of the mountains which he did not understand. And who can blame him?

Regarding the natural phenomena of the mountains from a different angle, it is easy to associate lightning, thunder, St. Elmo's Fire and similar phenomena with a friendly, though perhaps sometimes irritable God, instead of with dragons and demons. Perhaps Mohammed's vision of the Angel Gabriel during his solitary meditation on Mt Hira was merely a glimpse of the Broken Spectre – that rare and beautiful haloed shadow of oneself, cast by the sun onto a mist-filled abyss, which was feared in ancient times by the inhabitants of the Harz mountains.

Mt Kenya seen at dusk from the Teleki Valley

Himalayan landscape.
Below: the Thyangboche
monastery is situated at
12,700 feet on a wooded
ridge high above the Imja
Khola — behind is an icy array
of virgin peaks culminating in
Kwangde (20,320 feet).
Right: a young sherpa boy at
Namche Bazar; his heavily
laden sisters carry large loads
using a traditional head-band.
Centre right: the standard
beast of burden in the
Nepalese Himalaya is the yak
— a friendly docile animal.
Far right: an aerial view of the
still virgin Gaurishankar
(23,440 feet) in the
Rolwaling Himal

It was as natural too, to consider the mountains as sacred. Indeed, for many who frequent the mountains today it becomes an inevitable conclusion! Mountains are involved somehow in the 'myth' of almost all religions and civilizations, and often in similar ways on opposite sides of the globe. In the 'flood' story, the Ark comes to rest on Ararat – or is it Elbruz (Caucasus) or Kordyenes (Kurdistan), Mt Muto (Yunnan), Mount Pia (Tonking) or the Watzmann (Austria)?

The ancient Syrians believed that paradise was a walled garden 'on a mountain higher than all the others'; to the Greeks, Mt Olympus – a 9551-foot limestone massif in north-eastern Greece – was the home of the Gods, while to the North American Indians, Olelbis the 'Chief of the First Men' dwelt on Olelpanti 'the highest place on earth'. In Africa, the Kikuyu regarded Mt Kenya as the home of their great god, Ngai, and in recent times Mt Kenya played a significant part in the occult rites of the Mau Mau terrorists.

The ancient Israelites considered mountains were of particular significance: Moses collected the Ten Commandments from The Lord on the summit of Mt Sinai and thereafter met Him for regular conferences on mountain tops. King David wrote in Psalm 87 'His foundation is on the holy mountains'. And again in the well-loved Psalm 121 'I will lift up mine eyes unto the hills from whence cometh my help'. Even Amos (Chapter IV) described The Lord as a mountaineer: 'He that formeth the mountains and createth the wind . . . and treadeth on the high places of the earth. . . . His name is The Lord'.

Some mountains have always been routes to heaven. The Pillars of Hercules – Gibraltar and the Rif – supported the skies. The Tower of Babel was merely an artificial mountain, and might bear comparison in kind, if not in purpose, with Disneyland's model Matterhorn. Perhaps too the Pyramids of Egypt, Angkor and Central America were artificial mountains, reaching up to heaven?

Mountains are still sacred in many places, and modern mountaineers should respect this. The British expedition of 1955 which climbed Kangchenjunga (28,208 feet), the world's third highest mountain, promised the local Maharajah that they would not defile the actual summit should they reach it. The beautiful Machapuchare (22,956 feet) – 'The Fish's Tail' – on which Wilfred Noyce and David Cox reached to within 150 feet of the summit, is now 'off limits' in deference to the local religious feelings. In Tibet, Kailas (22,028 feet), a fine-looking peak explored by Ruttledge and Blakeney, is the Throne of Shiva and the Centre of the World to both Hindus and Buddhists.

It is easy to understand why the Himalaya of Nepal and Tibet have appeared as sacred mountains to many western travellers. On every pass tall white flags flutter their prayers to the wind. Chortens are silhouetted against distant ice-clad peaks, and other religious constructions – stupas, gompas and temples – are strategically situated so as to be conducive to such feelings. On the Roof of the World sacred graffiti are everywhere, carved on huge boulders, painted on rock faces

The sacred mountains. Right: Chorten and prayer flags at Thyangboche monastery in Khumbu, close by the foot of Everest, silhouetted at dawn against virgin peaks. Below: a prayer flag flutters beside a huge boulder, carved and painted all over 'Om Mani Padme Houm Hri' near the village of Pangpoche (13,000 feet) in Khumbu, the home country of the sherpas

Overleaf: Kancha, West Ridge sherpa sirdar with the 1971 Everest Expedition, examines the Yeti scalp which is carefully preserved at Pangpoche monastery (13,100 feet) close by the base of Everest

and inscribed on stone slabs and built into walls or cairns. The most frequent prayer is *Om Mani Padme Houm Hri*. *Om* is the Creator – the Eternal; *Mani Padme* is the jewel in the lotus – the dynamic life principle; *Houm* and *Hri* are war cries to terrorize demons. At least, this is the literal translation; although I have been told by Sherpas that a practical translation more on the lines of 'do unto others as you would they do unto you' would be fairer.

Every mountain has its legends, and some must surely be founded on fact. Alexander's army penetrated to the Indus, and the Hunzas of the Karakorum claim to be descendants of Greek soldiers. In Kashmir local legends label the nomadic Gujar hillmen as a lost tribe of Israel – and claim the prophet Jesus is buried among their mountains. King Menelik, son of Solomon and the Queen of Sheba, after conquering eastern Africa, camped on the Saddle of Kilimanjaro – between Kibo and Mawenzi. But feeling the approach of death he disappeared into the crater of Kibo, complete with his treasure. On his finger is the Seal Ring of Solomon, and one day it will endow the finder with the wisdom of Solomon and he will restore the glories of ancient Ethiopia! While in Wales, King Arthur sleeps with his knights in a cave on Lliwedd (pointed out as the cave pitch of Central Gully), close to Bwlch y Saethau, the 'Pass of the Arrows', scene of his last battle. Here he awaits the call to save Britain from the invader.

Besides gods and demons, other strange beings inhabit the mountains. On Mount Pilatus near Lucerne the ghost of Pontius Pilate is condemned to wander until the last trump. The appearance of the spectral 'Salt Man' of the Pennine Alps, who was once licked to death by salt-crazed sheep, foretells certain doom. In the Ledr River above Betws-y-Coed there once lived the Afanc, a monster which destroyed the fishing and was eventually captured by stout-hearted locals. Harnessed to a team of oxen, it was dragged over the mountains to Snowdon where it was banished for ever in the deep dark waters of Glaslyn – where it lives to this day. On the mountain slopes where it was dragged, its tears formed tiny tarns.

Local Highlanders know the Great Grey Man who haunts Ben Macdhui – the highest of the Cairngorms – as Ferla Mhor, and are reluctant to discuss him. He was seen by Professor Norman Collie, the well-known mountaineer and a scientist, a man not given to tall stories, who found the spectral presence in the Cairngorm mists sufficiently terrifying to prompt him to fly for his life.

The Sasquatch of south-western Canada and the American Pacific States has actually been filmed – or so it is claimed. In the dense mountain forests of the region there is enough cover to hide such a giant man-ape, which would appear to be similar to the Himalayan Yeti or 'Abominable Snowman'. Many reputable people believe the Yeti does exist; but although it is well-known to local mountain people, few westerners have sighted it for long enough to observe much detail. Don Whillans glimpsed one briefly by moonlight on

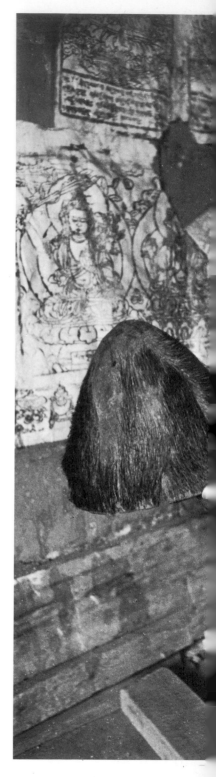

Annapurna in 1970. The Russians, from evidence they have collected in the Pamir, suggest that the Yeti belong to a tiny scattered relict population of Neanderthal man, and this theory would certainly account for its elusiveness. Contrary to popular belief, the Yeti does not live above the snowline; it only crosses it while travelling from one valley to another. In the thick montane forests that clothe the lower Himalayan slopes there is ample cover and food for an ape-man to thrive. Being fairly intelligent, the creature will obviously steer well away from the noisy western expeditions which seek for it, smelling of soap and aftershave and wearing bright clothes and living in orange tents. Put yourself in the poor Yeti's place! At least it all adds up. . . .

The place of mountains in our modern civilization had already been assured when Leslie Stephen described the Alps as 'the playground of Europe'. Between the age of 'Superstition' and the current age of 'Exploitation' there was a romantic period, which has still not altogether disappeared – although it has been popular for some time to denigrate those who see the mountains as more than a mere vertical gymnasium. The great romantics were poets and artists, writers and thinkers and often mountaineers too. It was not always necessary to climb the mountains to understand their appeal: Tennyson was surely 'turned-on' when he wrote, from the roof of Milan Cathedral:

I climbed the roofs at break of day:
Sun smitten Alps before me lay.
I stood amid the silent statues
And statued pinnacles mute as they.

How faintly flush'd, how phantom fair
Was Monte Rosa, hanging there
A thousand shadowy pencill'd valleys
And snowy dells in a golden air.

Some years earlier Byron had noticed that:

Mont Blanc is the monarch of the mountains;
They crowned him long ago
On a throne of rocks, in a robe of clouds,
With a diadem of snow.

A perfect description of the peak as seen from the outskirts of Geneva. Byron understood that relationship between man and mountains when he wrote in Childe Harold:

I live not in myself but I become portion of that around
me, and to me high mountains are a feeling . . .

That mysterious and prophetic poet William Blake was right perhaps:

Great things are done when men and mountains meet . . .

It is, however, the seventeenth-century Chinese poet, Hsu Hsia-k'o, who summed it up so perfectly:

The body roams the mountains;
And the spirit is set free.

13

2 The European Alps

Anglo-Saxons in the Alps

The British are not a mountain people: indeed few are even High-landers and it might therefore seem remarkable to claim that the British 'invented' the modern sport of mountaineering – alpinism.

The start of the British involvement in the Alps can be dated at 1787 – the year after the first ascent of Mont Blanc – when the fourth ascent of the mountain, the highest in the Alps, was made by an officer in the Coldstream Guards, a Colonel Mark Beaufoy.

The Jungfrau was climbed in 1811, and the Finsteraarhorn in 1812, both by the Swiss Meyer brothers, but mountaineering was still far from being a sport. In the early years of the 19th Century most of the men who climbed mountains, and there were very few, still found it necessary to invent scientific reasons to justify their climb – particularly on Mont Blanc. In fact when the first Americans, Doctors William Howard and Jeremiah van Rensselaer, climbed the mountain in 1820 they borrowed scientific instruments from the generous Dr. Paccard, who had made the first ascent and still lived in Chamonix. Seven years later when two Englishmen, Frederick Slade and Yeats Brown, unsuccessfully attempted the Jungfrau 'for the fun of the thing', continental critics expressed shock at the complete lack of any scientific justification for their attempt.

A pastoral scene on the slopes of the Lauberhorn above Grindlewald. A tourist studies the Eiger while behind is the Wetterhorn, whose ascent in 1854 by Sir Alfred Wills marked the start of the Alpine 'Golden Age'

Some, however, produced no such excuses. Among the steady stream of Britons to ascend Mont Blanc was one Frederick Clissold, who felt that he was '... in some measure prepared ... having frequently ascended Snowdon without guides ...'. Another, a Doctor Clark, buried an olive branch and a paper bearing the name of George IV on the summit! Shades of modern Soviet mountaineering!

Probably the first Briton to make a real impact on the Alpine scene was Professor James Forbes, a young Scottish geologist. He first came to the Alps in 1826, and for twenty-five years travelled incessantly among the high mountains, making scientific observations. In the course of his journeys he made the fourth ascent of the Jungfrau in 1841 and the first survey of the Mer de Glace. He became increasingly fascinated by the mountains for their own sake and eventually – by adoption, if not by original intent – a true mountaineer. His experience of moving over high mountain country and his engaging and popular books such as *Travels Through the Alps of Savoy* did much to make possible the 'Golden Age' and the birth of the sport that followed.

The growth of alpinism was influenced particularly by one other Briton of the period who indeed anticipated famous figures of the future, such as Frank Smythe and Christian Bonington. Albert Smith, a writer and dramatist, made the thirty-seventh ascent of Mont Blanc in 1851. For the next six years his resulting 'entertainment' – a sort of romantic Victorian illustrated lecture – ran continuously in London. Smith actually presented it twice to Queen Victoria herself.

The 'Golden Age' opened, it is said, with an ascent of the Wetterhorn by the young Alfred Wills in 1854, and it closed with the tragic conquest of the Matterhorn – the last great Alpine peak – by Edward Whymper's team in 1865. During these eleven years some 180 great peaks were climbed for the first time – half of them, virtually all the greatest prizes, by British climbers. Most of the great passes were crossed and scores of harder climbs and traverses were made too. Particularly notable British climbs on summits no longer virgin were the Guggi Route on the Jungfrau by the Rev. Hereford George and party, a classic ice climb still far from easy, and the famous 'Old Brenva' Ridge of Mont Blanc, the first route on the Italian side of the mountain, climbed in 1865 by A. W. Moore, William Matthews and the Walker brothers.

From an eccentric diversion, mountaineering had become a recognizable sport. The motivation of the British climbers to make it so was as much a product of the economic, social and mental circumstances of Victorian Britain as of their personal courage and initiative. These climbers were a mere handful, and all came from a similar professional, academic or ecclesiastical background. These were the men who founded the first mountaineering club of all, the Alpine Club, in London in the winter of 1857, and elected John Ball as its first President. Among the more persistent and successful members of the Club during this formative period were the Rev. Charles Hudson,

Edward Kennedy, Leslie Stephen, Professor Tyndall, Francis Tuckett and Edward Whymper besides others already mentioned. Many were men of responsibility, although not necessarily of substance: John Ball had been Under-Secretary for the Colonies, Tyndall was a Fellow of the Royal Society and Wills a Judge of the Queens Bench Division. But Dickens, when he wrote 'A society for the scaling of such heights as the Schreckhorn, the Eiger and the Matterhorn contributes about as much to the advancement of science as would a club of young gentlemen who should undertake to bestride all the weather cocks of all the cathedral spires of the United Kingdom', was voicing a popular sentiment of the time. And when, on the descent from the Matterhorn in 1865, a Peer of the Realm, Lord Francis Douglas, and the most gifted climber of his day, the Rev. Charles Hudson, were killed, the Times thundered out: 'Why is the best blood of England to waste itself in scaling hitherto inaccessible peaks?'

The pioneers of the 'Golden Age' climbed with guides, a growing body of local men who had originally been mountain peasants and hunters; a *corps d'elite* of skilled craftsmen with whom they developed a proud tradition of comradeship and teamwork. The skills and ability of both amateur and guide were complementary, a relationship which has now disappeared.

It is convenient, but inaccurate, to regard the succeeding forty years to the outbreak of the Great War as a distinct period. No longer were the British alone in the field, but in the Western Alps they still dominated it. The cult of winter mountaineering was initiated by Moore and Horace Walker crossing the Strahlegg and the Finsteraarjoch in December 1866. The Pilkington brothers and Frederick Gardiner started serious guideless climbing by spending the whole season of 1878 climbing difficult major peaks on their own, and repeating the experience the following year.

Americans were starting to show their faces in the Alps: between 1854 and 1878 there had been more than a hundred American ascents of Mont Blanc. But without doubt the greatest American mountaineer of the period was the eccentric expatriate Rev. William Coolidge. Many of his earlier climbs were made with his Aunt and his dog and by 1900 he had climbed 600 'grande courses' in the Alps. Together with Sir Martin Conway he edited the first series of climbers' guides to the Alps, as well as The Alpine Journal, and became *the* authority on alpine history. After one of his periodic quarrels with the Alpine Club he demanded that his name should never again appear in the Alpine Journal. The Editor replied: 'It would be as ridiculous for a man to speak of alpine matters without mentioning the name of Coolidge as it would be to discuss the Bible without mentioning God'. Coolidge died in 1926.

Now that all the major summits had been climbed, attention turned to new routes and minor summits. Eccles's remarkable 1877 ascent

The Matterhorn and its West Face seen from the Tête Blanche. On the left the Z'mutt Ridge, first climbed by the great Mummery in 1879, and on the right the Italian Ridge. Beyond are the Rimpfishhorn and the Strahlhorn

of the Peuterey Arête of Mont Blanc from the Freney Glacier was one landmark; the first ascent of The Dru in 1878 by Clinton Dent, a future A.C. President, was another. These and Mummery's great climbs with Alexander Burgener were just samples of what the British were doing throughout the Western Alps and elsewhere in the years following the 'Golden Age'. Mummery was the greatest alpinist in his day. His 1879 ascent of the Zmutt Ridge of the Matterhorn, his 1881 ascent of the Grepon and his 1887 ascent, with his wife, of the Teufelsgrat of the Taschhorn were great achievements. He disappeared on Nanga Parbat in 1895; but there were others to take his place.

The final years of the century were characterized by the difficult rock climbs being made on new ridges and virgin 'inaccessible' summits, such as the Requin, by skilled rock climbers who were also gaining fame on British crags – men like the Pilkingtons, Collie, Raeburn, Slingsby, the Abrahams and Hastings. Owen Glynne Jones, perhaps the best cragsman of his day, was another: he made the first Taschhorn–Dom Traverse in 1895, but was tragically killed on the Ferpecle Arête of the Dent Blanche in 1899.

Another alpinist worthy of mention was Norman-Neruda who, with his guide, Christian Klucker, specialized in ice walls. His 1890 season was remarkable. It included first ascents of the North Faces of Piz Roseg and Piz Scerscen in the Bernina, the North-east Face of the Lyskamm and the Wellenkuppe Ridge of the Obergabelhorn.

With the coming of the new century two giants were to dominate the scene; their influence is felt even today. One was V. J. E. Ryan, a gentleman who had resigned his commission in the Indian Army in order to spend more time climbing – almost invariably with the

The Dent Blanche, first climbed by T. S. Kennedy in 1862, dominates the Col d'Herens. On the left is the Ferpècle Ridge, where O. G. Jones died in 1899; facing is the easy South Ridge and to the right is the famous Viereselsgrat, climbed by J. Stafford Anderson's party in 1882

Top: Descending the Mountet moraines. Behind is the Obergabelhorn, first climbed by A. W. Moore and Horace Walker in 1865

Right: Climbing the 'Grand mere' crack on the East Ridge – the Ryan-Lochmatter Ridge – of the Aiguille du Plan

Lochmatter brothers. There are Ryan/Lochmatter routes scattered throughout the Western Alps, and all are classics well worth climbing today. His 1906 campaign was an incredible one. It included the East Ridge of the Plan, claimed by the Guide Vallot to be the best climb on its side of the Aiguilles, and not repeated for twenty years. They made the first ascent of the Santa Caterinagrat on Monte Rosa's Nordend, a mysterious climb unrepeated for seventeen years, and on the Dent d'Herens they climbed the East Ridge – one of the most formidable *arêtes* in the Alps.

Most important of all perhaps, they teamed up with Geoffrey Winthrop Young and his guide, Josef Knubel, to climb the South Face of the Taschhorn, a climb still rated as TD+, and a real tour de force. The following sixty years saw only seven further ascents.

The greater figure in fact was Young himself. In ten years, guideless with British climbers like H. O. Jones, Mallory and Herford, or with his faithful Knubel, Young achieved a brilliant series of first ascents. After the Taschhorn, he climbed the Younggrat on the Breithorn.

There were the three great faces of the Weisshorn, the long South-east Ridge of the Nesthorn and, in 1911, the Mer de Glace face of the Grepon. The Brouillard Ridge of Mont Blanc, the Frontier Arête of the Grand Jorasses and the descent of the Hirondelles Ridge are no less important. His last great climb, less than a month before Europe plunged into war, was the apparently impregnable Rote Zähne of the Gspaltenhorn in the Bernese Oberland. At the age of forty-one he lost a leg on the Italian front. It was a shattering blow; but he fought to master climbing with a peg-leg and managed, with extraordinary fortitude, to reach summits such as Monte Rosa, the Weisshorn, the Grepon and the Zinal Rothorn. He became one of the greatest mountain poets and writers, the elder Statesman of British mountaineering, President of the Alpine Club. Since his death in 1958 he is still remembered as one of the greatest of British climbers.

After the holocaust of the Great War, the British were not conspicuous in the Alps. In the ensuing twenty years British climbers made only a few notable achievements.

The first was immediately after the war in 1919, when Courtauld and Oliver, with their guides, Adolf Aufdenblatten and the Reys, made the first ascent of the Innominata Ridge of Mont Blanc. Then in 1927 Frank Smythe and Graham Brown, the two great names of the inter-war years, teamed up to open the great and beautiful Brenva Face of Mont Blanc – 4300 feet of sweeping ice and rocky ribs. Both were fine mountaineers; they climbed guideless, and their campaign on the Face was a methodical one. The Red Sentinel was its first product, followed in 1928 by the Route Major, well known as one of the finer routes in the Alps. The same year Dorothy Pilley and her husband, I. A. Richards, together with Joseph and Antoine Georges, climbed the North Ridge of the Dent Blanche, an obvious 'last great problem' involving one very difficult rock pitch of V + *.

But by the Thirties alpinism had become a mass-sport for the Europeans – a weekend sport even. There were national rivalries for the great north faces and new techniques on rock and ice were being perfected and used. The British could not – or would not – compete. The decade was one of great progress on British rock and great effort among the greater ranges, particularly in the Himalaya and on Everest.

Figures like Colonel Strutt, editor of the Alpine Journal for ten years and President of the Club in 1935, did little to help matters. Strutt had little sympathy for new continental methods or achievements and he wrote of the first ascent of the Grand Capucin: 'This sort of exploit is quite beyond the pale and is a degradation of mountaineering. Any steeplejack could have done the work better and in a tenth of the time.' The remark was typical of certain influential opinion.

However, with Smythe in the Himalaya, Graham Brown returned to Mont Blanc in 1933. Together with Graven and Aufdenblatten, he completed his exploration of the Brenva Face with the Pear

* See the explanation of the various grading systems for climbs in the Glossary, page 254, under **Grades**.

Opposite above: The Eiger in winter — photographed from the alp below Kleine Scheidegg. On the left is the great north face itself, while to the right — in sunlight — is the west flank, the 'voie normale' up the mountain

Opposite below: Les Dames Anglaises at dusk. These famous pinnacles are a feature of the Peuterey Ridge of Mont Blanc. Left is the Aiguille Noire and right the Pointe Gugliermina

The Dent Blanche, its north-east flank seen from near the Mountet hut. The Viereselsgrat is the left-hand ridge and the right-hand one is the N.N.W. Ridge, first climbed by Dorothy Pilley Richards and party in 1928

Buttress – the hardest of the Brenva routes and a magnificent and very serious climb. With Graven he made several other fine ice climbs in the Alps, notably the West Face of Piz Bernina, but none were comparable to his great climbs on the Brenva Face. His was one of the last of the fine partnerships between great guide and first-class amateur. Then came the Second Great War and Europe was in ferment again.

1947 was the first real alpine season after the war and it brought tragedy. Three of the most promising climbers who might have been expected to lead a British renaissance were killed: John Barford on the Ailefroide and 'Nully' Kretschmer and John Jenkins on the 'Old Brenva'. It took a few years to get going again.

The renaissance, when it came, was led by university men. In 1950 two Oxford University climbers, Tom Bourdillon and Hamish Nicol had a fine season. They made the first British ascent of the Dru North Face, in those days a very formidable undertaking.

It was the impetus that had been needed; there was a spate of activity the following year, with several British climbers repeating modern hard routes. Important milestones were Roger Chorley's climb of the big ice route of the Argentière North Face and McNaught-Davis and John Wilkinson's repeat of the Comici Route on the Cima Grande – one of those condemned by Colonel Strutt fifteen years before.

The British had found their feet again and proved themselves able to repeat difficult modern climbs on alpine rock and ice. In 1952 the Alpine Climbing Group was founded, originally a splinter group of

Previous pages: The Matterhorn – Ian Clough on the great ice ramp, the initial third of the classic north face. Zermatt is in mist below, and high cloud over the Mischabel peaks to the east indicates the approach of bad weather

Opposite: Winter on the Breithorn Plateau above the Theodulpass. In the distance is the Matterhorn, and to its left the Dent d'Herens. This picture was taken during filming for the BBC production 'Last Blue Mountain', a Himalayan reconstruction, hence the slightly out-of-place gear climber John Peacock – acting in the film – is wearing

Below: The ice-draped Brenva Face of Mont Blanc seen from Mont Blanc du Tacul. Behind the Frontier Ridge (foreground) of Mont Mandit is the ice arête of the Old Brenva, and beyond that Eckpfeiler rising to the upper section of the Peuterey Ridge

younger Alpine Club members. Its object was 'to encourage mountaineering of a high standard'; it was based loosely on the French G.H.M. and initially had a rule, since waived, making retirement mandatory at forty!

By this time the British were probably already the best free rock-climbers in the world. Those who had made this breakthrough at home were largely 'working' lads whose social background was such that before the war they would have been unlikely to venture abroad. These 'hard-men' started to arrive in the Alps. The big breakthrough into major league mountaineering was in 1954 when Joe Brown and Don Whillans descended on Chamonix. As Tom Patey put it:

He crossed the sea to Chamonix
To see what he could do . . .
He knocked three days off the record time
For the West Face of the Dru

This was the third ascent of the greatest rock-climb known in the Alps at the time.

On the unclimbed face of the Blaitière
The crux had tumbled down . . .
But he cracked the crux
By the crucial crack
Now known as the Fissure Brown!

This was the first ascent of a new route – the 'Voie Britannique' whose difficulty confounded continental climbers.

The next year, 1955, Bourdillon and Nicol repeated the Grand Capucin's East Face, a recent very hard route; Patey repeated the difficult ice of the North Face of the Plan, while Blackshaw and Downes forced the North Face of the Triolet. There was no looking back: the summit of alpine climbing was in sight again after nearly fifty years.

Great routes fell thick and fast. In '59 the Walker Spur of the Grandes Jorasses went to Robin Smith and Gunn Clark. In '61 Carruthers and Nally climbed the Matterhorn North Face. The same year, in the face of strong continental competition, the first ascent of the Central Pillar of the Freney Face of Mont Blanc was made by Whillans, Bonington, Clough and a Pole – Djoglosz. This was one of the last great problems of Mont Blanc and must rank as one of the greatest climbs in the Alps. In 1962 it was the turn of the biggest, blackest and most 'beyond the pale' of them all – The Eigerwand. Bonington and Clough climbed the wall in fine style although the first 'Anglo-Saxon' ascent had fallen to the powerful American John Harlin – climbing with a German – only a few days before.

The British were back at the top – second to none in the Alps, and for the first time since Coolidge there were first-class American climbers active also – men like Robbins, Hemming, Frost and Harlin. Five years later the ACG remerged with the Alpine Club. The cycle was complete.

The Eiger and the Monch in winter. Left is the dark cauldron of the Eigerwand, bounded by the white flank of the ordinary route — the line of the Eiger's first ascent by C. Barrington's party in 1858. The steep North Face of the Monch was climbed in winter by John Harlin and the ridge to its right is the famous Nollen

Days with the Doctor
Exploits at Chamonix

It was past four o'clock and the dawn was already filtering through the pine trees when Rusty shook me. 'Come on,' he urged. 'Great morning, not a cloud in the sky'. But getting up to go climbing was the last thing I wanted to do – two hours sleep hardly encourages dynamic decisions and even a large mug of hot tea can scarcely drown a hangover. 'Hell!', I thought. 'The bastard, how does he manage it?' I rolled over, comforting myself with the sure knowledge that Tom and Chris would be feeling as bad as I and no doubt just as unkeen.

But no. There was Tom, crawling blinking from his tent. He stood up, a mug of black coffee in one hand and running the other through his tangled hair. He looked pale and haggard. 'Aye – a grand morning – a fine day for great enterprises', he croaked, adding jocularly 'but Bonington's lost his socks!' Muffled swearing from the tent bore him out. There was no excuse for me now; anyway Rusty was already dishing up a foul brew of lumpy porridge. I struggled out of my sleeping bag.

However much you hurry in the early morning you can never get out of bottom gear. It will always take two hours to eat a sickening breakfast, to stuff enough climbing gear for a serious alpine route into your rucksack, and set off through the trees and the still sleeping campsite, past the Chalet Biolet and the Montenvers Railway Station and up the scruffy lane towards the Aiguille du Midi teleferique terminus. At least it does if you treat the whole enterprise with the nonchalance usually reserved for an easy stroll over the Welsh hills. It does if you're lazy and hungover and British. Chris strode purposefully ahead, his real feelings well disguised by his Sandhurst-trained stiff upper lip. Rusty and I tagged along behind, Rusty muttering Swahili swear words and myself breathing heavily, already sweating and wishing I was far away. Tom brought up the rear, stopping every now and then to re-tie a bootlace or adjust his rucksack or pour forth a stream of Aberdonian invective when he found that he'd forgotten a handkerchief. It was a dishevelled and evil-looking team that joined the chattering queue of French alpinists and their guides, edelweiss crawling up their clean stockings into their neatly pressed breeches and their white caps pulled down well over their dark-glassed and neatly shaved faces. We were too late for the first one, and it was after seven when we eventually shuffled into a cable-car and were swept upwards out of the shadowed valley into the morning.

It was all Tom's idea. We were after a climb on the 4500-foot North Face of the Aiguille du Midi, a pyramid of rock and ice which rises above the pinewoods to dominate Chamonix town itself. The famous Midi Teleferique, the highest in the Alps, sweeps up from the town in two huge bounds. The first a mere 4000 feet to Plan de l'Aiguille, an inn perched on a grassy knoll between the pine forest and the glacier moraines, and the second a dizzy 5000 feet to the needle-like summit of the Aiguille itself. Whatever the criticisms climbers may level at it, the cable-car is fine engineering and it does make possible, if you're a

33

very hard Scot, the sort of day's entertainment that Tom had planned for us. The classic route on the North Face is the Frendo Spur, a fine climb made by the famous French guide in 1941. To its right, however, another rocky spur rises from even lower in the Glacier des Pélerins and, unlike the Frendo, it leads directly to the summit. This is the Éperon Central. It was climbed by the aspirant guide, Yannick Seigneur in 1963; it had taken two days and was said to be harder and more sustained than the Frendo. It was still unrepeated.

The initial rocks were not steep and on the first little wall we were able to swing up on a rusty wire cable obviously discarded during the construction of the teleferique. Tom forged on ahead. 'If any of ye want the rope, give a shout', he cried. 'Ah don't think we'll need it a while yet'. The climbing was mixed, rocky ribs and walls linked by snow or ice patches. We moved at a breathless pace, always with Tom ahead leading round, behind and to the top of the next obstacle. I was always amazed at Tom's eye for a line and his genius which turned every problem into a feasible route upwards.

Eventually we caught up with him. Above was a steep dièdre. It looked hard. He was uncoiling his rope. 'Ah don't like the weather', he grunted and then he was moving powerfully upwards. The pitch was a good Grade V and ended on a snowy terrace where we stopped to eat. It was still early, not yet midday, and we must have been more than half way up the face, over two thousand feet in some four hours. For the first time I was conscious of the cable cars immediately above us, moving past swift and silent on the now almost vertical cable, apparently only a stone's throw out in space. By now the passengers would be tourists and massed faces were pressed against the windows eager to catch a glimpse of 'les alpinistes'. Maybe it looked quite exciting from up there. But the weather was not so exciting. As we had climbed the crisp morning light had dulled and the shadows had lost their edge. There was no longer a light mist below us but a layer of grey cloud into which the teleferique cars plunged out of sight. As we munched our chocolate the watery sun faded for good and it was suddenly cold. I fumbled in my rucksack for my cagoule.

The buttress had now melted into the face itself, and roped-up in two pairs, we moved right across a steep ice couloir into a maze of short walls and icy slopes. I had led our rope across the couloir, but for some reason unknown I had not yet taken my mittens from my rucksack. It started to snow and while Chris fought his way up the verglassed wall above I brought Rusty across. I remember weeping in the agony of the 'warm cold' as my hands regained their feeling in my newly donned mitts.

Mist and falling flakes drifted round us and visibility dropped to a few yards. Thunder rolled ominously over towards Mont Blanc. Conditions were difficult and we had to move very carefully. From the exhilaration of swift movement on warm rock the climb had suddenly degenerated into a slow, cold and uncomfortable clawing upwards.

My back was sticky with cold sweat and I was really aware of the sore throat I had had for several days. I felt ill and wished now I had stayed in bed.

And then, right above us, through a rent in the swirling mist, was the teleferique station. A vertical wall of black and evil-looking ice-plastered rock guarded our goal. Only a few hundred feet, so near and yet so far! It would be the true finish, but not today. The vision faded. We moved left into a white world of seracs and snow slopes that we knew were somewhere near the top of the Frendo Spur. We could move together again now, but we paused momentarily for breath and Tom consulted his watch. 'Last tele's in half an hour', he exclaimed. 'We'll never all make it at this rate and Ah'm buggered if Ah'm going to bivouac! Ah'll push on alone and try t' hold the last car for ye'. And with that he was gone, cramponing off into the swirling whiteness at a steady lope.

Tired and almost despairingly the three of us slowly wound our way through the ice walls and crevasses and then the angle started to ease. Suddenly there was a black hole ahead – a door in a snow bank – and a line of lights leading deep into the mountain. 'This is it', shouted Chris. 'Off with your crampons quick and run', and we went pounding down the echoing corridors into the smell of tourists and humming machinery. 'Vite! vite!', shouted a muffled figure in blue uniform and then there was Tom standing by the cable-car door, a huge grin on his face and snow plastered in his hair. 'Ah just made it, but Ah told them Ah couldna leave ye to bivouac on yer own', he grinned. And we were swooping downwards through the grey murk and the gathering darkness.

The next night there was a great party at the squalid clearing in the woods where we were camped. Paul Nunn and the Sheffield lads were with us, Martin Boysen and Mags, Gary Hemming, several Austrians and some of the hard French lads of the Mountain Gendarmerie, the ones responsible for bringing down the dead bodies. From the log fire the sparks flew upward through the trees, wine flowed like water and Tom's accordian was never silent.

Soon after midnight a plaintive bald-headed figure, clad only in polythene sandals and a nightshirt was discovered muttering at the edge of the throng by one of the Scots lads. 'If ye want tae join us bring yer bottle', he was told but it turned out that this was not his purpose. 'If ye wish tae complain put yer trews on first', our lad advised him before he rejoined the party.

At ten o'clock next morning there were only three of us in camp. Most of the team had repaired to the Bar National for a 'hair of the dog' breakfast, but my throat was still bad, and together with Beardie and Ian Jock, I had stayed to drink strong tea and clear up the mess. A few hundred yards away through the trees I noticed two well known middle-aged English alpinists tidying up their own camp. As I watched two tall gendarmes appeared and sidled over to the Englishmen. They wore combat boots and battledress, huge floppy berets crowned their small heads, and both carried slung sub-machine guns. I wondered what was up. One of the Englishmen gesticulated towards our camp, 'Yes officer – up there officer – they're the ones officer!', I could almost hear him saying. The gendarmes nodded to each other purposefully and came striding up towards us through the trees. 'Jock! Beardie!', I cried. 'Here comes trouble'.

They strode into the campsite and said nothing. They wandered round it, kicking at the dixies and poking at the tents. *'Sale . . . dégoutant!'* grunted the one with the little moustache, then *'Où est l'accordéon?'*, he demanded. I shook my head unco-operatively and Jock muttered 'Ah don't understand ye'. Then they started to search the tents and immediately found what they were looking for. Tom's big shiny squeezebox lay on his sleeping bag amid a pile of dirty clothes. *'Aha'*, cried the one with piggy eyes, triumphantly. *'Nous allons saisir cela'*, and he picked up the offending instrument. It was plainly time to do something. In my best French I tried to explain that the musician was not in camp and that they had no right to confiscate anything without first seeing the owner. The gendarme too must have realized that he was acting outside the rules. He threw down the accordian and turning to me he shouted provocatively 'La Reine Elisabeth, she steenks'.

There was a moment's silence. But Ian Jock had met that ploy before. He squared his shoulders and grinned. 'Aye', he said brimming over with Scots republican fervour, 'Aye – she does too'.

Moustache shook his head. He had obviously hoped for a fruity answer concerning de Gaulle's ancestry and a quick arrest for insulting the Head of State. The other gendarme nudged him. *'On va'*, he muttered and with a final pronouncement of *'Jamais musique encore!'* they strode off back down the track. 'Eee Jock – that was a good 'un', said Beardie. 'You deserve another cuppa tea for that'.

Tom's Black Book was legendary. It was handled with reverence and spoken of with awe by those privileged few permitted to see it. A large black ledger, reinforced in strategic places by strips of pink National Health Service plaster, it contained all Tom's far reaching research into potential new routes in the alpine areas which tickled his fancy. It bulged with photographs, sketches, 'topos', foreign press reports and cuttings from climbing magazines from all over the world.

We had just been stormed off one of the Black Book's secret lines on the Italian side of the Rochefort, and sitting over a brew in our Val Veny campsite, Tom produced the Book again. 'Ah know a great wee line on the Plan', he confided. 'Ah canna think why nobody's seen it before. Look here it is. What d'ye think, John?' Because of the bad weather, Chris Bonington had disappeared to the Vercors with Lionel Terray, so we conscripted, to make a foursome, tall, lean Martin Boysen, the gentle rock genius, and drove post-haste through the tunnel back to Chamonix.

It was dark when Tom came rushing into the camp. 'Damn Bonington', he cried, 'He's back from the Vercors and what's more he's already off and away up our route! Left this afternoon with Lito, that American manny, and planned to bivouac at the bottom. Ah should never have shown him ma book!' Rusty gave a grunt of disapproval at so base an action. Obviously the spirit of friendly rivalry had been overdone. Tom continued 'Look Ah've an idea . . . We'll catch the first tele' again in the morning and burn him off before the bastard's awake!'

We made the first cable-car this time and by eight o'clock we were kicking steps as fast as we could up the steepening *névé* of the Pélerins Glacier below the West Face of the Aiguille du Plan. The face is square and massive, a tangle of shattered pillars and ice patches, its centre defined by the wide broken buttress of the famous Gréloz/Roch route of 1946. On its left a slender and well-defined rib rises high to butt against a vertical wall that appears to guard the summit. That rib was

On the West Face of the Plan — delicate slab climbing below the cracked roof

our line. 'Hey, Tom, let's stop and put on crampons', I called breathlessly. The *névé* was hard and steep and I had visions of a long and painful slide back to square one. 'Och ye don't need yer crampons here. There's no time to be lost', he called back. We reached the rimaye safely and, without pausing to put on the rope, carried on at a mad pace up the easy rocks.

The first difficulty was a tall slab roofed by a big cracked block. We roped up and enjoyed some delicate climbing followed by a strenuous pitch hand-jamming round the crack beneath the roof. To Tom's dismay there was no sign of Chris or Lito. We broke out of the shadow and into the sun and whatever Tom's feelings about the rivalry, I am sure the other three of us had forgotten it in the sheer delight of moving smoothly up warm rock beneath a cloudless sky. There were more slabs and a series of steep steps split first by an icy chimney and then by a series of grooves. We were almost at the base of a steep upper wall when we heard from above the unmistakeable sound of hammer on piton. 'There they are', cried Tom, pointing up to a huge chimney immediately above us, and sure enough there were Chris and Lito hanging in étrier in the dark confines a couple of hundred feet up. We sat down on a small ledge, Rusty got out some food and Tom stroked his chin. 'Aye', he said, 'There's no point in going up there behind them. They'll take days nailing that thing and it's dark and cold in there. We've only been climbing Grade V so far and it seems stupid to do an A3 finish! Look there's an obvious line going right . . . It should lead without too much difficulty into that smashing dièdre that Joe and I did two years ago; now that would make an admirable finish. Let's try for it!'

So we shouted good luck up to Chris and Lito and got moving again, traversing rightwards below the steep upper wall via a series of rocky terraces and sloping icy gangways. Four or five pitches found us half way across towards the top of the Gréloz/Roch buttress and below an incredible-looking smooth dièdre. Water dripped down the right wall, sparkling in the sun, and the left wall overhung. There was a thin crack up the back. So this was the famous Dièdre Brown/Patey of which we had heard! It looked, as the French would say, formidable. Martin set off up it. He moved with remarkable grace, his lithe form silhouetted against the deep blue sky above. He was obviously not finding it too hard. I watched an avalanche on the North Face of the Midi across the way and eventually it was my turn. With big boots and a large rucksack it was far from easy. The exposure was exciting and so steep was the wall that the rucksack was pulling me back the whole time. It was very strenuous. After one long pitch of 150 feet the angle eased slightly for a second pitch. The third pitch was difficult again with a short sharp overhang near the top, and then we were on easy ledges and snow slopes. Martin was licking his lips. The Dièdre Brown/Patey had been a memorable experience. Joe and Tom had found it in '63 when they'd done the Gréloz/Roch route and this was

39

probably a third ascent. Tom was in great form. 'Ah hope they freeze tae death nailed in their bloody chimney', he cried and without more ado he set off at the trot up the wide snowy couloir towards the sharp summit rocks. The three of us stopped to put on our crampons and then gingerly followed Tom's footsteps. 'That man is quite incredible', Martin exclaimed. 'Do you realize he didn't even bring his crampons?'

The descent from the Plan is easy. First a snow arête leads down to a little col from which a steep head-wall drops to the Envers du Plan Glacier. When we reached the col Tom was already far below on the glacier and running still. 'Oi, Tom', shouted Rusty. 'Get a brew on'.

High on the West Face of the Plan rocky terraces and icy gangways lead towards the base of the Dièdre Brown/Patey – Tom Patey in action

Right: The Dièdre Brown/ Patey – Rusty Baillie silhouetted against the deep blue sky

The tiny figure paused and waved an arm before continuing his mad downward progress.

The Envers du Plan Glacier is never steep but there are several bands of crevasses and there are route-finding problems among the seracs near the bottom. Several years later while descending it fast with another friend we were roundly abused by an elderly guide for moving unroped on what appeared to us to be fairly safe ground. As we ran on my companion tripped over his crampon, and describing a complete somersault in the air over a small crevasse landed neatly on his feet at the far side, continuing with his run as if nothing had happened! The astonished guide sat down in the snow and stared. It was, of course, unintentional and a chance in ten thousand, but then that's the way things go! This time there were no epics. We too moved downwards at a steady trot, but Tom had long since disappeared into the distance.

There was a welcome pause at the Requin Hut, perched on a scree-covered *rognon* above the confluence of the Plan and Tacul Glaciers. True to our instructions Tom had a brew waiting, but it was already evening and the hut was crowded with sweaty climbers swilling bowls of coffee and stuffing spaghetti. Tom had us out on the path again very soon, jogging down the unpleasant scree slopes that lead to the dry glacier below and the long walk back to the Mer de Glace.

It's an uncomfortable walk that four miles down the gritty ice of the Mer de Glace, weaving between piles of boulders and rotting moraines and navigating around groups of gaping blue crevasses. But at least it is just downhill! By the time we had turned the corner below the Aiguille de la République it was dark. Nobody had a torch and we were soon completely lost in the intricate maze of twisted crevasses, below the place where the steep iron ladders lead up the lateral cliffs to the hillside path and Montenvers. There was no moon and we were very tired. Martin sat down on a boulder and wiped his brow. 'What a place to bivouac after all that', he growled. 'Hell, Tom, why didn't we stay at the hut?' 'Never fear, Patey's here', advised Tom. 'Follow me'. And miraculously he led the way round gaping holes and over shifting piles of moraine and in fifteen minutes we found ourselves at the bottom of the ladders. 'How did he manage that?', Rusty asked me. 'I thought I knew the place, but that was quite impossible'. I shook my head. 'The Doctor is a genius', I whispered.

Once we were on the easy path the thought of a drink spurred us on, but the Montenvers Hotel, dark and gaunt on its grassy promontory above the ice, was barred and bolted. There's no call for night life at 6500 feet! So we continued down into the steep zigzags beneath the aromatic pines; the night smell of the forest after a hot day was soothing, but our feet were sore and dusty. A brew was all that Rusty and I desired. We staggered into camp about one in the morning, and dry though we were, we fell straight asleep onto our sleeping bags. A day with the Doctor was bound to be memorable!

The Dolomites
Playground for the rock climber

The great chain of the Alps curves from the Mediterranean coast through central Europe and into the Balkans. Well towards its eastern end, almost twice as far from Dover as are the snows of Mont Blanc, lies a large area of dramatic limestone mountains. The whole region is as large as Wales and for all practical purposes lies completely in Italy. This is the Dolomites.

The area is a complex one. To the average mountaineer accustomed to the valleys and ridges of more usual mountains, the topography will often seem confusing. Above the twisting valleys the great massifs seem to rise through the pine forests without rhyme or reason. Then fairy-like spires and impossible walls soar from acres of white scree, their colours changing through red and pink to yellow and black as the day wears on. Below the scree are lush meadows, bright with a profusion of wild flowers, and deep valleys which descend to the hazy plains and lakes of the distant Venetian littoral. The Dolomites are famous for their landscapes and the Germans, tourists, walkers and climbers alike, flock to the area in their thousands each summer.

Historically the area is interesting. Until the Great War, the South Tyrol, as much of the area is known, was part of the Austro-Hungarian Empire. Then the tide of battle swept back and forth across the Dolomites. Troops of both sides, Italian and Austrian, were subjected to fantastic hardships. Even in winter the fighting was bitter and more soldiers were killed by avalanches than by the enemy. Some of the fiercest fighting in the whole conflict – on either eastern or western fronts – took place on the Colle di Lana. Parts of the Dolomites are still littered with the flotsam of war: there are tunnels and gun positions carved into the mountain sides and old mess tins and boots still lying in the scree. Even in 1958 Lothar Brandler's party had to climb through barbed wire at the top of their Direct route on the North Face of the Cima Grande – perhaps an unnecessary fortification for 1916! The Treaty of Versailles gave the South Tyrol to Italy, although much of it is still German speaking, and the area has remained a source of friction between Italy and Austria ever since.

The history of climbing in the Alps too is clearly linked with that of the Dolomites. Although the British were among the first to travel in the area, particularly the painters Josiah Gilbert and G. C. Churchill, whose book *The Dolomite Mountains* was published in 1864 and contains some very fine and accurate illustrations, the first ascents of most of the peaks were left to continental parties. Pride of place should perhaps go to Grohmann, a Viennese, who scaled the Cima Grande, The Cristallo, The Marmolata, Tofana and Langkofel. An exception to the rule, however, was John Ball, the first President of the Alpine Club, who climbed Monte Pelmo (10,398 feet) as early as 1857. It was the redoubtable Leslie Stephen who wrote in 1869, when he too was President of the Club, 'I hoped at the time that some of the peaks might turn out to be inaccessible!' But it was to be many years before the last pinnacles were eventually climbed.

Looking south-east from the Civetta towards the Venetian Dolomites that rise above Belluno

43

After the summits came the steep buttresses and faces, and it could be claimed that steep wall climbing started in the Eastern Alps. Pioneers like Hans Dulfer and Paul Preuss pushed the first routes up the vertical limestone of the Kaiser and Karwendel Ranges between the Inn Valley and Bavaria, before turning to the higher Dolomite walls. Preuss climbed the North Face of the Crozzon di Brenta in 1911; his famous 'Kamin' on the Cima Piccolissima was in the same year. Angelo Dibona, whose name graces many fine climbs throughout the Alps, was active too, climbing the South West Ridge of the Roda di Val in 1908 and the North East Ridge of the Cima Grande – the left-hand bounding arête of the great North Face – in 1909.

Before the Great War, difficult vertical rock climbing was in full swing in the Dolomites; soon after it, continuous artificial climbing was to develop from the same sources. This next generation of Dolomite specialists included Italians like Ricardo Cassin, Gervasutti and Emilio Comici, or Germans and Austrians like Fritze Weissner (who later emigrated to the U.S.A. and made the first ascents of the Devils Tower and Mt Waddington). Armed with the skills and techniques developed in the Dolomites, they laid siege to the great buttresses and faces of the Western Alps in the twenties and thirties, and finally conquered them. On the continent today, most of the great names associated with climbing ice, snow or rock in the Western Alps have served an apprenticeship on steep Dolomite limestone.

And so the 'Dollies' have the reputation of being a playground for the hard-men. But there is also much for the less ambitious climber and mountain walker . . . and the skiing too is exceptional. There are no real glaciers excepting for two square miles of ice draped across the northern flanks of the Marmolata, the 'Queen of the Dolomites' and the highest summit, at 10,968 feet. The weather tends to be milder and the atmosphere more hospitable than further west. First-class huts abound and hut walks are usually short or even non-existent. There is also a network of excellent high and long-distance paths, many of them a legacy of the Great War.

Perhaps the most popular areas with the British are the Tre Cima, Civette and Sella groups. Other worthwhile areas include the Marmolata itself, the Catinaccio or Rosengarten groups, the Tofana and the extensive Brenta group, isolated from the rest by the deep Adige Valley and the most westerly of the Dolomites. Eastward the limestone spills into Yugoslavia to such mountains as Triglav; these are the Julian Alps.

The Tre Cima di Lavaredo, or Drei Zinnen as they are known in German, offer a wealth of difficult rock climbing on sometimes dubious rock. The *voie-normale* on the Cima Grande, the South Face, is an easy scramble up a complex mountainside, the awkward route-finding eased by a succession of empty chianti bottles and tin cans and loud with cursing guides and the rumble of falling stones kicked from the scree-covered ledges by their clients. The classic route on the Grande

is the Comici/Dimai, 1600 feet of climbing that is still considered a fair Grade VI (V.S+) and the original line up the blank and largely overhanging North Wall. It was put up in 1933 and has since become a trade-route for 'hard-men'. Much of the climbing is supposed to be artificial; but the pegs are a disconcerting couple of moves apart, and it can be done without étrier altogether if your fingers are strong! The lower 750 feet are continuously overhanging and the rest merely vertical. The exposure is stunning; not just downwards, but sideways too across this huge wall.

There are three other major North Face lines and two are almost completely aid-climbing, the Via Camillotto Pellisier which lies close to the Dibona route on the North East Arête, and uses 340 bolts, and the Saxonweg, which was first climbed in the winter of 1963 amid a fanfare of publicity, and required 16 bivouacs. An apocryphal story is told of a youthful pair from Newcastle on their first visit to the Alps, who climbed the Saxonweg by mistake for the Comici. They had heard so many stories of the excessive use of pegs and bolts on the Continent, and were such good rock climbers, that it was only when confronted with the large roof towards the summit that it dawned that they were on the wrong climb! The third route is the Brandler/Hasse. It is a magnificent climb with both hard free and artificial pitches. It is said that it is necessary to fall from the crux before discovering how to climb it, and Gunn Clark, who made the first British ascent of it with Chris Bonington in 1959, told horrifying tales of bolts wedged into their holes with old newspaper. For some time the climb had a reputation for bad pegs and loose rocks, but it is now justly popular.

It is probably because of their fame, their dramatic shape and easy access by car along a very rough and hair-raising track, that the Tre Cima are the most popular group in the Dolomites. Perhaps an unpleasant experience of mine is typical? It was our first visit to the Dolomites and Rusty Baillie and myself were keen to sample the Comici Route which, despite having been superseded both in directness and difficulty, is still a climb well worth having done and by no means easy. As we were fit and climbing fast, we decided that we would almost certainly better the time of eight to ten hours given for the climb in the English guide book – so we would not bother to make an early start and would behave in a leisurely way as befitted English gentlemen. What we did not realize was that the day we chose – our last day before returning to Britain – happened to be an Italian Bank Holiday!

Only when we had scrambled up the initial easy pitches to the ledge where the real climbing begins did it dawn on us that we were the last party at the end of a long queue, all waiting patiently their turn to start on the overhangs. High above our heads the wall was dotted with struggling figures and every now and then a karabiner or a fumbled étrier would go whining past to the scree already some distance below. We decided to wait. It was not a wise decision. Several other parties appeared on the ledge – only to shake their heads and disappear

Civetta, the towers of the north west face mirrored in the tiny Lago di Coldai. Nearest is the Torre Alleghe and highest the Civetta itself

49

muttering. To cut a long story short, although we spent only seven hours actually climbing we spent twenty-four hours on the mountain. Seven hours we spent waiting on tiny ledges while climbers who were obviously climbing beyond their safe limits, fought their way up the pitch above. Eventually, caught by darkness, we bivouacked near the top, on the uncomfortable scree of the 'Ringband', in our shirt-sleeves and wrapped up in our ropes. In the interests of speed, and sure of our ability to move fast, we had not even carried a rucksack! There were several other parties bivouacked between us and the summit, and on the easy ground descending the southern flanks. But we learned our lessons – the most important being that Bank Holidays are better spent at Blackpool than on a popular route in the Eastern Alps!

The Cima Ouest also has a fabulous North Face with one classic route, the Cassin, a bit harder than the Comici, which was the original route up the Face, and five different and most spectacular artificial lines breaking through the incredible roofs that bar the entire face

below it. The first of these were the Swiss/Italian and Desmaison/Mazeaud routes of 1959, the latter being slightly the harder at A.4, but both requiring over 300 pegs and several expansion bolts. The latest and most difficult is the Bauer/Rudolf, which far from seeking a natural line, attacks the overhangs at their widest point, actually crossing one horizontal roof for over a hundred feet on continuous aid. This climb had its fifth ascent – its first British – in 1969, by a team led by ace aid-climber Doug Scott. All these routes of course take several days. More suitable for moderate parties are the excellent lines on the East Face, the Via Della Disperazione of 1909, 1500 feet at Grade IV, and the North East Ridge of 1933. This is Grade V and has one aid pitch, but the situations are fantastic and the views across the Face spectacular.

The other two peaks of the 'trinity' are the Cima Piccola and the Cima Piccolissima. These have shorter climbs, many on the sunny southern faces above the Lavaredo Hut, which is accessible by car.

The Tre Cima di Lavaredo — an unusual view of the group from the south-east, showing the Cima Piccola, the Punta di Frida and the Cima Piccolissima. The famous 'Spigolo Giallo' (Yellow Edge) is the vertical arête in the centre of the picture

So accessible is it in fact, that recently a climber emerging from the hut after an excellent meal supplied by the friendly guardian, discovered his Volkswagen squashed flat beneath a large boulder which had fallen from the Piccola above!

Perhaps the most famous climb here – a climb which ranks among the very best in the Dolomites – is the 'Spigolo Giallo' – the Yellow Edge. It is graded V+ and is a serious route – not one to fall off. In fact, several people have died after falls on the climb or have slowly strangled while hanging free in space on the rope. So steep is the climb,

Mo Anthoine in action on the 'Yellow Edge', the first pitch of the Spigolo Giallo. The Lavaredo Hut can be seen already some way below

High on the Spigolo Giallo of the Cima Piccola an Austrian team are seen at work on the difficult dièdre, — the crux of the climb. Two British climbers are close behind them

that the Yellow Edge has even been parachuted by a sky-diver leaping from the summit. It is a magnificent line, almost 1000 feet high, which starts up a steep dièdre, pulls over a small roof and moves up steep walls towards a hairy traverse which leads into an impressive yellow groove on the crest of the bulging Edge itself. It is much more interesting than the Comici, for instance, because the climb follows a series of different features, and the route-finding is not just a question of following an obvious line of pegs.

Another exciting climb is Preuss's original 1911 route, The Preuss-

Kamin on the Piccolissima. Several pitches, including a short one of Grade V, lead into the bottomless chimney which cuts 800 feet through most impressive surroundings. Bridged across it, high out over space, one can look down at the tiny ants of tourists far below crossing the Forcella Lavaredo between the Lavaredo and Locatelli huts.

The Tre Cima group is no place for a novice, but the Sella group is a good place to learn Dolomite climbing. It lies further east near Bolzano and is close above the road at the Sella Pass where there is a C.A.I. hut. Besides the four Sella towers themselves there is plenty of other good climbing in the area, particularly on two other impressive towers, the Torre and the Gran Campanile del Murfried some two miles further north round the edge of the escarpment. Both have classic and not too difficult north face routes; that on the Torre is some 1300 feet and grade V, and rejoices under the name 'Camino Obliquo della

The great North-West Face of the Civetta towers behind the village of Caprile. The Quota IGM is the slight rounded step just left of the summit shoulder, the location of the famous Dièdre Pillip/Flamm

Morte' – 'The Slanting Chimney of Death'! The Sella Towers themselves dominate the pass and demand to be climbed. There is little of difficulty on any of the four towers; but perhaps the pleasantest route is the North West Face Direct of the second tower, an 800 foot route on excellent rock graded at V – and put up by the two Messner brothers in 1968. It should take about four hours.

The other side of the Sella Pass from the Towers is the Sassolungo group, climbed from either the Sella Hut or the Vicenza Hut in the centre of the massif. Among the routes for the 'hard-man' there are several grade VI lines of over 3000 feet, including the mysterious 'Esposito Nose' put up in 1940. Esposito and his companion Butta were killed shortly after completing the climb, and they left no complete description. The exact line they took can only be guessed at – although it must run over most impressive and difficult ground. But Sassolungo is a large and high mountain, over 10,000 feet high, which often holds snow and ice. Even the easier routes demand a certain amount of mountaineering skill. The best of these is probably the grade IV East Tower of the North Face, an old line put up in 1907 but a fine one and with little objective danger. At the south east corner of the group is the Cinque Dita or Funffingerspitze, a clump of weird spires like an upstretched hand. These are particularly dramatic when seen from a distance, and the classic route, again a grade IV, is the traverse of all the fingers by the South West Arête, an old route dating to 1906 but a very popular one giving exciting situations in airy surroundings.

Some ten miles to the south west is the Rosengarten or Catinaccio, containing, on its western side, the famous Vajolet Towers. The three towers are named after early Dolomite climbers, Delago, Stabeler and Winkler, while there is a smaller Torre Piaz as well. The Towers are not high, only some 400 feet, but they offer spectacular and exposed climbing of no great difficulty, and rising immediately behind the Vajolet Hut, itself within easy access of the main road, they are justifiably popular.

Although many alpinists consider the Dolomites as lacking the seriousness of the big mixed routes further to the west, no one can deny the Civetta to be a real mountain. It presents a great face to the north west some three miles long, a face battlemented with pinnacle-like summits and holding a hanging ice-field, the Cristalo, high on the wall immediately below the highest top. There is a hut at either end of the range, another below the North-West Face towards its centre, and a fourth just below the 10,558 foot summit, which can be reached by an easy path and a series of iron ladders. Apart from the *voie-normale* to the highest summit, at Grade II one of the most worthwhile easy routes of the Dolomites, there are no easy climbs on the Civetta and the great North-West Face holds nothing easier than a grade V +. This is the Solleder route, one of the greatest in the Alps and first climbed in 1925. It usually involves one bivouac and is a mountaineering route with real objective dangers; route-finding is difficult and

Peak after peak fade into the
dusk as if cut from cardboard.
From left to right the Sasso
Levante group, the Cinque
Dita and the Sasso Lungo
group seen from the Civetta

there is liable to be some stone fall: bad conditions can make the route much harder and it is over 3500 in length. A few metres to the north is another classic – the 3000-foot Phillip/Flamm Dièdre, a very conspicuous and direct line up the Quota IGM, one of the great buttresses of the Face. It was first climbed in 1957, the third ascent in 1962 by Crew and Wright being the first British ascent. Most parties are forced to bivouac; but in 1963 Paul Nunn and Martin Boysen completed the route without a bivouac after an epic climb during which Paul, his leg broken by stone fall, must have gone through considerable agony! It is still considered to be one of the hardest rock climbs in the Alps.

Besides the problems of route-finding, once on this vast wall, it is so steep and complex, and so foreshortened when seen from the scree below, that it can be difficult even to locate oneself correctly. John Wharton and I once attempted what we thought to be the North Face of Pan di Zucchero – a summit towards the northern end of the Wall. We climbed for six or seven hours, the climbing seeming to fit the description in the guide book, until suddenly nothing seemed to tally. The way was barred by a series of caves, and it was obvious we would have to climb out over the roofs – this surely merited a few words in the guide book? After several attempts we were unable to break through, and had to make an unpleasant descent by abseil. Still mystified the next day, it was only after careful sitings and meticulous map reading, that we realized we had been climbing the wrong mountain! We had attempted an un-named, but similar-shaped summit, between the correct one and the Valgrande a few hundred yards further north. According to the guardian at the Coldai Hut, that particular part of the wall as yet had no line on it – and we knew why!

At the southern end of the range there are some 'fun routes' on a series of small pinnacles, among them the leaning Campanile di Brabante, first climbed by King Leopold of the Belgians in 1933, and grade IV. The descent is a spectacular free abseil – much photographed and prominent in the publicity literature of certain German camera companies – onto the top of a lower pinnacle which rejoices in the incredible name of 'Boccia della XLIII Legione Alpina Piave'.

And there is plenty more! From almost any viewpoint the Dolomite Peaks stretch away as a blue forest of dreaming spires. A photographer is tempted to spend the day photographing and not climbing: visually, dawn and dusk are particularly exciting. Even the smell, that dry dusty smell, usually with a whiff of wild thyme or heavy with the scent of the lusher flowers peculiar to high limestone country, is evocative. In contrast to certain areas of the Alps the local people are especially friendly and, certainly for the British, Italy is an excellent and in-expensive place in which to eat, drink and live. Leslie Stephen claimed the Dolomites were mountains bewitched. Certainly, once having climbed there, no one could forget the enchantment of their spired landscape.

North Face

A line of sparks through the night, echoed crashes and a dull thump of rock on ice, and almost silence again. Silence but for the moan of the wind through the teeth of the ridge three thousand feet above, where St. Elmo's Fire flickers across the wet curves of black granite. 'Biggest bugger yet!' growls Wharton.

I pull my sodden pied d'elephant further over my arse and try to forget that I am very wet and very cold. At least the rain has stopped but I am too gripped-up to sleep.

We are bivouacked on the North Wall of the Piz Badile, a vast curl of smooth granite high above the Val Bregaglia in S.E. Switzerland. We started the climb in the evening and stopped at dusk on the last ledge before the difficulties begin in earnest, to give ourselves a full day to climb the face and retreat down the southern flank to the sanctuary of an Italian climbers' hut. We pulled on our eiderdown jackets and windproof cagoules, our gloves, balaclavas and crash-helmets. We stuffed our feet into our pied d'elephants, and then into emptied rucksacks. A quick brew of soup on our little gas cooker, and we tried to sleep. But by then the night was swirling with cloud and lit by the first flashes of lightening. The rain started and turned to sleet. The thunder rolled and crashed round hidden spires. And the acres of overlapping slabs became a vast waterfall, sweeping away the stove and spare food lying beside us on the ledge.

Rocks, falling from high above, spin unseen through the darkness. At dawn the upper face will be plastered in ice and new snow – and unclimbable. We grit our teeth and pray for morning. We are thankful that we are no higher, where retreat might be impossible. We've tried the Badile four times this year. What a way to spend the summer!

The North Face of the Piz Badile is one of the six alpine north faces 'collected' by the famous French guide and author, Gaston Rebuffat, into his book *Starlight and Storm*; consequently these have come to be regarded as the classic six. All provide routes of great character and interest on some of the most imposing mountains in the world. There are harder climbs and other north faces, but these are among the *pièces de résistance* of the alpine world. The Grandes Jorasses and the Aiguille du Dru are in the French Mont Blanc chain; the Eiger in the Bernese Oberland, the Matterhorn in the Valais and the Badile in the Bergell are Swiss; while the Cima Grande di Lavaredo is in the Italian Dolomites. Because of their position on the sunless flanks of the peaks the northern faces are higher and steeper and often more icy than the warmer slopes. Many are simply ice-walls, but not the classic six; not for nothing are they known jocularly among the 'hard-men' as 'The Big Black Walls'.

The Alpine summits were first climbed by their easiest routes, usually easy-angled ridges or gentle snow flanks. Only then did attention turn to the more difficult ridges and steeper slopes. Always the north faces flaunted their special challenge, their size, their situation and their mystery. Although two of the greatest climbers of their day,

The North Face of the Matterhorn seen from the Wellenkuppe. On the left is the Hornli Ridge and on the right part of the Italian Ridge appears over the Zmutt Ridge, on which the dark bulge indicates the famous Zmutt Nose. The line of the standard North Face route ascends the steep ice ramp on the left of the face, bears right up the obvious shallow couloir into the centre of the face and then makes straight for the summit

Overleaf, above: On the great ice ramp of the Matterhorn North Face, Hamish MacInnes in action. Beyond is the improbable curl of the Zmutt Nose. Below: Nikki Clough (right) and her husband, Ian at work on the ice ramp of the Matterhorn North Face — looking straight upwards

Ryan – an Indian Army officer, and Winthrop-Young – an Eton schoolmaster, had attempted the north faces of the Dru and Jorasses respectively in 1904 and 1907, they were thirty years before their time. It was not until after the Great War that the era of the *Nordwand* began.

By 1930 the north faces of the classic six were among the outstanding problems of the day. But there were new men, Germans, Austrians and Italians trained on the steep limestone crags of the lower Eastern Alps. Brilliant climbers, they were familiar not only with new techniques on rock and ice but also with the psychological problems of living in a hostile and vertical environment for several days at a time.

In a raging storm at two o'clock in the afternoon of August 1st, 1931, two unknown brothers, Franz and Toni Schmit, reached the summit of the Matterhorn after 33 hours on the Face. While Zermatt rocked with the news, the two lads mounted their bicycles and peddled back to Munich. The great decade had begun.

Emilio Comici climbed the wall of the Cima Grande without incident in 1933. He had said, 'a drop of water falls from the summit, that is the line I will take . . .'. In '35 the Frenchman, Pierre Allain climbed the north face of the Dru and in '37 it was the turn of the Badile. A strong team led by Riccardo Cassin spent three days on the face and reached the summit in a blizzard. The two youngest climbers

died of exhaustion. Such was the reputation of the climb that it was not repeated until 1949 by Rebuffat and Jean Franco.

Peters in 1935 had climbed the north spur of the Point Croz, a secondary summit of the most beautiful mountain of the six, the Grandes Jorasses, but it was not until 1938 that Cassin finally led his party to the highest summit by its northern buttress – the Walker Spur. The same year a four-man Austro-German team, after a five-day epic climb, surmounted the North Wall of the Eiger, the biggest and blackest of the lot. Already notorious in the Press after eight deaths on previous attempts, this face was at one time under a climbing ban by the Swiss Government.

There were many, both in Europe and Britain, who feared that a fanatical motive lay behind the bold courage of the climbers, and fancied they saw a dark political shadow hanging over their achievements. Had not Hitler presented Olympic gold medals to the successful Eiger team? Col. Strutt, retiring President of the Alpine Club, thundered into attack in his 1938 valedictory address: 'The Eigerwand continues to be an obsession for the mentally deranged of almost every nation ... the most imbecile variant since mountaineering first began ...'.

More recently, Tom Patey, the finest Scottish climber of his time and a great humourist, summed it up in lines from his song, The Eigerwand:

For two desperate days and a terrible night
They spurred themselves on in their desperate fight;
Let the Valkyries howl in the pitiless sky –
But the Führer has ordered: You will conquer or die ...

A climber has fallen, but why let us mourn?
For each one that dies there are two to be born.
Ready to rise at the Führer's command,
To conquer or die on the grim Eigerwand.

The old men were shouting, but the young men were climbing – and today we can look back and laugh.

Of the six routes the Cima Grande, the Badile and the Dru are rock-climbs; but the Dolomite peaks are lower and have better weather than further west, while the Badile and Dru are subject to severe storms and ice-plastered rock. Often the north face of the Dru is unclimbed for a whole summer because of the verglas.

On the other hand the Jorasses, the Matterhorn and the Eiger are all high peaks notorious for bad weather. In perfect conditions the Jorasses can be little more than a long and difficult rock-climb, but the other two are as much ice as rock, and all three are liable to bad stonefall. We were forced to retreat from the Matterhorn North Face after being hit by a rock salvo which had actually shattered one of the team's crash-helmet in the summer of 1966, while Mick Burke from Wigan claimed, after his 1967 winter ascent, that the face was only held together by its ice-glaze. Michel Darbellay actually time-tabled the rock avalanches before starting his solo Eiger climb in 1963.

61

The five classic North Faces –
Right: The Cima Grande di
Lavaredo, with (left) the
Piccolissima and the Piccola,
(centre) the Cima Grande
and (right) the Cima Ovest.
The North Face of the Grande
is about 1600 feet high

Far right: The Petit Dru. The
North Face line leads to the
snowy niche, the West Face
reaches the niche from
directly below and Bonatti
Pillar runs up the shadowed
edge

Below left: The Piz Badile
with new snow plastering the
top of the North-East Face.
The famous North Ridge
leads directly into the picture

Below centre: The North
Face of the Eiger appears
dark and menacing through
the clouds. The White Spider
is the obvious small ice-field
high on the Face

Below right: A tele-photo of
the Walker Spur of the
Grandes Jorasses after a
summer storm

The mountains are the same but the men have changed again. They come not only from the alpine countries now but from Glasgow and Paris, from Manchester, Warsaw, California and Cologne – even from Tokyo. They train hard. Herman Buhl who made the first solo ascent of the Badile North Face would carry a snowball in his fist all winter, and John Harlin, the top American climber killed on the Eiger Direct in '66, always skied without gloves. Certain British lads I know spend winter nights bivouacked in the garden to prepare for the real thing. It is Scottish ice and our highly developed free rock-climbing that have made British climbers second-to-none in the Alps once again after sixty years.

Now we climb in wind-proofs of man-made fibre and wear light-weight crash-helmets against falling stones. We sleep in down-filled clothing and eat concentrated scientific foods. Our nylon and perlon ropes are immensely strong and half the weight of the damp and frozen hemp they used in the thirties. The pegs we hammer into rock-cracks

The Eigerwand – a winter view. The line of the John Harlin Direct route is dotted white, the original 1938 route on the Face is marked in black, and the Death Bivouac is where the two routes cross at the top of the 'Flat Iron'. On the left of the face is the recent Scottish route and on the right the Japanese Rote Fluh route

for protection or aid are chrome-molybdenum aircraft steel and our crampons are twelve pointed and tungsten tipped. Gone are the long wood-shafted ice-axes.

Yesterday we used short-handled North Wall hammers, designed for cutting ice holds high above the head and for hammering home pegs in rock and ice, while today even these are obsolete as the American Chouinard Hammer and Scottish all-metal Terrordactyl come into more general use. These are highly specialized tools, scientifically designed; on big ice slopes we no longer cut steps but climb swiftly, a tool in each hand, like daggering automatons. Times for big routes have been slashed and speed is safety. We can even carry transistor radios and check with Geneva Airport for the latest weather forecast. And if all goes wrong our friends will get a chopper sent out to pluck us off the face – at a price.

So what then is the lure of the six north faces today? Or, for that matter, of the many other harder and more dangerous *grandes courses* in the Alps? Most have lost their mystery, and all six of the classic north faces have become 'trade-routes'; even ladies' ascents are considered nothing unusual. The walls are still big and steep, dark and difficult, but with our new-fangled gear and our polished techniques we have reduced their difficulties to our own level. We have not made ourselves better climbers. There are more of us and we are better informed than forty or even twenty years ago. We are no longer exploring the mountain: now we explore only ourselves. But there is still a great thrill in measuring up to Cassin or sharing the experience of the Schmits. Today we can only marvel at these men and their boldness. Even if it is no longer virgin, even if it is a 'trade-route' and even if the guide-book has been translated into Japanese, a climb is always a fresh experience to those who venture on to it. It is exciting to climb difficult ground safely, to carefully avoid objective dangers and to beat the weather, and afterwards to look up with satisfaction at a great face, to trace out the route on it, and laugh wryly that one was so scared.

Perhaps it is this rational conquest of fear that gives the alpine climber his greatest pleasure on a difficult route. The blind suppression of justified fear makes heroes, but vastly reduces a climber's life expectancy. The great alpinists, those who have achieved most, know exactly the limits of their fear and climb to those limits. They know just when to retreat and not before. They have achieved but survived.

We climb because it is compulsive and we enjoy it. Why probe for deeper meaning? Serious alpinism would become pretty deadly were we unable to laugh at it. Tom Patey had his tongue in cheek when he wrote as the first verse of his Eigerwand song:

Two tiny men on the ghastly north wall;
And a hungry great bergschrund just ripe for a fall;
The avalanche roars and the thunder-clouds boom,
And the black shiny rocks are like walls of a tomb.

Incident on the Lenzspitze

The door flew open with a crash. Snowflakes whirled thick down the shaft of yellow lamplight. Two men, their balaclavas rimmed with the white flakes, paused blinking in the brightness, then clumped on into the hut, swinging off their huge rucksacks.

From his stool beside the stove the guardian, an elderly unshaved peasant, frowned over his shoulder at the newcomers, before turning back to continue his conversation with the group of guides who were sucking at their pipes and swilling the Fendant, that thick white wine of the Swiss Vallais.

As mere foreigners, we had a corner of a table furthest from the stove and nearest the door. Well wrapped in our duvet jackets, we were huddled round a steaming two-litre jug of tea.

Kris turned to the newcomers, who stood panting over their mammoth sacks, shaking off the snow from their clothes. 'Here mate, want a cup of hot tea?' 'Ach so – Englanders? Ya! hot tea, das ist good – tank you.' The three of us shuffled along our bench to make room for the two tired Germans, who slumped down beside us. They were obviously exhausted and delighted to share our tea. There was no reaction from elsewhere in the hut. It was almost time to turn in and the other occupants were busy with their drinking and their gossip. Over everything hung a pungent blue cloud of tobacco smoke.

Tony spoke fair German and the lads had a smattering of English and we soon got into conversation. They must have been very tough characters indeed: it seemed that they had come that very day from the Ruhr, crouched low across the handle-bars of their mopeds. 500 miles down the autobahn into Switzerland, then up the Rhone Valley and the Saasertal to Saas Fee, before slogging over 5000 feet with their incredible rucksacks up to the Mischabel Hut, perched high on a shoulder of the Lenzspitze at almost 11,000 feet. It was small wonder that they were all in. 'It is necessary zat we make best use of our time', Fritz explained. 'Ve have only ze two week leave from our factory'.

Life in an alpine climbing hut starts before dawn, at that time of the night when life is at its lowest ebb and all sensible human beings are fast asleep. It is a time when the comfortable resolution of the previous evening is easily swamped by an overwhelming desire to sleep on, and a well-planned expedition is in jeopardy in the face of a barbaric awakening and a stomach-turning attempt at breakfast. The next morning was no exception; there was no sign of our German friends. Outside a myriad of stars pulsed in a clear sky, while eastward a faint flush gave shape to ridge upon ridge of saw-toothed peaks. Underfoot, however, the new snow lay deep. First one guide then another crept outside and returned shaking his head, while their clients muttered their thankful disappointment, knocked back their coffee and straggled back to bed. Today the mountains would be dangerous, there would be a serious avalanche risk and the going would be hard. Any idea of climbing was absurd!

It is early morning above the Mischabel Hut; a cloud sea fills the Saastal, on the far side of which rise the peaks of the Weissmies

Deep new snow on the North North-East Ridge of the Lenzspitze

But we too were on holiday, and we had a tight schedule to keep on our traverse of peaks and passes all along the Pennine Alps to Mont Blanc. Besides, there were friends expecting us in Zermatt next day, and as experienced guideless climbers we were confident in our ability to move safely over potentially dangerous terrain. We decided to press on with our plans and dawn saw the three of us moving steadily up the narrowing shoulder that becomes the E.N.E. ridge of the Lenzspitze.

The climb, like so many standard routes in the Alps, is technically no more than a scramble for an experienced rock-climber. But it can be made serious by uncontrollable factors such as length, weather, loose rock and ice. Today everything was plastered in powder snow; the going was slow but the morning was beautiful.

Once we paused for breath and looking down saw far below a pair of tiny figures moving slowly up our tracks to the start of the ridge. 'I reckon its those two Germans', said Tony. 'I'll bet they're the only ones keen enough today!' 'Can't keep a good man down!' grunted Kris.

New snow makes the traverse
of the Grand Gendarme high
on the North-North-East
Ridge of the Lenzspitze
slightly awkward. Beyond are
the peaks of the Weissmies

Later on, when the sun got warm, we stopped for a second breakfast. We were sitting relaxed on a rock ledge and Tony was peeling an orange when Kris grabbed my arm. 'Christ!' he said, jumping to his feet. 'Just look!'

Below us the ridge was a narrow snow arête. A small figure was sliding down the ice slopes of its northern flank. As we watched the body shot out over an ice cliff and went spinning on down the steepening slope. Again the figure shot over a serac, a bigger one now. He hit the ice and broke in half. Tony groaned. Two black blobs swept on down the slope and out – far out – into the snow basin of the glacier, before finally coming to rest.

Kris broke the silence at last. 'Poor bugger', he said. 'What do we do now?' I asked. 'Nothing for him!' replied Tony, ever practical. 'We finish our breakfast and then wander down and alert the guides to collect the bits. No rush'. 'Thousand feet', Kris shook his head. 'Not surprising he broke in half! But there are worse ways of going, eh?' We sat down again but no one felt much like eating, so we got out the bivi-stove and proceeded to brew-up.

Eventually we felt it was time to move and get on with our morbid task. But we were still pushing gear back into our sacks when two large hands appeared over the rocky edge of our ledge followed immediately by a tousled head wearing a large pair of snow-goggles. 'Guten tag Englanders!' cried Fritz.

Kris stood up astride his sack. He pointed down towards the two motionless dots on the distant glacier. 'But your friend – he is dead – kaput!' 'Ach, ja ja, Heini is tot! But I come to ze summit no?' 'Hey, wait a minute'. Tony was cross. 'You can't just go on like that. We must all go down to alert the rescue – the Bergwacht!' 'Nein Nein – I make ze top'. Fritz sounded emphatic. 'Heini would vish it . . . I go all ze way with you . . . I conquer ze peak!' 'We'll take you down with us', insisted Tony. 'We will tie you onto our rope'. 'Ze summit – ze summit', insisted Fritz.

Suddenly Kris grabbed my arm again. He was pointing down to the glacier. Abruptly Tony and Fritz fell silent. One of the black dots – half the mangled body – was moving! In dumbfounded silence we watched. The dot moved erratically and painfully slowly towards the other dot lying in the snow some distance away. It merged with it. The bigger dot seemed to flail around a bit and then, in a series of crazy zig-zags, it seemed to stagger down the glacier towards the distant moraines beyond which the hut lay out of sight.

It was Fritz who broke the silence. 'Ach so, Heini is OK! I sought he vas broke but it vas his grosse rucksac vich fell off', he grinned at Tony. 'Vierzig kilo – vierzig kilo in der sac. Now I go down. Zank you for offering to take me to ze summit on your corde! Now it iz not necessary! Danke schön, Auf wiedersehen!'

He swung down over the ledge and disappeared and five minutes later we heard him yodelling far below.

Disgrazia
Love affair with a mountain

A Landrover is not the most comfortable of vehicles in which to be bumbling along the straight road that runs eastward from Lake Como up the monotonous Valtellina. We were approaching Sondrio when Wharton grunted and pointed up to the left, where the steep scrub-covered hillsides ran into a leaden roof of grey cloud. 'Italian friend of mine in New York's got a chalet up there', he said. 'A place called Chiareggio. Says there's an incredible mountain up there. Completely isolated, great north ice face and one of the best ice ridges in the Alps. No-one in Britain seems to know anything about it!' I nodded; my legs and backside ached, but the facts registered. We bowled on towards Bolzano.

Several years later Springett and I climbed the delightful West Arête of the Ago di Sciora in the Swiss Bergell, and settled down among the summit blocks for a lazy lunch. The weather was perfect and the view superb. To the south-east it was dominated by a shapely spire, perhaps ten miles away; the ice glinted on its faces and it stood considerably higher than the spiky tangle of intervening tops. It was a fine looking peak. We consulted our map and it was obviously Monte Disgrazia, just over 12,000 feet high and by far the highest peak in the Bergell, but isolated and aloof from the main chain on a long subsidiary ridge leading down into Italy. I remembered what Wharton had said. This must be the mountain. Springett and I resolved to have a closer look.

A week later we had found our way to the Porro Hut high above the little Italian village of Chiareggio and just below the snout of the long Ventina Glacier that pours down the eastern flank of Disgrazia itself. Obviously English visitors to the hut were rare, for we were wined and dined and treated as special guests in the best Italian alpine tradition. The helpful guardian spoke no English and we no Italian, but we gathered that the famous ice arête was called the Corda Molla and we decided that we would try to find it. It seemed that the approaches were long and complex and that first we must find a pair of tiny bivouac huts, hidden in a maze of subsidiary rock peaks and steep ice falls.

The weather was not hopeful, but we left the hut three hours before dawn expecting to waste several hours route-finding. Lost in the pre-dawn darkness in a maze of moraines on the west side – the wrong side – of the Ventina Glacier, feeling bleary, hollow and slightly sick (the standard alpine pre-dawn syndrome), we had eventually to stop and wait for the first light. We were hopeful that it was fine weather mist which obscured the stars, but we knew deep down that the clouds must be clinging damply to the summits around us. How often has that forlorn dawn ritual been performed since men first climbed the Alps? Dawn never came: it was merely a fitful grey light that slowly happened. We found ourselves at the bottom of a shattered rock face rising into the damp overcast. We could either retrace our steps, or venture up a steep and evil-looking couloir of stone-scarred ice, in which a series of peeling 'schrunds gaped open onto streaming black slabs –

Monte Disgrazia rises aloof and separated from the main chain of the Bergell. This telephoto from the Ago di Sciora some ten miles away shows clearly the route from Monte Sissone to the Passo Cecilia and up the arced snow arête of the North-West Ridge

Overleaf: Two British climbers seen at work on the North Face of the Cima di Rosso, a classic ice climb in the Bergell area. The picture is taken from the North Face Rib of the mountain

obviously a swift entry into the underworld. Rather than go home we climbed the face. It was scrappy, rather loose and not particularly difficult; but it was about 1300 feet high and at least it was exercise. Springett was very excited to discover great veins of raw asbestos, grey fibrous stuff like somebody's long-lost rotting sweater caught in a rock sandwich. 'Hey man', he shouted, 'if they'd only a run a railway up here it would be worth a lot of money'. Springett happens to be a mining geologist.

We reached a damp and unpleasant summit and set off through the drizzling mist to a wet snowfield. Suddenly we saw it – a little tin bivvy hut at the base of the snowfield – and we made for it. Now we knew where we were. It was the Bivouac Taveggia and we had climbed the north face of the Sentinella della Vergine, for our sins. Disgrazia was as far off as ever. We stumbled down the ice-fall to the Ventina Glacier and, wet and cold, made for the Porro Hut. Within a few hours we were heading fast south-westward towards the blue Mediterranean and the warm limestone of the Calanques.

The following year I met up briefly with Springett again and we made the first ascent of the North Face Rib of the Cima di Rosso. It was my first route of the season and his last. From the north side the Rosso is a fine-looking mountain and the climbing was mixed, the sort that I enjoy; we were feeling pretty clever when we got to the top. Immediately southward, rising high and icy from the deep shadows of the Val Sissone, a patchwork of dark pinewoods and grey moraines, was Disgrazia. The sight was stunning. We were spellbound. The great ice pillar of the North Face swept upwards from a skirt of incredibly tangled glacier to a triple-spired summit. The Face was bounded on its right by the shiny black-scaled pyramid of Monte Pioda while to the left the curling arcs of what was obviously the Corda Molla swept downwards into a jumble of minor rock peaks. Even as we watched a large avalanche peeled itself from the ice pillar and spilled down in a cloud of white dust into the hungry maze below. The rumble of the falling ice took several seconds to reach us. We were both silent. Avalanche always has a very sobering effect. If you are sitting in the sun on a safe mountain top, experiencing the 'high' that only a first ascent can generate, it swiftly brings you down to earth. To hell with the North Face, I thought. You can keep that! But it was the most beautiful mountain I had ever seen. I was determined to climb it.

My chance came exactly a week later. I was very fit, with three more good climbs slotted in, one a long mixed route, and one a plum first ascent. But my partner, Pete Crew, had an appointment to keep in Chamonix while I had time for just one more climb before flying home to my wife and three-week-old baby. Alone in the late afternoon I walked up the long dusty glen to the Forno Hut – a friendly place then run by the cheery Yorkshire wife of Hans Phillip, a young and well-known local guide. I knew I was sure of a welcome. The hut had pleasant associations, for it was from there one night that I had watched

the moon, full and round and hanging low over the crenellated black shape of Castello, as the first men were setting foot on it and the live broadcast crackled out from a transistor loud and clear into the frosty air. I was pleased to note that I had taken only two hours for the dusty seven-mile slog up from Maloja, half my time of a week before.

Hans expressed no surprise at my plans, but suggested that I might need to use the Mello bivvy hut, strategically placed on the long rocky ridge linking Disgrazia to the rest of the Bergell. I was away from the still-sleeping hut at 3.30 a.m., into the silent and velvet night.

Moving steadily uphill before drawn is a bittersweet experience. Your body is hot, but under the rucksack the sweat on your back is cold and clammy. Your stubbled face is raw to the crisp air and your lips are dry. Only your eyes watch the dawn arrive, for your mind is slow and, when in the cosy flush of the new sun, it catches up, the dawn is gone. Three miles and three thousand feet of easy but crevasse-strewn snow fields took me through the dawn to the summit of Monte Sissone. From there I could plot the major features of my route, thrown into sharp relief by the early sunshine. Then I was scrambling down the short southern crags onto steep *névé* which gave an exhilarating glissade towards the misty blue abyss of the Val di Mello. Somewhere down here I knew there was a path, the Roma Traverse, a high-level route connecting the huts in the southern Italian cwms of the Bergell, via a series of passes in the jagged intervening ridges. Finding it should guarantee finding the passes, but I didn't find it. Perhaps I kept too high, for I was anxious to lose no more height than was strictly necessary. I found myself traversing awkward and broken ground along the flanks of the ridge leading to my mountain.

Eventually I found myself below a rock needle, a smaller edition of the Grand Capucin, which I had seen from Sissone; in front rose the steep glacier that hangs from the western flanks from Monte Pioda. Somewhere above me was the Passo Cecilia, a secret passage in the ridges like the staggered entrance to an Iron Age hill fort, leading onto the Preda Rossa Glacier in the main south-west cirque of Disgrazia itself.

On with crampons, and a steep rhythmic 1600-foot plod to find the Passo with no difficulty. For the first time since the dawn I allowed my mind to wander. Contrary to what people may imagine, the excitement of solo climbing is a subconscious thing. Moving fast over difficult ground demands great concentration, and although there is an incredible delight in being alone, indeed an excitement akin perhaps to fear, the business of navigation allows no time for idle musing. The mind is totally involved with the job in hand. Not so, however, on that long methodical plod, where the only break was the occasional crevasse that required negotiating or the quick about-turn from leftward zig to rightward zag. For the first time I could consciously analyze the pleasures of my loneness and explore its motivation.

The snow on the Preda Rossa Glacier was already soft and sticky. A well-trodden line of footprints rose from where the Ponti Hut lay out of sight below towards the lowest point of the ridge ahead – the North West Ridge of Disgrazia itself. The south west face of the mountain, flat and red in the morning sun, rose to my right, a jumbled mass of small buttresses and facets and steep weeping-snow patches. I could see a couple of parties high on the Ridge, hardly moving dots against the cobalt emptiness of the sky.

I passed a struggling party of three with a cheery 'Buon giorno', negotiated a couple of awkward 'schrunds and arrived on the Ridge. There was a slight breeze and I rolled down my sleeves and slipped on my cagoule. And now only 1000 feet to the summit.

Right: Climbers descending the North-West Ridge of Monte Disgrazia. Below them are the final slopes of the Spigolo Inglese

Above: The Forno Hut, a typical Swiss Alpine Club mountain hut, above the Forno Glacier in the Bergell Alps

Far right: Monte Disgrazia seen from the summit of the Cima di Rosso. The long snow and rock ridge of the Corda Molla drops left from the summit; below the summit is the icy North Face and on its right the obvious rib of the Spigolo Inglese

This was the route of the first ascent in August 1862 by Leslie Stephen, Edward Kennedy, Thomas Cox and Melchior Anderegg. It is easy climbing, but very exposed and continuously interesting. A narrow rock ridge alternates with a snow or ice arête. At times I paused to let a descending party pass, or to peer over the edge at the unfolding northern face. I recognized the steep Spigolo Inglese, the ice rib on the west side of the Face and the first route on it. It was climbed in 1910 by the great Scottish pioneers, Harold Raeburn and W. N. Ling; it is said not to be easy. Then I could see the upper section of the Face proper – a band of steep rock at the summit above a hanging icefield sweeping down towards the top of the great pillar. Below that only the dappled depths of the Val Sissone.

The summit was small and rocky, and to reach it I had to make an exposed step – a wide and awkward bridging move – over an icy

chimney. It was 10.45 a.m. and I dug out a little food and took some photographs. In a zinc container below the metal cross was the summit book, and reading through it I was able to find only two other British entries over the past dozen years. One was Eric Shipton and his son; and the other – it was no surprise really – John Wharton with an American friend. So he'd made it at last, and beaten me to it!

I was back at the Forno Hut for a quick brew, just after 4 p.m., much to Hans's surprise, and then I trotted down in the dusk to Maloja and gallons of tea, and home.

All winter that Face haunted me and the 'high' of that fabulous day lingered in my mind. Come summer again, with our equipment already in Moscow, the Russians withdrew our visas for the Caucasus,

At dusk the North Face of
Monte Disgrazia looks
forbidding — on the left is
the Bivouac Oggioni and the
snow arc of the Corda Molla
leads up towards the summit.
On the far right-hand side of
the face is the Spigolo
Inglese and further still
Monte Pioda

but I knew exactly where I wanted to go instead. And so the 1st of
August found me back at the Porro Hut with 'Pin' Howell, who had
been coming to Russia with me and is one of my closest friends. With
us also were Pete Biven and Alison Chadwick, friends from Devon
and south-western sea-cliff specialists.

The guardian warned us that the snow that season was poor and
everything was hard blue ice. The Face he said was 'unthinkable',
but the Spigolo Inglese might go, though it would involve arduous step
cutting and might perhaps be rather dangerous. Pete and Ali had
planned for the Corda Molla anyway, and Pin and I decided that we'd
see what we'd see.

There was no difficulty finding the Taveggia Bivouac again by the
easy way, or in continuing to the Bivouac Oggioni. It was perched at

At dusk the North Face of Monte Disgrazia looks forbidding — on the left is the Bivouac Oggioni and the snow arc of the Corda Molla leads up towards the summit. On the far right-hand side of the face is the Spigolo Inglese and further still Monte Pioda

10,300 feet on the crest of the ridge that eventually became the Corda Molla, in most impressive surroundings, above a huge drop. There was even a short, but very exposed ice pitch to reach the hut door, and before dark Pin and I recce'd the route down to the glacier below and fixed abseil ropes for the morning. The hut was cosy, but Alison lost a contact lens and spent half the night searching for it by the light of a guttering candle, while Pin dreamed of drowning in a sea of porridge.

We abseiled into the dawn and cramponed across alarmingly steep slopes to reach the little ice sanctuary below the face. Here the ice was smooth, but behind us were acres of most twisted icefall I had ever seen. The Spigolo Inglese looked a fine line but it led nowhere near the summit. Much of last year's great ice pillar had fallen away, revealing a steep rock rib leading high into the face, but menaced by the hanging ice. We both felt that it looked promising and I led off across the 'schrund and up 100 feet of ice to reach the jutting bottom of the rib. The rock was blank so I tied onto a good ice screw. Pin came up and, still wearing his crampons, started powering his way up the rock. It was smooth and the holds sloped awkwardly but he managed to place a large nut some thirty feet up. Suddenly there was a cry. He was off. The loose block came whining past my ear. With a crash Pin hit me. I held him. We untangled ourselves – he was shaken but unhurt. My breeches and thighs were torn by his crampons but the nut was still in place. He must have hit me on the stretch of the rope. More stones came whirring through space and the air was filled with a stomach chilling sulphurous whiff of rock dust. The sun was on the summit and rock fall was starting in earnest. 'Let's get out of here', I shouted. 'Too damn right', cried Pin.

Back down on the glacier we took stock of the situation. Time was getting on and there were three alternatives. We could retrace our steps to the bivvy hut and waste the whole expedition, for it was far too late to embark on the Corda Molla. We could attempt the Spigolo. Or we could return to the Face. We studied the line carefully. The whole upper face funnelled into a wide couloir to the right of our rib, down which there was now regular rock-fall, but what had frightened us seemed to have been an isolated salvo straying from the couloir. Valour got the better part of discretion and we returned to the rib.

Without crampons the first rock pitch proved no problem and was followed by several more before we arrived at a small snow patch beneath a steep bastion. Here there was a rusty piton but we could see no possibility above it. Pin led left into a sort of ice runnel between the rock and the remains of the great pillar; it was completely overhung by shattered ice but led easily upwards. Gaining height is important for morale.

Eventually a weakness in the bastion led back right, but it was difficult and Pin climbed without crampons, the rock loose and shaly and seamed with asbestos. There was no friction at all and I followed wearing my crampons, which was comforting for they bit into the

79

stuff; but I pulled out his only protection peg easily with my fingers. Several more long rock pitches followed with the rib narrowing all the time until, leading, I found myself at the rope's limit, kneeling on a smooth wet mantleshelf, my face pressed into the bulging ice above, from beneath which water streamed. Awkwardly, the rope tugging back at me and my balance critical, I placed an ice screw and tied on. What was left of the rib tailed away diagonally rightwards, a series of rocky outcrops and islands disappearing behind the curve of the ice slope which hid the couloir. Above, the remains of the pillar bulged, drooling icicles. Scrabbly mixed climbing in crampons again led to the last outcrop right on the edge of the couloir. I looked at Pin. 'It's your lead', he said reassuringly. It was wide, two pitches at least, and the ice was scored into deep runnels and blackened with stones and rock dust. As I watched another salvo thundered down it. It was a frightening place but there was a hopefully broken looking rock rib on the far side. About 300 feet above us the ice bulge barred the slope right into the funnel of the couloir. 'It's narrower up there', I pointed out. 'Might only be one pitch and if I play it right it'll be yours!' A scatter of small rocks jutting from the ice led upwards and marked the final demise of the rib.

The second pitch up this dangerous ground was mine and as I climbed stones came spinning out of the funnel and across my path. I was terrified. A climbing fall is one thing, that's your own fault; but objective dangers never seem quite the same! A sort of cave appeared beneath the ice bulge and I thought it might provide a little cover, a brief respite before facing the bombardment in the funnel. I crawled into a sort of chimney, choked with powder snow but reassuringly subterranean. Pin came up, and while he dug out some chocolate I explored the back of the chimney. It led through – and up – and round and – suddenly we were on a big ice ledge. It was the lip of the upper hanging ice field and there were the summit rocks deceptively close above.

The tension eased. The apprehensive excitement of climbing into the unknown disappeared as the way ahead became clear and apparently safe. But experience reminded us that the most obvious lines hide the most unexpected difficulties. There can be no relaxation until safety is reached again at the bottom of the mountain. The slope was steep but covered with crisp snow, perfect for quick cramponing; we made height swiftly and easily. Soon we came to lines of narrow 'schrunds stretching right across the face. Always the upper lip overhung, but either to right or left there was a weakness. A short steep climb ending in a bulging pull-out on good finger holds in the firm snow above led us over the difficulty each time. It was the top 'schrund. I leaned out on my left hand, reached over the lip and stabbed hard with my fingers into the snow above. An explosion of pain. A red haze in my eyes and I was falling backwards.

I struggled upright in the soft powder of the 'schrund bottom and

ripped the mitten off my right hand. My middle finger was bent back along itself from the joint. It had been hard blue ice above the 'schrund. Suddenly I was sick and crying like a child. Round and round in my mind went the thought 'I was born with that finger . . . it's mine and I've lost it'.

Eventually I got a grip of myself and brought Pin up unbelayed. He was very comforting and together we straightened out the finger and lashed it together with a torn handkerchief. The hand was already swelling noticeably and it was obvious that I would be unable to take any serious part in the rest of the climb. And it was ice – hard ice. Pin was the rock specialist and the ice had been all for me! And now it was late afternoon.

Pin led off again, but now he cut steps and placed ice screws every so often. I joined him on a tight rope, feeling very sick and wobbly, my right arm tied across my chest with a spare tape sling. We reached the summit cliffs where there seemed to be a weakness and the climbing got difficult again. The rock was steep, plastered with verglas, and the climbing was strenuous, athletic and interrupted by a series of icy mantleshelves. Pin was magnificent. He held me on a tight rope while I bodged up as best I could, using my right elbow where I really needed a right hand. The hand itself was merely a delicate throbbing mass that had to be kept well out of the way.

With great relief we crawled on to the summit ridge a few yards from the top. Wisps of cloud drifted round and, now that the tension was off, and we were still, it was very cold. The light was beginning to fail. We looked beneath the cross for the summit book, saw that Pete and Ali had completed the Corda Molla and descended hours ago, and scratched our own names in it – luckily I am lefthanded. Then we looked for a bivvy site and found a smooth sloping ledge, well out of the wind, a hundred feet below the ridge. We had the communal gas stove with what was left of the cartridge from last night's brew, but Pete had the pot. Pin found a rusty beer can and we struggled into our duvets and started a brew. It was only tepid water with a dissolved boiled sweet, but it was nectar and I lapsed into a troubled sleep.

Sometimes I awoke, if that is what the transition from half consciousness to three-quarter consciousness is called, with thunder in my ears, to feel mist blowing round my face and see the flashes of distant lightning over the Bernina. Once it started to snow. Then it was dawn, bleak and grey. We struggled with another brew before packing up and searching for a route downwards. We were already on it – a ramp line leading eventually to the upper *névé* of the Ventina Glacier, by a series of easy abseils which were painful and awkward one handed. Down and down and still down – rock, snow, glacier and moraine. Distance seemed nothing, moving with mechanical steps till there on the meadow by the glacier snout was Biven, come up to meet us. 'Hey man', he called, 'we thought you were dead'.

My love affair with Disgrazia was over.

Entertainment on the Matterhorn

It was bound to be an epic season after the journey out. We raced hell-for-leather for the midnight boat, threw a fanbelt somewhere in the depths of rural Kent, and in disgust climbed over the roadside wall to bivouac. Dawn found us in the lush summer grass of the village graveyard! It was a very auspicious start.

We drove via the tedious autobahns to Munich, where we fortified our luck by shopping for crash helmets at Sporthaus Schuster. In those days nothing was available in England but caver's helmets and we felt these would be a little infradig on world-wide television. We proceeded to Innsbruck, where we met up with Austrian friends Rusty had met in Kenya and enjoyed an excellent day in the Karwendel. We needed the exercise. Then down to Lecco: a visit to Cassin resulted in a 'deal' which filled the van with cheap pitons, and an excellent day followed exploring the Grigna and lazing on the limestone in the sun. But this was little better than Dorset – except for the excellent ice cream to be had in the town!

At last we were in Switzerland, and we set off to Zermatt to link up with the BBC expeditionary force. The first Briton we saw, striding nonchalantly down the main street, hands in the pockets of his dirty jeans, was none other than Davy Crabbe, MacInnes's apprentice. 'Och, you'll no get by in those boots', he greeted us. 'They're dreadful! Yon hill's plastered and they'll no keep the water oot. It's just like the Ben on a wet Hogmanay'. Indeed, he was right. The snow on the 'hill' lay right down below Schwarzsee and the paths leading upwards through the woods were running with melt-water.

Perhaps I should explain: the year was 1965 and on July 14th was to fall the 100th Anniversary of the tragic first ascent of the Matterhorn. The occasion had prompted the Swiss to declare '65 as 'The Year of the Alps' to be marked by frolics, fun and festivities throughout the country, and by exhibitions as far away as London. The BBC, in conjunction with Radio Geneva, had decided to mark the anniversary with a most ambitious project – nothing less than an ascent of the Matterhorn televised live, and scheduled for transmission by landline throughout the Eurovision link and by satellite to America. It was hoped the climb would be seen by millions of viewers, unfolding instantly in all its reality, as it happened and when it happened. In all seriousness 'live television' is very different from film or even from telerecording, and the BBC's Outside Broadcast Department had, by the mid-sixties, brought the practice of this most fraught of television techniques to a fine art, second to none. Its previous two live rock-climbing broadcasts, particularly the most recent on the great limestone roof of Kilnsey Crag in Yorkshire, had proved highly successful. Now the Matterhorn was to be attempted – with the full backing of the Swiss and the participation of the Swiss Army Signals Corps.

Television on the Matterhorn. The nearest full size television camera to the action was this static cable-operated one placed just above the Hornli Hut. Above is the Hornli Ridge leading to the summit of the Matterhorn, still a mile away

It seemed a bold concept then, but looking back on it, and knowing the mountains as fickle partners and the Matterhorn as bigger and more fickle than most, it can only seem foolhardy in retrospect. But nothing ventured nothing gained – and so there we were in Zermatt.

Up at the Hornli Hut the snow was deep and crisp and even, but all was not silent. The Belvedere Inn next door had been turned into a television control-room and it was packed with television people – engineers, technicians, directors, producers and personalities, British and Swiss. Few had ever been on a mountain before; most were suffering from the altitude, and all were shouting in their own language at no one in particular. The smell was bad, worse than usual, but

The cameraman's camp on the Hornli Ridge. Rusty Baillie and Hamish MacInnes relax with a 'wee dram' outside the tent. In the distance the South Face of the Obergabelhorn catches the evening light

we had already decided to camp. We found two good tent platforms among the boulders on the north side of the ridge, a few hundred feet above the Hut, and there we pitched our tent in the falling snow.

There were four of us: Hamish MacInnes, the 'Fox of Glencoe', and myself – both freelance cameramen, assigned to operate portable radio-cameras on the climb to the summit; and our respective assistants, or 'tweakers', climbing partners who were expected to both hold the ropes and tweak the knobs – Davy Crabbe and Rusty Baillie.

The snow fell for several days and as we learned more of our jobs and the plans for the programme we began to realize more and more how impractical were the arrangements to carry them out. There was a big TV camera with a very long lens on a railway flat-car on the Gornergrat line more than five miles from the mountain, and another big camera which had been airlifted onto the ridge just above the Hut but still a mile from the summit and four thousand feet below it. These could picture the mountain and set the scene. But everything that was to happen during the climb, all the detail, the chat and the close-ups, was dependant entirely on our two portable cameras sending back radio pictures to the control-room at the Belvedere. And it was uncertain if they would even operate at the ranges and altitudes necessary!

Naturally transmission times had been scheduled weeks ahead and, come what may, we must be 'on the air' at six specific periods throughout July 14th. The schedule of transmission times bore little relation to the mountaineering involved. There was a lot to be carried: besides spare television equipment, batteries, cables and radios and suchlike, there was the normal gear needed by climbers on an easy route up a 14,700-foot Alpine peak . . . spare food, climbing gear and bivouac equipment. The loads we had to carry proved to be crucifying and porters were booked to assist with the logistics. However, it was the 'Year of the Alps', the best men were otherwise occupied, and our helpers did little to endear themselves to us. Some of them, we felt, would have been hard put to get to the summit of Tryfan! And to cap it the mountain had not yet been climbed that season! There had been a late spring and continuous storms.

In order to fit the scheduled transmission times, Hamish and I had decided, after the easy first transmission leaving the Hut at dawn, to leapfrog our respective teams up the mountain. I would handle the second transmission at a place we called 'The Wymper Bivouac', a photogenic site where a rocky step bars the ridge. We could easily reach it in time to get set up and get the camera tuned in before our 'cue'. Meanwhile Hamish would push on and select a likely site. By the time the next transmission was due, he would be operational and the 'stars' would be hurriedly approaching, suitably breathless and harassed. While he was 'on the air' my team would be dismantling their gear and moving up close behind the commentators, eventually to overtake them and get set up again at a photogenic site I would select just in time to meet the next transmission. And so on. We hoped it would work but it meant only one camera covering each 25-minute transmission – aided, of course, by the long lenses from far below. But it was the only answer to the dilemma.

One day there was a Press Conference at the Schwartzsee Hotel, on the alp half way down to Zermatt. Despite the TV personalities who were to make the climb up the Hornli Ridge and do the commentary, and the team of ace Swiss climbers who were to attempt the North Face at the same time in the hope we might see them en route, the four of us seemed to be the focus of the party. This seemed a little premature; but since we were to do the hard work, it seemed fair enough for free meals and plenty to drink, and it turned out a good laugh. One of the German newspapermen wished to discover something of our own climbing records, some of which were quite formidable: MacInnes had done a remarkable route in the Caucasus, the traverse of Shkhelda and, in typical Scottish style, had climbed for thirteen days on this particularly arduous route fortified only by enough food for three! He had also attempted Everest with a two-man team. Rusty Baillie too was a climber of distinction. He had made the second British ascent of the North Face of the Eiger with Dougal Haston and had many fine climbs in the Alps and in East and Southern Africa to his credit. 'And

High on the Matterhorn –
rotten and dangerous snow
on the Hornli Ridge just
below the Solvay Hut

vat ees your best climb plise Meester Crabbe?' There was a pause before Davy answered the question. 'Tis the traverse of the Cuillin in winter', he muttered eventually. 'But plise Meester Crabbe', said the reporter, 'Vere is ze Cuillin? Perhaps zis is Patagonia?' 'Nay mon, it's in God's own countree', said Crabbe aggressively. 'But plise Meester Crabbe', replied the puzzled German, anxious for his quote, 'Plise Meester Crabbe, vot do you zink of ze Alps?' 'Ach mon, 'tis good training fur Scotland in winter.' The last I have heard of Davy is that, after a short but meteoric alpine career and some considerable achievements on Scottish ice, he has given up climbing and turned to ski instructing! I suppose such a fate could happen to any of us.

July the 14th was a Wednesday. On Tuesday a complete rehearsal had been planned with the whole programme to be recorded on video-tape against the possibility – or indeed probability – of bad weather or disaster on the following day. On Monday it was planned that we should reach the summit, transmit pictures and make our final plans but with no worry about actual timings. But Monday was a catastrophe. The sun was too hot and the 'hill' was dangerous, knee deep in slush lying on ice. Our porters muttered and grumbled and became particularly unco-operative. Vital linking cables had been forgotten, important equipment broke down. Eventually we fought our way to the Solvay Hut but the cameras didn't work and we transmitted no pictures. We got back to the Hornli about six in the evening, it had been a very long day and we felt disappointed and frustrated. Luckily there was a plentiful supply of refreshment.

Allan Chivers, the BBC 'Supremo', a most inspiring man to work for and highly respected by the whole team, was not discouraged. Indeed he oozed confidence, whatever he must have felt himself. Anxious to do all he could to ease our problems on the mountain, he had sent his men through the Zermatt streets that day, contract forms in hand, and recruited the only two likely looking English climbers that could be found, as 'sherpas' to augment the unreliable porters. We were relieved to have Barry Whybrow and his companion with us, for at least here was somebody we could trust.

Tuesday was another grim day – but all was under control for the second transmission. I had time to select a good camera position beside the rock step and work out stage directions with 'Mac-the-Telly', Ian MacNaught-Davis, a well-known climbing 'spokesman' who had taken commentator Chris Brasher's place after Chris had been laid low with that occupational hazard of athletic mountaineers, piles. Mac was climbing with Heini Taugwalder, great-grandson of Wymper's guide on the first ascent, and Zermatt's chief guide that year. We all knew exactly what we were to do and where. Then came Chiv's steady voice crackling over my headphones 'Okay John, we've got you . . . good . . . nice picture – zoom in a bit . . . that's fine, we're on you now . . .'. Everything worked smoothly. Heini and Mac moved along the ridge crest silhouetted against the distant valley and the far

peaks of the Mischabel. They arrived close to camera, Mac panting a little and sweat dripping off his brow. He started to explain that even though the climbing was not difficult it was a big serious mountain they were on and this was where Wymper had bivouacked on the eve of his successful ascent exactly a hundred years ago. He was now close in front of me, standing against the rock step and right beside a bronze plaque bearing the inscription: 'Ici quatre hommes moururent dans un tempête 18'. I held his face full frame, and as he explained that four men had died in a stormy night right here, I zoomed wider to show the plaque to which his finger was now pointing. As I zoomed, the view finder was filled by four rotund little men sitting below the plaque wearing goblin-hats and eating sausages. There was a burst of indignation in my headphones and a shout of 'Cut – what the hell's going on'. I yelled at Rusty 'Who are they anyway? Get them out of the way'. Rusty scrambled off across the steep snow and started shouting and gesticulating. The four little men were rather cross; it seemed that they were the official Italian commentators, but as they had not arrived for the briefing they had not been briefed! We managed to communicate with them eventually and explained what was happening. They took it all with good grace and the transmission was able to proceed. It was lucky we were only on tape!

But the sun was still hot and the mountain still dangerous. Again equipment broke down and, although they knew that the summit sequence was scheduled for 3.0 p.m. on the morrow, our local porters refused to go high after midmorning and ultimately struck. Our brave 'sherpas' were doing a terrific job, but the complete enterprise seized up. There was nothing we could do and even our radio links with base were cluttered with jabbering voices in languages we couldn't understand. It was obvious that there was a shambles down there too. Finally Chiv, still sounding calm through the crackling radio, suggested that we call off the whole shambles and return to the Hut.

Drowning our frustrations in good Swiss beer outside the Hut, and awaiting the usual debriefing session with a now noticeably white-haired Chiv, a hush fell on the assembled party. Stepping daintily barefoot through the snow under a large rucksack was Mary Stewart. 'Who's that?', I heard someone whisper to Davy. 'A Scots mother of five', he answered loudly. 'She'd show those lazy bloody porters'. Mary was indeed mother of five bonnie children in Glasgow – a tough redhaired vet and a friend of ours. Close behind plodded other Glaswegian friends – Ian 'Jock' Martin, Johnnie Wright, Chris Patterson and . . . wonders never ceased . . . Eric Beard, the Leeds fell runner and known in ACG circles as 'The Alpine Clown'. 'Grab them Chiv', shouted Hamish. 'Sign them on quick'. And so at the eleventh hour help arrived. With Beardie to keep us laughing and the others to augment the 'sherpa' party, only the weather could stop us now. Perhaps our luck was turning?

And on the day everything went according to plan except, of course, there was no plan. The first transmission went off without a hitch at dawn. Everything went smoothly for the second transmission and my party leap-frogged Hamish and arrived at the shoulder just in time to set up, net in and work out 'stage directions' with Mac and Heini. Then we were in cloud and the next transmission was to be from the summit at three p.m. One of the camera outfits had blown up but we got the other to the top with little trouble and now, against the clock, started to net in. We were delighted when, only a minute before we were due on the air, Chiv's voice came excitedly over the radio and told us that they had pictures and good ones too. We were operating now at more than the designed range of the camera.

I remember little about that transmission. The 'stars' arrived, back-slapping and handshaking, while Michel and Yvette Vaucher, Hilti von Allmen and Paul Etter arrived over the convex curve that hid the North Face and joined in the mutual congratulations. Hamish bore the brunt of the transmission and I remember that towards the end the sherpas had actually to hold him up. The fierce concentration and physical effort required to hold the heavy camera to the eye, keeping millions of viewers all over the world glued to their screens, made for a gruelling half hour. But as far as I was concerned the crux was to come. The next transmission, the final one, was mine; it was supposed to cover the site of the accident where, a hundred years ago, Douglas Hadow had fallen. The rope had broken and he had dragged Lord Francis Douglas, Rev. Charles Hudson and the guide, Michael Croz over the North Face to their deaths, leaving a horror-struck Wymper and his remaining two guides, Taugwalders, father and son, alone on the mountain. The actual site must have fallen away long ago but we had selected an appropriate looking place in about the right position, somewhere below the fixed ropes and out to the right of the Shoulder

Climbing camera team on the shoulder of the Hornli Ridge. The author is using the radio while Rusty Baillie, in crash helmet, adjusts the transmitter pack

on the edge of the Face. Unfortunately, with only one camera operational we could no longer apply our leap-frog techniques.

As soon as Hamish was off the air, my team descended on the equipment like vultures, packed it and set off at a run back down the 'roof' to the steep ground above the fixed ropes. But the piste ploughed in the snow was already occupied by a slow-moving caravan of commentators, celebrities and guides of several nationalities. The transmission was due to start in forty minutes; now every second was precious. There were angry scenes as we tried to pass. Rusty even exchanged blows with an obdurate guide. Admittedly, unroped as we were – for speed – and loaded with 50 lb packs, we could not have seemed a very good insurance risk! But we made it – just – and we came on the air exactly on time.

Mac was marvellous. Moving gingerly down what was particularly unpleasant and exposed ground, and held on a short rope by Heini, he was in the process of explaining that this was where the accident had happened, when suddenly his own feet shot from beneath him and he fell, only to be held easily after a few feet, by Heini. Afterwards Mac claimed that it had not been an intentional fall and that the rock really had been loose and slippery, but it was good television! The tension was unbearable. I was exhausted by this time and the camera was getting very heavy. Chiv came over the radio and asked if I was prepared to 'over-run' for a further ten minutes as a special request from London. Naturally we agreed and followed the progress of the other parties down over the dangerous ground and back to the shoulder. At long last the radio crackled again and Chiv said 'Great John, that's fine, we're off you now. Thank you, my boy, thank you.' And it was all over. I let the camera fall on to its strap and collapsed against the rope. There was a rumble as the big boulder on which I had been propped tumbled away with a whiff of sulphurous smoke and went plunging down the North Face. Rusty grabbed me and pulled me back to safety and a big mug of tea, which the sherpas had been brewing. We'd done it!

But it was not quite the end. It was now late afternoon and the mountain was swirling in cloud. As we descended a thunderstorm hit us. Verglas coated the rocks and lightning flickered and crashed into the mountain around us. We dumped a lot of equipment in the Solvay Hut so that we could move down more easily and safely. Mac claims he saw a porter swing off his rucksack – heavily loaded with BBC electronics – to remove his crampons. These must have pierced a charged capacitor or something for he received a hefty electric shock and with a cry of 'Himmel, the BBC has bewitched me', hurled his rucksack and its expensive contents far over the black void of the Face. But I cannot confirm the story. We reached the Hut at last; a drink was waiting, there was backslapping all round and then a fast run down, down through the falling snow to Schwartzsee, where the last teleferique had been held waiting for us. Down through the night to the twinkling lights and fleshpots of Zermatt.

Left: On the summit of the
Matterhorn, Ian MacNaught-
Davis interviews Heini
Taugwalder, the Chief Guide
of Zermatt in 1967. Heavy
radio camera to his eye,
Hamish MacInnes – almost
exhausted – is supported by
British 'Sherpa' Barry
Whybrow

Above: The final transmission
at the 'Whymper accident
site'. The author, supported
by Rusty Baillie, fights the
'overrun' specially requested
by London

3 North America

Previous page: Mount Hood (11,245 feet) is a beautiful ice-plastered extinct volcano in north-west Oregon; it provides some entertaining climbing

Top left: Impressive sandstone buttes and spires on the east bank of the Colorado River in the Canyonlands near Moab in Utah

Top centre: Fine climbing on extremely rough granite near Laramie in Wyoming

Top right: Rusty Baillie in action on the excellent rock of the Granite Dells near Prescott, Arizona

Below: On Beckey's Wall in Lower Cottonwood Canyon just a few miles outside Salt Lake City

Below right: In the Shawangunks of New York State — the direct finish of Thin Slabs. These crags are extremely popular with climbers on the East Coast

Introduction to a new world

North American climbers are lucky. A wide mountain system fills much of Alaska and most of western Canada. It extends south throughout the western third of the United States and deep into Mexico. In the near-arctic north rise giant mountains of Himalayan proportions – including Mount McKinley at 20,320 feet, the continent's highest summit. In south-western Canada three major ranges contain many fine glaciated peaks of alpine style: Mount Waddington in the Coast Range is 13,260 feet and Mount Robson, in the Rockies, 12,972 feet. In the U.S. a huge variety of mountains extend over eleven States, from ice-plastered extinct volcanoes such as Mount Rainier (14,410 feet) and Mount Hood in the Pacific North-West, through a myriad rock peaks in such ranges as the Cascades, the Olympics, the Sawtooths, the Tetons, the Wind Rivers, the Wasatch and the

Colorado Rockies, to the weird sandstone spires of the south-western deserts. They culminate in Mount Whitney (14,495 feet), a granite wedge in the Californian Sierra Nevada. Unfortunately, apart from the north-western volcanoes, there is little glacial ice in the contiguous United States.

Even in the East there are the hilly ranges of the Appalachian Mountains, which extend from New England into the deep South and contain many fine crags. Across the border, Mexico too has worthy mountains, including volcanic cones such as Citlaltepetl (18,700 feet) and, almost untouched by the cragsman, the Sierra Madres and the Sierra Juarez of the Baja Peninsular.

As a mass sport, however, mountaineering is young in America. Despite early visitors to the Alps, expatriates like Coolidge, and the founding of the Williamstown Alpine Club in 1863 and the famous Appalachian Club in 1876, much of the early exploration and first ascents fell to soldiers and surveyors – men engaged in extending the 'frontier', rather than in mountaineering for itself.

Gannet Peak (13,785 feet) in the Wind Rivers fell to a Captain Bonneville in 1833, and it seems Lieutenant Kieffer bagged the Grand Teton (13,766 feet) sixty years later. Clarence King, the famous surveyor, made many difficult ascents in the sixties and seventies, notably California's Mount Tyndall (14,018 feet). He became a fine mountaineer and it is evident from his excellent book *Climbing in the Sierra Nevada* that he greatly enjoyed his work among the mountains.

Alpine mountaineering in North America began in the Selkirks, one of the interior ranges of British Columbia. The catalyst was the arrival of the Canadian-Pacific Railway in 1885. Suddenly spectacular peaks such as Sir Donald (10,818 feet) were easily accessible and gentlemen from the Alpine Club, the Swiss Alpine Club and the Appalachian Mountain Club were quick to exploit the fact. By 1899 two Swiss guides, Feuz and Hasler, were resident in the area and subsequently played an important part in the development of Canadian mountaineering.

But mountaineering evolved slowly in America. Serious rock climbing developed in Yosemite during the thirties; men like Charles Houston and Terris Moore were active in the Himalaya and Sikang; great mountains were climbed in Alaska and the Yukon – but it was not until after the Second War, and more particularly after the 'ecological revolution' of the sixties, that mountains and climbing found popular appeal. Young Americans went abroad to climb while foreign climbers visited America. Yosemite was the 'mecca' where, with little outside influence, Americans had themselves developed the most advanced aid-climbing in the world. Ideas crossed the Atlantic – both ways – thick and fast.

One summer Sunday in 1972 Park Service rangers in Yosemite counted 2000 roped climbers active in the Valley. Climbing had 'caught on'.

Far left: Yosemite — the
3000-foot buttress of El
Capitan (7042 feet) towers
over the wooded valley floor.
In the distance Clouds Rest
and (right) Half Dome

Left: Half Dome — this
spectacular 8842-foot peak
dominates Yosemite Valley.
It is well seen from Glacier
Point against a summer
thunder storm brewing over
the High Sierra. On the left is
the 2000-foot north west
face

Above: Granite — on El
Capitan. Heart Route goes
somewhere up here

Royal Robbins
Hard man from Modesto

It must have been about 1960 that the British climbing public became first aware of serious climbers and real climbing in that most bountiful of the lands across the Atlantic – the U.S.A. We all knew that the Americans could do many things, and do them well, but somehow we had not suspected that climbing was one of them. Whispered and mispronounced at first, a name synonymous with that other mountain valley of Shangri La came to climbers' ears. A name invested with romance and legend: Yosemite, where rock walls dwarfing the Empire State Building were said to overhang for thousands of feet and where the weather was supposed to be eternal spring. And linked with Yosemite were men's names. One in particular was Royal Robbins.

I first saw Royal in the Bar National at Chamonix, that little cafe in the main square that replaces the Padarn Lake for the alpine season and where the impecunious English-speaking climbers gather to gossip, play table-football and get drunk. It must have been just before his 1965 Direct Route on the Dru because he was sitting plotting with John Harlin, the 'blond god', and certainly the most outstanding American mountaineer of the day; we were introduced briefly by Bonington. It was not until the following year that I met him to talk to and then it was at a far more improbable place – Holyhead Railway Station, platform one. It was the spring of 1966 and his first visit to Britain. Coming direct from snow-plastered Switzerland he was still impressed by the little green fields and stone walls of Anglesey and the mist-hung Carneddau rising behind the coastal railway. He strode across the platform, tall in a ski jacket and Levi cords and the famous flat white hat, a bulging rucksack on his shoulder. He was slim but with very wide shoulders and although he'd shaved off his beard I recognized at once the tall forehead and the shrewd blue-grey eyes behind the horn-rimmed spectacles. Although his hand when he shook mine was powerful, a real rock-man's hand, he looked more a gentle academic than a legendary 'hard-man'.

At my suggestion, the BBC had invited Royal to appear as 'guest star' in a TV climbing 'spectacular' which was scheduled to be transmitted live from the then virgin sea-cliffs of South Stack, Holyhead, on Easter Saturday. He was to join Joe Brown, Ian MacNaught-Davis and Tom Patey in an epic which Tom well described in his excellent book *One Man's Mountains* as 'The Greatest Show on Earth'. He soon made an impression on the team of climbers assembled for the project; not just on the other stars, but the 'sherpas', cameramen and commentators alike. His rock-climbing was delightful to watch and as superb as we had been led to believe. We soon discovered that his outwardly thoughtful and serious demeanour concealed wry stabs of humour and an occasional disarming smile. Royal best remembers this week as his introduction to the social life of British climbing, a scene which he greatly enjoys and in which he now regularly partakes. It was, as he told me later, such a pleasant contrast to the American scene where most climbers take themselves in deadly earnest.

Little Yosemite Valley seen from Washburn Point. The Merced River pours over the 200-foot high Vernal Fall, and on the left rock walls rise towards Mt. Broderick

101

My own particular memory of the programme was at the end, when Royal, belayed on the cliff top, was bringing Tom Patey up the final vertical wall. It had been aid climbing, and Royal had swung up through the overhangs with his usual effortless ease, while Tom, a brilliant ice climber, but not at home with 'mere gadgets', was fighting and suffering every inch of the way. He finally emerged, rope draped and breathless on the cliff top. Royal looked hard at Tom's raw and bleeding hands. 'Back home in the States', he remarked, 'they say you can always tell a good Aid-Man by his hands'. 'Lots of scars?', suggested Tom hopefully. Royal shook his head gently 'No scars', he said.

Royal Robbins was born in 1935 in West Virginia, but when he was six his family moved out west and settled in Los Angeles. At school he was never interested by conventional sports, and at an age when small boys set their sights on being engine-drivers or baseball stars, young Royal saw himself as a Robin Hood character and had decided to become a professional adventurer. It was this desire for adventure which took him out into the countryside of Southern California, where at the age of fifteen he was first consciously aware of the intense physical delight he found in surmounting a difficult move on rock. It was a mere bridging move in a small canyon but it left a lasting impression on his young mind. This is, after all, one of the things that rock climbing is all about.

1950 was a milestone year. Robbins was fifteen, he left school and decided that he wanted to ski. Although Southern California is not the world's best ski area, there is good snow not far distant in a country where travel is easy, and he found a job in a ski resort. Royal enjoyed the physical pleasures of skiing; it was wild and fast and needed boldness and determination, but most of all it required co-ordination and control. Soon he was good enough to be chosen to represent California in the Junior National Championships. Since then skiing has played a very important part in his life. To take up skiing was, he considers in retrospect, the wisest decision of his life.

Most important, however, was his decision to take up serious climbing. For some years he had been reading widely about mountaineering, but it was James Ramsey Ullman, and in particular his book *High Conquest,* who inspired this desire to climb. In America today Ullman is considered a passé mountain writer, much as Frank Smythe and his 'spirit of the hills' style has been considered here of late years. But while it is easy to denigrate popular writers of the recent past, there is no doubt that they did capture the atmosphere and feeling of the mountains that has inspired so many tyro mountaineers. Robbins was no exception: spurred on by Ullman and by a belief that here was a pastime which was both romantic and personal, which could harm nobody but oneself, and which demanded total commitment both physical and mental, he started to climb, solo at first, at nearby Tahquitz Rock. At once he found that rock climbing came

A telephoto picture of the great North-West Face of Half Dome taken from the high country north of Tenaya Canyon

easily – he was a 'natural'. Within a couple of years he had put up America's first 5.9 climb on The Rock.

It was as a boyscout that Royal first visited Yosemite, the valley with which his name was to be so inextricably linked. It was not long after he started climbing that he returned, this time with a young friend and an old rope. They had no ambitious intentions and as Robbins emphasizes, The Valley is no place to go just scrambling. As it happened his companion was terrified just to be there and they climbed nothing, but Royal remembers being acutely conscious of the huge virgin walls arcing into the sky and more inquisitive than overawed.

He was 19 when he climbed his first Yosemite route; he had teamed up with Jerry Gallwas and together they made the second ascent of Yosemite Point Buttress, a 1200 foot classic close by the Yosemite Falls and Lost Arrow pinnacle. It was a two day route with some hard free climbing which had been put up the previous year by Al Steck and Bob Swift. It was quite an achievement, but was soon to be dramatically overshadowed by his first 'big' route in the Valley, the second ascent of the Salathe-Steck route on the North Face of Sentinel, a line still considered by many to be the best climb in Yosemite. The first ascent three years before in 1950 had taken 4½ gruelling days, and the climbing was 5.9 and A3. Royal and his companions, Gallwas again, and Don Wilson, reckoned to take five and were very surprised to complete the route in two days. Looking back he feels that they managed some pretty inspired climbing but cringes at the thought of some of the dangerous antics they got up to, particularly a 50 foot uncontrolled pendule which left him battered and breathless. Quite obviously a second ascent of this sort must have come to the notice of the leading climbers in the Valley, but Royal claims that in those days there was no thought of prestige or fame in their minds. For a start there was no competition, so few other people climbed; and he and his friends were climbing purely for thrills.

Despite the fame and size of El Capitan, Yosemite is dominated by a real mountain some 1800 feet higher which stands isolated and aloof above the head of the Valley – Half Dome. Royal and his friends were attracted to it by the very fact that it was a mountain, but they were especially interested in its great North West Face, over 2000 feet high, virgin and plumb vertical. In 1955 Royal, Gallwas and Wilson were joined by Warren Harding for a first attempt on the face. Harding already had a reputation for hard and aggressive climbing but it was an audacious idea at that time and the attempt petered out, as much for psychological reasons as any others, after only a short way. It was not until 1957 that Royal eventually completed the climb, this time with Gallwas and Mike Sherrick. It turned out to be quite an ordeal: in July the face is in the sun soon after mid-day and the climbers suffered much from the heat, but there was also an underlying current of fear for they had brought along a thousand foot abseil rope in case the upper face proved impossible. The sack hauling was very strenuous. Gallwas had made some special pegs, copies of Salathe's hard-steel ones, and these proved extremely useful; but twenty bolts still had to be placed. The climb took five days – it was the first Grade VI in America, and Royal Robbins was famous.

There was soon to be another crossroads in Royal's life – two years service in the Army. But even as he was drafted, Harding's team had started work besieging the next great problem of Yosemite – the Nose of El Capitan. Royal was posted to El Paso in Texas as a clerk. It was an easy job and the Army worked a five day week, and although he did some climbing on the surrounding desert spires, Royal spent many of

Below left: El Capitan towers above the forest at its foot – the line of the 'Nose' follows the edge of the shadow in the middle of the picture. To its right is the fearsome Wall of the Early Morning Light, which took Warren Harding and Dean Caldwell 26½ days of continuous climbing in 1970

Looking down from Glacier Point into Tenaya Canyon — the upper left fork of the Yosemite Valley. On the left are the curling roofs of Royal Arches and beyond Washington Column and distant Watkins. On the right is Half Dome (8,842 feet)

his weekends back in California — climbing of course. Often he was able to beg a lift on a military aircraft heading west on the Friday night, but he always had to hitch-hike back to Texas. In uniform the 800-mile journey used to take him about 20 hours, and this meant spending all day Sunday on the road. These sort of weekends were not conducive to serious climbing.

When in '59 the Pentagon dispensed with his services, Royal returned to banking, this time working in Berkeley so as to be nearer Yosemite. But his military incarceration had crystallized his ideas, and in the deliberate and calculated way in which he had always approached life he saw that banking would not take him where he

wished to go. After six months he quit and started work in the mountains as a ski instructor. Now Royal was able to spend most of the summer season climbing and he returned to Yosemite. Great things had happened in his absence, and in particular Harding and his team had eventually completed the Nose after a total of 47 days climbing spread over a period of seventeen months. Bongs had not yet been invented and they had been forced to use old stove legs in one crack. In the fall of 1960 Royal, climbing with Chuck Pratt, Joe Fitschen and Tom Frost, attempted the second ascent, but in one continuous push. It was exhausting work but they emerged in six and a half days with considerable admiration for Harding and his companions and in particular for the stove legs! Royal says that by then

Royal Robbins enjoys an uncomfortable bivouac in the bottomless alcove of Black Cave on the sixth day of the North America Wall ascent. The ground is 1600 feet straight below the hammock. 'We felt we had climbed into a cul de sac'

Overleaf left: Robbins on jumars on the final pitch of the Muir Wall

Overleaf right: Robbins in action at Wambello near Fresno in California

he was climbing competitively, success felt good and not only was competition fun but it spurred him to greater efforts. But in those days it was without rancour – one didn't steal routes from one's friends.

What came next was, Royal considers, his greatest achievement. The South West Face of El Capitan, to the left of the Nose, was vast and blank, but on close examination it seemed that there might be a line on it, rather meandering it was true, but it seemed to follow cracks most of the way. One hundred and twenty-five bolts had been used on the Nose, and Royal could see little point in forcing a new route up a bolt ladder; not only were the ethics questionable, but placing the bolts was hard work! In September 1961 Royal, with Chuck Pratt and Tom Frost, reached the top after spending nine days on the Face over a period of three weeks. They were delighted with the route, much of it was really excellent free climbing and they had placed only 13 bolts. Royal had dubbed the whole South West Face 'The Salathe Wall', but this was the first route on it and the climb itself was soon known by that name. But he was not content; he and Frost returned a year later to make the second ascent in one continuous push of four and a half days. It was certainly a climb to be proud of.

Other routes on El Cap followed, but competition was now intense and Royal admits that other motivations than pure fun had crept into his climbing. Desire for recognition and respect from those he himself respected might well describe the new reasons, he says looking back. New routes on El Cap were good for the reputation, and he completed three more in the next five years: the West Buttress in '63, North American Wall in '64 and the West Face in '67. North America Wall has become a route of international importance, but the climbing is mean and difficult and there are several pendulums which cut off retreat. Royal, Frost, Chouinard and Pratt spent nine apprehensive days on the ascent after several reconnaissances and the climb was undoubtedly an apogee of American climbing.

Meanwhile Royal went to Europe. In 1962 he took ship on a Yugoslav freighter bound for Tangier and hitch-hiked to the Calanques. There he met John Harlin, relaxing before his successful Eiger North Face ascent – and incidently the first American one – later that same summer. Royal progressed to Chamonix and teamed up with Gary Hemming, an old acquaintance from the States. Gary was a mystic, he would slouch around Chamonix with a bushy beard, wearing an old threadbare raincoat, his toes sticking out from the end of his worn out kletts. He was a man of turbulent emotions and climbing was his answer to them; he was a brilliant mountaineer.

Hemming suggested that they should try a new line on which he had his eyes on the Dru, and in four days they completed a direct start to the famous West Face Route. This avoided the dangerous couloir that leads into the face and it joins the standard route at over half height at the bottom of the crucial thirty-foot dièdre. The free climbing is very hard and Royal found it an enjoyable introduction to the Alps.

107

When Harlin left the USAF in '63 he went to work for the American School at Leysin, a little Swiss ski resort above the Rhône Valley, as organizer of their outdoor programme. In '64 he left to set up his own climbing school, The International School of Mountaineering, just down the road, and Royal came to Europe to take over the job for a couple of years. Mostly it involved ski instruction, but there was scope for climbing in the spring and autumn. It was with Harlin, in 1966, that Royal made his most serious climb. Once again he spent four days on the Dru, this time on a direct line from top to bottom up the blank wall between the West Face Route and the Bonatti Pillar. This route has been described as the hardest aid climb in the Alps; there are several pitches of A.4 with sky-hook moves. Matters came to a head when, on the second day, Harlin's leg was damaged by a falling rock. The situation was obviously critical, but Royal plays this down by emphasizing that they were lucky that the weather didn't break while they were still on the climb. It broke near the summit, however, and when they got there a storm was raging and six inches of snow had fallen. Royal says that the climb down the S.W. ridge and across the steep and highly crevassed little glacier to the Charpoua Hut was 'horrible'. I can quite believe it!

Royal must always be in complete control of a situation; he is certainly the most calm and collected person I know, and the exper-

ience on the Dru set him thinking. Not only was he dissatisfied that he was so tired when he got down to Chamonix – feeling that he had little strength in reserve, but he realized how deadly serious big climbs in the Alps can be. By this time he had climbed in other mountain ranges, the Tetons and the High Sierra for instance, but they were forgiving by contrast. The price of a small mistake in the Alps – with such fickle weather, heavy glaciation and high altitude – could well be the 'big chop'.

Survival he says is not luck. It is being fit for the climb to be attempted and prepared both physically and mentally to face any eventuality that might happen on it. There is no merit in trusting to luck. Mistakes do happen but one should learn from them and make sure they do not happen twice. He cites an occasion during an early reconnaissance of the Salathe Wall with T. M. Herbert. Royal rolled a large stone off a ledge but it didn't fall where he had expected. Instead it nearly removed his second's head on the wall below. No longer does Royal roll stones!

Although he is one of the world's greatest rock-climbers Royal does enjoy big mountains, but he claims that he has never climbed a really difficult snow and ice route. Four or five years ago he climbed three 8000 foot peaks in the Kichetna Spires region of the Alaska Range and he has climbed in the Logans, and other areas of the Canadian Rockies. Typical perhaps of the man is his solo ascent of the North Face of Mount Edith Cavel in 1968. He had heard a lot about the face, which had only recently been climbed: it was mixed, with rock, snow and ice, and he had little experience of the latter. He was in the area with no one to climb with. The year was good, the weather was fine and he was fit. Besides, the experience would be new to him. So he climbed it. It was quite hard, bad snow and poor rock with no possible protection, but there was no rush and all was under control. He enjoyed it immensely.

Royal has always enjoyed solo climbing, right from the early days at Tahquitz. His best solo climb was the second ascent of the West Face of the Leaning Tower, just behind Yosemite's Bridal Veil Falls, in the spring of '63. The nailing was extremely arduous, retreat might well have been impossible, and there were continuous storms during the four day ascent. The first ascent two years before had taken eighteen days over ten months with fixed ropes the whole way. It was a remarkable effort. He looks back, however, with little pride or pleasure on his far better-known second ascent of the Muir Wall on El Capitan. Perhaps he was less in control of the situation during this nine day epic? At any rate he won't tell! But he summed up his attitude to solo climbing in a nutshell when he wrote:

The thing about a solo climb is that it's all yours. You are not forced to share it. It's naked. Raw. The fullest expression of the climbing egoist. It's also a way of exploring oneself. A solo climb is like a big mirror. You are looking at yourself all the way up. If it is a way of showing off, of proving something, it is also a test, a way of finding out what you are made of.

Gary Hemming had advised Royal to come to Britain to sharpen up his free climbing back in 1962, but it was not until '66 that he managed his first visit, initially for the BBC programme and then for a lecture tour. He now visits regularly, both for business and pleasure, and as a brilliant technician and master of aid-climbing he enjoys the ethics of free climbing as practised here – although at present these are sadly being eroded away by the popularity of the sport. In '66 he was struck particularly by Joe Brown and his mastery on rock – it was beyond anything he had ever seen he says – and by Tom Patey's humour and the fun he engendered. For Don Whillans he has the greatest respect: here is a man after his own heart – a survivalist always on top of the situation. He considers him one of the world's very best mountaineers.

In 1963 Royal had got married. Liz is an attractive brunette and she comes from Modesto, an agricultural centre of some 70,000 in the Central Valley of California, rich irrigated orchard country below the Sierra and directly on the route from San Francisco to Yosemite. The careers of many promising climbers have been shattered by marriage but it has had little effect on Royal's climbing. For Royal climbing is a need and a means of expression and Liz knows better than to meddle with such an important part of the man she married. In fact, although she is not passionate about climbing, Liz does enjoy good routes and has climbed up to 5.9 standard. She and Royal have shared many climbs together including the N.W. face of Half Dome.

When he was working in Switzerland, the French boot manufacturers, Galibier, asked Royal if he would develop for them a specialist lightweight rock-climbing boot. This he did – the famous blue suede R-R, designed specifically for Yosemite-style rock work. Naturally he started to distribute the boots in the States himself, and quite soon other lines followed. Eventually Royal and Liz found themselves with a part-time import and distribution business on their hands and Liz's father lent them an old warehouse in Modesto in which to store the

The Muir Wall is completed and Royal relaxes with Liz on the summit of El Capitan

merchandise and from which to operate. Aided by Liz's excellent business sense, the project mushroomed. The idea of eventually joining Liz's family paint firm had never appealed and so soon after Tamara was born in 1971, the couple decided to go full-time into climbing equipment and opened a retail shop 'Mountain Paraphernalia' in the Modesto warehouse in July 1972. The shop is panelled in beautiful, naturally weathered boarding, colours and textures are subtly matched and much fine equipment is laid out. It is worth a visit just to sample the atmosphere of that shop; Royal gives all the credit for the design and selection of decor to Liz. Luckily the opening of the new venture coincided with a tremendous upsurge in public interest in mountains and climbing and the shop has been spectacularly successful. In 1973 they opened another in Fresno.

What of the future? Royal says, in a rare unguarded moment, that he half wishes the business would collapse – it's a hassle and like all successful businesses it occupies large quantities of time and energy. It has been a very personal thing for the two of them and he does enjoy making it a success. But he adds that unless he is able to take more time from the business in the future he will sell out and go back to climbing, guiding and writing – all things he does so extremely well. 'Do what you really want to do', he says 'Whatever makes you live most fully'. Recently Royal and Liz have taken up white-water canoeing. It is something that they can do together and a famous white-water river, the Stanislaus, is only an hour's drive from Modesto. Canoeing is something that involves the same sort of control over natural elements as do climbing and skiing. They both enjoy multi-day expeditions down the great canyons, and recently spent three weeks running the Green River, but that sort of time is difficult to find.

He would like to climb further afield more; to return to the Alps where – but for the summer queues – he rather fancies the Walker Spur. He would like to do a big wall in Alaska – a game he knows, but played in hostile surroundings. Patagonia seems poor value for money, despite its spectacular rock towers. He went there in the spring of '73 and climbed nothing; the weather, as seems normal down there, was terrible. Australia beckons with excellent rock-climbing and weather as good as that of California. He has no particular Himalayan aspirations. What is the point, he asks, of huffing and puffing and struggling up a really big mountain just to ruin your health? There is something in that, of course; but he has been invited to join an expidition to Kashmir in '74 and he may go. Just to see the countryside, he explains!

Asked about his autobiography, a slow smile spreads over his face. It's difficult, he explains, because he hasn't been in the same sort of 'grip-ups' that other famous climbers have been in. It would be about enjoyment rather than adventure – and that doesn't make the best reading. The fact is that Royal Robbins has always been very much in control of the situation.

In the Valley
Legacy of iron

It was hot. It was August. In high summer the Valley is peopled by tourists, for all self-respecting climbers have retreated to the cool meadows up at Tuolumne. But we were tired. Last night, bivouacked in the long grass of Leidig Meadow, we'd been woken by bears – so we dozed in the shade beside the idling waters of the Merced, oblivious to the continuous muffled roar of the traffic which plagues Yosemite Valley at this unfortunate season.

The high country above Yosemite Valley in the California Sierra is studded with granite domes offering tremendous scope for climbs. Landscape near the head of Tenaya Lake

Perhaps it was a particularly noisy motorcycle that finally stirred us to action. Leo struggled to his feet. 'I need a beer', he said. I yawned. 'Why don't we climb?' 'Okay,' he said. 'But a beer first, huh?'

We slid into the Triumph, the hot leather singeing our bare thighs, and drove down the tunnel of pine trees towards the village with its large, unpleasant supermarket.

The late afternoon was cooler – and so were we – and we climbed out of the Triumph at the dusty forest edge below one of the most amazing expanses of rock I had ever seen – the Apron of Glacier Point. Like a vast skirt, the smooth grey granite curved away to left and right while sweeping upwards at a steady incline for a full 2000 feet. And then the rock reared into a dark vertical tower for a further thousand feet to the tiny pines on the summit of Glacier Point itself. Despite the easy angle of this huge slab, about 50 degrees I suppose, I was under no illusions as to its difficulty. Yosemite granite is smooth and ice-polished and I was aware of the reputation of these almost holdless acres for improbable and highly specialized friction climbing.

'. . . they don't go all the way . . .' Leo was saying. 'Only a few pitches then you rappel down. I know just the route for us in our present state of health. Not too hard – about 5.7 – and if we move fast we'll be down nicely before dark.' 'What about pins?' I asked. 'I guess we used some for belay and protection last time – but that was several years ago – and the cracks are good! We'll take a full set of nuts; we don't like using iron in the Valley nowadays', he said. We plodded out of the pines up the scree towards the waiting rock.

There was a triangular pillar of darker rock leaning against the Apron. It was the only feature on the whole expanse and, although dwarfed by the arching slabs, it must have been 400 feet high. We stopped below it.

'Monday Morning Slab,' volunteered Leo. 'Easiest climbs here – very popular – and a rather good 5.8 up the middle.' 'Where do we go?' 'Climb starts near the top – we gotta get up there first – but we don't need the rope, it's just third-class for three hundred feet.'

He set off up the flakes and cracks that formed the right side of the Slab; I started up behind him. It was scrambling, easy but strenuous, and I soon began to feel the exposure. A very easy place to die if you were slightly careless. Eventually the flakes became a shallow chimney capped by an awkward bulge, and Leo was waiting for me, slightly out of breath, on the platform above. 'Excellent', he said. 'We're almost there', and he stepped out rightwards onto a narrow ledge. I followed him carefully. The ledge was particularly narrow and I was very aware of being a tiny dot far above the ground on what must be the biggest slab in the world. Two hundred feet out the ledge stopped. There was a small stunted pine tree and Leo was uncoiling the rope.

'There's three pitches, man', he said. 'The second is the best as far as I remember. Like to lead it?' 'Okay', I said. 'So you'll lead one and three?' 'That's it', he replied.

113

There was nowhere to belay but the tree, and when he had carefully racked the nuts on one of those wide and fancy-embroidered gear-slings the Americans seem to like, he started frictioning delicately upwards and across the slab. After thirty feet he disappeared behind a slight curl in the rock and the pace slowed. It was obvious he was having to work things out. I hoped he would place some protection but I couldn't see what he was doing. Either the climbing was very hard, which seemed unlikely, or he was being particularly careful. Then he called down 'Can't get a bloody nut in anywhere . . . but don't worry it's not very hard'. I looked at my anaemic tree and hoped he was correct. Eventually he came into view again moving slowly back across the slab above to what was obviously a good ledge line.

'Only fifteen feet', I yelled. 'I need twenty', he called back. 'Can you unbelay? I'm on easy ground.' 'And not a runner between us', I thought unhappily. 'Might as well solo.' 'Good stance', he shouted, 'Come on.' And, pleased to be moving at last, I stepped cautiously on to the slab. It was delicate, frictiony and fun and I soon reached the shallow dièdre which had hidden Leo. There was a crack all right, but I soon realized why protection had been impossible. At each likely place pegs had been pounded in and smashed out, and the crack was blinded and gaping. Nowhere at all for a nice harmless nut. Protection would have been very reassuring here, I thought. A 200-foot peel would be most unfair on a second belayed to that precarious tree!

I reached the ledge. It was a good one, a wrinkle about three feet wide with rocky flakes and cracks along the back. Leo was sitting, his feet braced against a small flake, taking in my rope. 'Sorry I couldn't get a belay', he explained. 'But there was no more rope. It's a pretty good stance.' I grunted, 'I don't like psychological belays'. But I had to admit that it was a sound stance. 'All the damn cracks are smashed', he went on. 'Too many people done too much nailing; pity we didn't have nuts five years ago! But you'll find something along the end of the ledge I guess. Then that's where you go.' And he pointed upwards. Thirty feet along, the ledge curled upwards and became a series of flaky cracks leading vertically through the blankness above. Where the angle changed it looked very broken. There'd surely be a nut placing over there?

'It's a long pitch', said Leo. 'But it looks harder than I thought. I don't remember it looking so strenuous.' I looked up at it. Certainly those flakes would need some energy . . . and just how steep was it? At 60 degrees it would be really hard but if it was 45 degrees . . .? The angle was most deceptive.

I scrambled to the end of the ledge. I spent a very fruitless half hour pushing nuts into every possible – or impossible – crack, but they were all rounded and scarred white with the hammering and beating of chrome molybdenum steel. I climbed as far up the rearing flakes as I dared without a belay, but vandals had been there too. I was worried. 'I'm not prepared to lead this without a belay, Leo', I shouted. 'Why

Fine little granite peaks — all of about ten and a half thousand feet — rise from the snow fields above Budd Creek on the south side of Tuolumne Meadows

don't you come and have a look. You're more at home with this rock!'
'All right', he replied, and I scrambled along back to the stance. I
handed him the gear sling with a glum look and he set off towards the
flakes. Five minutes was enough to convince him that I had been right.
'Well I'm not going to solo that either', he protested. 'We'd be okay
if we'd brought some iron – but that would smash the rock even more.
It's a vicious circle. Now that nails are obsolete they're all you can use!'

I was fed up. It was starting to get dark and clad in only jeans and a
teeshirt I was no longer warm. 'Let's get the hell out', I suggested to
Leo. 'If we can't go up we've got to go down.' 'But how are we going
to get down?' he asked, and then I realized the predicament we were in.

No belay to climb from meant no belay to rappel from. We would
have to down-climb the way we had come, and virtually solo to boot.
It would be slow and the last man – the dangerous one – would be
climbing in pitch darkness. Leo had an idea. 'Look', he said, 'I've led
that pitch below twice. Hard bit's at the bottom – the last forty feet.
It's 150 feet down and we have a 150-foot rope. If you rappel on the
single rope, I'm prepared to down-climb with you belaying me from
that tree – if I peel it'd only be a short tumble down the slab. It'd be
much quicker with you rappelling and there'd still be light for me to
climb.' 'But there's nothing to rappel off', I protested. He patted the
rounded boss he had been sitting on. 'We put a long tape round this',
he explained. 'Plenty of friction and if I hold it on it'll take a downward
pull. But you'll have to go very gently', he emphasized.

Two minutes later I'd arranged my karabiner brake on the rope
and was lowering myself gingerly over the ledge. The dangerous part
was the first bit where the rope was not yet running steeply. 'How's it
looking', I breathed. 'It's okay', said Leo. 'Keep going, I'll shout if
it's coming off.' Heck of a lot of good that would be, I thought. I
remembered the climbers who had died rappelling – friends and
strangers – some of the best climbers in the world, and I took it easy
and tiptoed carefully down the smooth, polished rock. I reached the
tree with a big sigh of relief. I belayed firmly on to its now reassuring
trunk. I felt a sense of security at last – the first for a couple of hours.

Leo came climbing down into the dusk, he moved calmly and it took
time. Frictioning delicately backwards down the last thirty feet was
very heart-in-mouth, but he reached me safely. We scrambled back
to Monday Morning Slab and found a large pine tree, a really safe-
looking one, and rappelled almost carelessly into the darkness. Below
us there were lights winking through the pine trees and the sound of
music drifting up from Curry Village and the acres of campers and
mobile homes, TV and all, plugged in beneath the trees. I had forgotten their existence for a few precious hours.

'We've earned a beer', I said to Leo as we stumbled blindly down
the scree. 'Huh', he grunted. 'We've survived the mountain, and now
if the bears don't get us, the fleshpots will.'

The Fish-hook of Mount Russell

The grass was soft and green and sprinkled with flowers, the creek was cool and clear and reflected in its blue mirror the tall pines and the puffy clouds sailing between the snow-streaked towers.

I munched at my cheese. I liked these mountains, they seemed friendly and welcoming, unlike the moody Alps. Yesterday the southeast buttress of Cathedral Peak had been superb. Cool forests, crisp snow and warm rough granite. A fine introduction to the Sierra Nevada of California – the High Sierra. I finished my cheese, lay back in the grass and shut my eyes.

Last night the great eastern wall of the Sierra had risen pink above the dusty defile of the Owens Valley as we drove into Bishop, and at dawn these same ramparts had drifted fairylike 10,000 feet over the dusty sagebrush, as we had passed through the one-horse township of Independence.

At Lone Pine we had turned up out of the deep valley and there, as the road curled through the dark swellings of the Alabama Hills, framed high above us by lesser peaks, was Mount Whitney – the wedge of its east face white in the morning sun and buttressed on the south side by a jagged crest of sharp rock needles. I recognized the view Ansel Adams had made famous, but now those faces were shadowless in the bright June glare, and it was not the time for moody pictures.

Up at 8000 feet Whitney Portal was a bit cooler. It had been a surprising transition from desert to aromatic pines and cool streams. We left the VW bus at the road-head and slogged up the steep and tortuous trail beside the roaring torrent of Lone Pine Creek's north fork. And so, three hours later, here we were – the four of us – with our big heavy packs, stretched out on the grass beside Lower Boy Scout Lake, some considerable distance and a lot of hard sweat above Whitney Portal. It was good to be here.

The trail crossed the creek and led on through the silent foxtail pines to lose itself in steep scree and wide snow patches. We battled a tangle of dwarf willow to pace up huge rock sheets flooring the valley. Torrents poured down them and we revelled in their jewelled spray. They led to Upper Boy Scout Lake, cradled in a wild cwm beyond which rose the tangled ridges and spires of Mount Russell – the mountain we'd come to climb.

But we branched off left, climbed a steep slope and entered another unsuspected cwm. The prospect that unfolded was stunning. Hanging above us, already black silhouettes against the westering sun, were the jagged spires of Whitney, Keeler Needle, Day Needle, Third Needle and Pinnacle Ridge. It must be one of the finest high valleys in the world!

But it was already late, and Leo and Mike and I were exhausted – the office is no place to train for 12,000 feet slogs. We decided it was time to bivouac and, as we collapsed onto the warm gravel, Gary – already fit and acclimatized – had the brew going. The fires subsided

Mount Whitney (14,495 feet) – the highest peak in the contiguous United States, towers some 10,000 feet above the arid Owens Valley near Lone Pine in eastern California. The east faces of Whitney, and of the Keeler and Day Needles to its left, give excellent rock-climbing

Overleaf: Colorado River – a raft expedition approaches the Tilted Park area in the Colorado's Cataract Canyon in S.E. Utah, immediately after a summer thunder storm. To the connoisseur of mountain form the pinnacles and canyon-cut plateaus of the desert provide a never-ending spectacle of shape and colour not found in the classic mountain ranges

behind the pinnacles and the shadows crept down the valley floor. We were too tired to talk much as we stretched out in our sleeping bags. As the first stars glittered in the dusk we drifted into sleep: the last thing I remembered was the spark of a satellite tracing its bright path from horizon to horizon. I woke once. The cwm was flooded with soft light. The sky pulsed with stars and the Milky Way writhed across the heavens.

The sun woke us, but it takes time to struggle into full consciousness, brew and eat and move off, and Leo had had a rough night. Beneath the tall beckoning spires we went, crested a rise and reached Iceberg Lake, its frozen surface cracking to reveal patches of turquoise water. Snow slopes led to a narrow rocky col, and suddenly there ahead was the great south flank of Mount Russell, across a wide snow-streaked desert of scree.

We gazed at the spiky summit ridge – a mile long – and at the half-dozen ribs and spurs which buttressed it on this southern side. As far as we knew they were all virgin. 'West face – the profile left of the highest top – is the route Galen Rowell and Chris Jones did in '71', said Gary. 'Fred Beckey did a line on the North-East Face, but they're the only modern routes. Which line shall we try?' 'It's obvious isn't it?', I countered. 'You mean that hooked rib dropping from the highest point, straight towards us?' 'That's it.' 'Okay then, we'll climb together and Mike can climb with Leo.' We sat down and waited for our friends to arrive.

But they were slow. Leo still felt poorly, and he and Mike decided to opt out of the heroics. Gary and I were both excited and we ran down into the shallow valley and started the tedious climb up scree and snow to the steep lowest rocks of our rib. The bottom 'hook' section is knife-edged and rears up in a gargoyled prow. We turned this by overlapping grooves on its shadowed left flank. Gary led two awkward pitches, while I shivered on the stances in the strong wind which funnelled coldly up the couloir. We reached a sharp ridge crest, its right flank dropping sheer to the scree already 300 feet below, and an interesting pitch *à cheval* led to a dark niche below another over-hanging prow. Guessing it might be difficult, I again declined the lead and Gary stepped cautiously round the corner into the sun on the invisible right wall. The rope went out very, very slowly and the wind blew and I shivered. Obviously the climbing was very hard. But I found my concentration wandering. I remembered Everest – the last place Gary and I had climbed together – and thought with pleasure how good it was to be climbing together again. I willed the sun to move quicker towards my frigid sentry-box. And still the rope crept imperceptibly round that blasted corner.

Finally it went tight, and there was a vague shout above the wind. I unclipped and stepped stiffly onto the corner and into the sun. What I saw took my breath away. I was looking 80 feet across a smooth and vertical wall bounded on the far side by a wide and bottomless dièdre.

The Maze is an incredibly complex canyon system rising in the Land of Standing Rocks and eventually joining the Green River near its confluence with the Colorado in S.E. Utah. The picture is taken looking down one of the dry river beds of the Maze from a cave in which we found probable Indian remains. There is a natural arch in its roof and difficult rock climbing was necessary to enter

The most impressive mountain
above Budd Creek is
Cathedral Peak (10,940 feet).
The left skyline is the
South-East Buttress, an
excellent 500-foot route on
flawless granite

Gary Colliver on the opening
pitch of the South-East
Buttress. Below: Looking up
the Buttress — 500 feet of
curling slabs

The far edge of this dièdre rose into a tower – over the top of which Gary's head was silhouetted against the deep blue of the sky. The rope arced to three runners in its diagonal path across this sheet of rock, before disappearing round the far edge of the dièdre some forty feet below Gary. No wonder he'd taken his time!

I cursed my heavy rucksack, the full water-bottle, the food, the iron for emergencies, the spare clothes and – most useless of all – my cameras. I cursed my big alpine boots. I foresaw an epic and uncontrolled swing into potential disaster.

I launched out – at first upwards. It was a mantleshelf, on tiny fingerholds at full stretch, with nothing but crystals for the feet, but somehow I stood up on them. Another similar move and there was a perfect nut to hang on and rest.

Damn! – I had passed a long runner round the edge on my left. I lowered myself down on a sling and wasted a lot of energy fighting to rescue a large and well-jammed nut. I was well aware that we were over 13,000 feet. The diagonal fingery traverse up the wall that followed was steeper than it looked but at least there were holds. Surprising! Then there was a runner. I touched it – it came out. It was the last one before the rope disappeared round the corner forty feet ahead. I stood with a toe on a tiny flake and a finger in a small hole and breathed a sigh of relief that I was still on the rock. A slight wrinkle led across the wall but stopped short before the dièdre. The dièdre itself was obtuse and smooth, until there seemed to be a small knob of rock on its right edge some fifteen feet above.

I was aware of Gary shouting instructions down to me. '. . . it's very thin into the dièdre', he was saying. 'And you have to bridge up it, feet on the left, arms and shoulders on the right until you can get your hands round the knob. That's a perfect hold. Swing round the corner and you can rest. Then the final wall to me is straightforward.' 'Oh God', I groaned. 'It looks appalling.' My knees quivered. I wanted to go home. 'Hold on', yelled Gary. 'I'll flick the rope over the edge.' And he flicked it over his tower and into the top of the dièdre.

Nothing ventured nothing gained. I tiptoed boldly across the wrinkle, palms flat and sweating on the rough granite. Then the wrinkle faded away and I pushed myself out of balance and reached across to the far lip of the dièdre – I touched it – but it was all wrong and I managed to fight myself upright again and back into balance on the wrinkle. I was tense and my fingertips oozed fear. That's not the way! I tried again, more cunningly this time, slapping my left foot high and allowing my body to fall across the gaping void. I caught myself with my outstretched right arm and lowered my shoulder on to the rock. Now I was horizontal, wedged precariously across the dièdre. With my left hand I fumbled for a crack. None. I worked my feet up a few inches but it was a terrible mistake. I couldn't move my shoulder. Suddenly my feet were above my head . . . my shoulder was sliding down . . . I was off. A great lurch into space. The scree spinning

below me. A flood of relief that the issue had decided itself. And there I was hanging – like a sack of coals – several feet out in space and a long way from the dièdre. Everything was overhanging and I hadn't realized it.

Luckily I'd arranged a crutch sling on my swami belt and the swinging and struggling to regain the rock was not too painful. I reached some holds and tried to relax, my heart pounding fit to propel me into space again, while I tried to be calm and think constructively. It wasn't much help but at least I knew what not to do – I was learning the hard way.

'Okay?', shouted the voice from above. 'Just about', I blurted back. 'But it's bloody hard.' 'Sorry I can't help much but a tight rope's no use.' I was very tired and I realized there was a limit to the number of times I could fall off before exhaustion. Apprehensively I launched out again. This time I bridged with my hands on the far wall and not with my shoulders. It felt perilous but certainly more powerful. I eased my way up inch by inch, working first my hands and then my feet. It was a terrible strain on my burning arms. Then unexpectedly there was the rock knob close above. Could I reach it? Would my left arm hold while I tried with my right? It reached. It was a perfect jug. For a split second I hung with my right arm as my feet dropped into space and my left hand slotted in beside the right. I swung my feet onto the tiny nicks on the corner of the dièdre and stepped round onto a small but extremely comfortable ledge.

'Well done', shouted Gary. 'By God', I breathed. I looked up at his grinning face. The wall between us looked easy. I rested and then assaulted the series of short cracks which led up it. It wasn't easy but I would have enjoyed it thoroughly had there been enough strength remaining in my arms to use the holds properly. I reached Gary and collapsed panting onto a large ledge.

Above left: Morning light on the incredible spires of the Mt Whitney cirque. On the left is the Pinnacle Ridge, then Third Needle, Day Needle, Keeler Needle (14,240 feet) and the East Face of Mt Whitney itself, 14,495 feet

Centre: Gary Colliver on easy ground approaching the towers on the Fish Hook Arête of Mt Russell. The chimney splitting the 'Blank Tombstone' is clearly seen some way above

Bottom: The westering sun drops towards the spires of Mt Whitney

Above right: The vast and tangled South Face of Mt Russell seen from the Russell-Whitney Col. The Rowell/Jones route runs up the shadowed face left of the summit, while the 'Fish Hook' falls immediately below the summit, shaped like a letter 'J'

I was streaming sweat and my knees were shaking but I was glowing inside. 'Gary, that was an incredible lead', I managed to gasp. 'Yeah, guess I'm quite fit', he laughed. There were easy pitches now to a couple of rock towers. Then, at a narrow gash, the ridge turned abruptly through ninety degrees to become a steep spur rising direct to the summit of Mt Russell. We were in the wind again and I'd cooled off. But we stopped briefly in the lee of the second tower for lunch.

'Looks interesting', I observed as we studied the buttress above. 'Probably quite hard.' 'Uh huh', Gary answered between mouthfuls of raisins. 'Sure interesting – but probably not too hard. Surprising what goes on this rock . . . it's a helluva difference from Yosemite!' I remembered that this was the High Sierra. The granite more like Skye than Chamonix, the difference between chalk and cheese. High cirrus was drifting in from the west and I mentioned it to Gary. 'No hassle', he explained. 'Summer weather's settled – it don't mean nothin' here.' What a place, I thought; a climber's paradise.

Crossing the gash provided some pleasing little moves and then a succession of steep cracked walls and little mantleshelves led up the series of great flakes that formed the crest of the spur. Eventually, several pitches later, we arrived at a small ledge on the edge of nothing, below the biggest and most obvious flake of the lot. A great blank tombstone with a crack line up the middle. But I'd misjudged the scale badly. What had looked like a narrow crack was a chimney you could climb right inside, and the tombstone was only eighty feet high. There were one or two anxious moments as Gary by-passed two chock-stones that might have wiped me out, had they been loose, and then I followed. My only difficulty was extracting some firmly wedged hexentrics. The climbing was superb: pitch followed pitch, never hard, never easy, always sustained, interesting and athletic (as the French would say!). We moved fast and enjoyed every moment.

125

Top left: 'What had looked like a narrow crack was a chimney you could climb right inside, and the Tombstone was only 80 feet high

Top right: Gary Colliver surmounts a small tower at the end of the first section of the Arête. Beyond, frozen tarns in the deep valley lead to Whitney Creek and Crabtree

Bottom right: Gary Colliver and the author on the summit of Mt Russell – in the distance to the right is Owens Lake, and beyond that the Inyo Range and Nevada

The northern flanks of Mt Whitney, the highest peak in the contiguous United States

Then the angle eased back; over a last short wall the summit was in sight. 'Last pitch', said Gary as I arrived at his stance. 'Your lead!' 'Hell no', I protested. 'It's your climb!' But he insisted: 'It's *our* climb, we're a team, remember. You've earned it – off you go!' And so I climbed a beautiful hand-jam crack and scrambled a few feet and found myself on the summit blocks on Mt Russell.

Among the boulders, in a metal box, was the summit book. Entries went back forty-five years, the earliest being soon after that great Sierra pioneer, Norman Clyde, had made the first ascent by the East Ridge on June 24th, 1926. We could understand why Russell was one of the last of the Sierra peaks to be climbed; even the East Ridge looked a good scramble. Beyond it, across the deep purple trench of the Owens Valley, rose the Inyo Range and beyond again ridge after blue ridge stretched to Death Valley and into Nevada. But west lay

the Sierra themselves – a vast desert of granite pyramids and dark forest – streaked with snow fields and jewelled with tarns glinting in the late afternoon sun. Several hundred miles of high and roadless wilderness. It was bewitching. I'd come again.

But it was time to go down. We scrambled along the summit ridge towards the east peak and climbed carefully down a loose gully in the head wall of the second great southern couloir. We ran down steep scree and snow patches and, somewhere near Russell-Whitney Col, paused to look back at the mountain and at our hooked ridge, edged now with gold, falling through the blue shadows towards us.

'It was a great climb – we must name it', I said to Gary. 'Any ideas?' 'Let's call it Fish Hook Arête?' he said and, as we ran down the darkening snowfield to Iceberg Lake, we were very happy.

The ice revolution

The rumpled mountains of the Scottish Highlands stretch some 215 miles from the granite peaks of Arran, rising from the sheltered waters of the Firth of Clyde, northward to the white quartzite screes of Foinaven behind Cape Wrath and the pounding Atlantic. East from the black spires of the Cullin, jagged over the Hebridean island of Skye, mountains sweep into the distance for 135 miles to the prominent cone of Mount Keen, not far from Stonehaven and the bleak North Sea shore. The Highlands cover more than one-fifth of the land area of the United Kingdom – the greatest wilderness in western Europe. They lie on the latitude of Labrador or the Alaska Panhandle.

Ben Nevis, the highest summit in the British Isles (Nevis – Gaelic for 'venomous' or 'hellish'), rises a mere 4406 feet above the sea at its base, and yet the climate on the mountain itself is Arctic. Snow lies for at least six months of the year and white wreaths linger in the corries into the autumn. The mean annual temperature on the summit is below freezing point.

But 'The Ben' is by no means unique. Of the 543 summits of over 3000 feet in Scotland, there are twelve that are over 4000 feet. Nine of these are in the Cairngorms, a high twisted plateau gouged with deep corries which hold snow throughout the year and where, because of their location, further east from the warm Gulf Stream which caresses the west coast, an even more Arctic climate prevails.

The Scottish mountains are at their most interesting and beautiful under snow, but it is not just the subtlety of winter colour that attracts the winter mountaineer. The Highland weather is fickle, and the clashing of Atlantic depression and Arctic airstream results in winter conditions almost unique in countries where climbers climb. The everlasting rapid succession of snowfall, thaw and frost, coupled with a strong and constant wind, fills the gullies with ribbons of hard ice and plasters the crags with snow-ice and verglas. The heavy snowfall, which may give excellent skiing conditions in Speyside or Glenshee, must first avalanche and thaw and freeze and consolidate before it is in a good condition for climbing – and if and when this happens the Scottish Highlands provide the best ice climbing in the world.

Ever since Whymper's time and the alpine 'Golden Age', which ended with his first ascent of the Matterhorn in 1865, the accepted technique for climbing steep snow or ice had been to cut a ladder of steps up it. The angle at which it became necessary to cut the steps was determined not only by the boldness of the climber but also by the introduction first of more sophisticated boot nails and then of the crampon, that frame of steel spikes strapped to the boot and perfected some eighty years ago by the English alpinist Oscar Eckenstein, the most technically minded mountaineer of his day. Old customs die hard, and it was many years before the crampon became universal. As late as 1960 the very capable climbers of Aberdeen still favoured the old tricouni nailed boots to the crampons worn over a Vibram sole by rival winter climbers from Glasgow and Edinburgh.

Hamish MacInnes uses terrordactyls on steep mixed ground on the Buachaille Etive Mor in Glencoe. Typically he is wearing a 'flat 'at' and gaberdine trousers

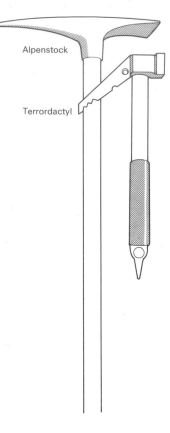

Alpenstock

Terrordactyl

The actual cutting of steps was done with an ice axe. Over the years this had evolved from the steel-shod staff of the early alpine crystal gatherers to the five-foot alpenstock of the pioneers and, by the time of the Second World War, to the handier three-foot ice axe, its steel head comprising an adze and a straight pick and its ashwood shaft tipped with a metal ferrule. The head was usually forged by primitive methods in an alpine smithy. The design was what one might call 'evolved-traditional'.

For obvious reasons Scottish climbers have always exploited their winter. It seems that they would agree with the mighty Gervasutti who wrote: 'A climber who is strong and sure of himself should prefer winter ascents because these more than any other give him a chance of measuring his strength against mountains in severe conditions'. The first winter climbs were up the gullies – an echo, of course, of the way in which rock climbing was developing at the same time, both north and south of the Border. The highlight of the climb would be an ice pitch or two, followed by some good entertainment surmounting the cornice at the top. A few of the bolder climbers did venture out of the gullies – a notable ascent was that of Ben Nevis's 2000-foot Tower Ridge in 1894 by a team led by Professor Collie. Even today this is a Grade III climb and was a redoubtable effort for its period. So although some remarkable ascents were made in those early days, between the foundation of the Scottish Mountaineering Club (S.M.C.) in 1889 and the outbreak of the First World War, they were mostly rather lacking in variety: for gullies, until they are of the highest order of difficulty, tend to a peculiar sameness.

The undoubted father of Scottish winter climbing was Harold Raeburn, who had already a record of bold leads before he joined the S.M.C. at the age of thirty-one in 1896. Raeburn was a fine rock climber and a brilliant alpinist. Often climbing with fellow Scot, W. N. Ling, he made the first British guideless ascents of the Viereselgrat of the Dent Blanche, the Zmutt Ridge of the Matterhorn and the East Face of Monte Rosa. It was he who first climbed the Spigolo Inglese of Monte Disgrazia, described later in this book. In 1919 he made a daring solo traverse of the Meije. He climbed in Norway and the Caucasus and his climbing career reached its zenith perhaps with his visit to Kangchenjunga in 1920 and to Mount Everest in 1921 as the climbing leader of the reconnaissance party. After this he was troubled by ill health and died in 1926 at the age of sixty-one. Many climbs, both summer and winter routes, bear his name, and he recorded no less than thirteen first ascents on Ben Nevis alone.

One of Raeburn's noteworthy climbs was the gully that bears his name on Lochnager, that fine mountain – a Cairngorm outlyer – whose great northern corrie hangs over Balmoral and Deeside. It was 1898, and it is interesting to note that one of the vertical ice pitches was climbed by pulling up on an ice axe – in those days a long one – the pick precariously hooked over the glass-like mantleshelf at the top.

Although there have since been rock changes inside the gully, it is still considered a fine and entertaining route, not easy, and with a steep and difficult exit. A winter climb he made on the Comb Buttress of Ben Nevis has not since been traced, but of it he wrote: '. . . I must confess to a feeling of helplessness for a moment as I stood on my ice axe, driven horizontally into the vertical snow wall, some hundreds of feet of little less than vertical ice-plastered rocks stretching away down into the depths of the mist beneath, while my fingers slid helplessly from the glassy surface of the cornice *névé*, in the vain attempt to find or to make a hold by which I might haul myself up . . .'. Raeburn claimed that this route was far harder and more sporting than the Zmutt Arête of the Matterhorn which he climbed the following summer. What is intriguing, in the light of his experience and ability, is that he suggested using a 'light tomahawk-like hatchet' for difficult ice climbing! It was to come.

In the thirties Scottish winter climbing again experienced a resurgence in the best Raeburn tradition, and standards of difficulty were constantly pushed upwards. Several climbers were setting the pace. One was Graham MacPhee, who, working at weekends from his home in Liverpool, made many fine winter ascents on Ben Nevis. His best was perhaps Glovers Chimney which he climbed in 1935 – an extremely steep and ice-choked rift leading to the famous 'Gap' high on Tower Ridge. The bottom pitch was a single 120-foot ice fall which actually overhung at one point, and MacPhee took two gruelling hours of one-handed step cutting to surmount it.

The most important group however, were Bill Murray and his friends, who were particularly active in Glencoe. Like MacPhee and J. H. B. Bell, another pioneer of the day, Murray and his friends discovered that any summer rock climb – provided it is suitably plastered in ice – will make a good winter climb. Buttresses, ridges and faces offered more interesting and varied lines than the old conventional gullies. If conditions were bad they learned to adapt their techniques to meet them, climbing as necessary on ice, *névé*, powder snow, verglas or frozen vegetation. Murray's efforts encouraged a new attitude towards climbs, in which mere length and difficulty were considered irrelevant, and they would climb on into the night using torches if necessary. Great ascents of the period were the Deep Cut Chimney of Stob Coire nam Beith in Glencoe by Murray and his friend, Bill MacKenzie, MacKenzie's own first ascent of the now classic Crowberry Gully on Buachaille Etive Mor in 1936, and the route that is probably the prototype of the modern ice climb, the Garrick Shelf on the Crowberry Ridge of the Buachaille – a real epic by Murray and MacKenzie in 1937.

To venture where they did was an indication of changes to come, but the equipment Murray and his friends used and the techniques with which they climbed were little different from those of fifty years before. Climbing steep ice still necessitated a ladder of holds, and the

Standard Ice-Axe

Chouinard

Overleaf: MacInnes at work in his Glencoe workshop — ice axes and climbing tools, prototypes and production models litter the work bench

131

only innovation was the introduction by Bill Murray of a short slater's pick. With this it was easier to cut holds above the head and its length was no encumbrance, unlike the current three-foot ice axe. Twenty years later little had changed. The only radical development was the introduction by Austrian and German alpinists of the 'lobster-claw' crampon with its two forward-pointing spikes enabling the climber, with a dagger or ice axe pick in each hand, literally to claw his way up slopes of fairly steep ice, and so do away with tiresome step cutting. Rigid crampons such as the Marwa and later the Chouinard made the footwork less tiring. Independently, the French had evolved a technique known as *'Pied à Plat'*: this did not require twelve-point crampons, merely an extremely flexible – some would say *impossibly* flexible – ankle! It necessitated the feet being placed flat so that all the crampon spikes bit into the ice and involved a crab-like diagonal movement of little use on a vertical or confined ice pitch. While the French preferred a fairly long ice axe for their technique, the Scottish ice climbers who swiftly adopted the front-pointing method, took to the short-handled North Wall hammers, where the adze was replaced by a hammer-head, or cut down the shafts of their regulation axes. An eighteen-inch shaft seemed fairly standard in Scotland.

This was the position in the mid-1960s when a score of brilliant climbers had pushed the upper limit of Scottish ice climbing as far as it could go with the equipment and techniques then at their disposal. Prominent among the great winter climbers of the decade were Jimmy Marshall, Len Lovat, Bill Brooker, Robin Smith and Dougal Haston, Hamish MacInnes and Tom Patey. There was often intensive competition for first ascents between rival groups – the Aberdonians, the Edinburgh climbers, the Glasgow J.M.C.S. or the Creag Dhu 'gnomies'. In Glencoe and on Ben Nevis they had climbed virtually all the great lines, often necessitating multi-day epics or, in the case of Ben Nevis's Point-Five Gully, twenty-nine hours of siege tactics spread over five days. This last was by a team of English 'invaders' led by Ian Clough, who was also a prominent figure in Scottish winter development. Creag Meaghaidh, a huge winter cliff in the Central Highlands, had been opened up, while in the more remote Cairngorms there had also been great happenings presided over largely by Tom Patey. When he moved from Aberdeen to Ullapool Patey started an incredible series of exploratory climbs, often solo, in the previously untouched and wild corries of the far north-west. In 1960 he wrote:

. . . the summer months in Scotland are not the off-season, but a period when hungry tigers sharpen their claws for the winter onslaught. . . . the scope for original winter exploration in Scotland is still enormous. . . . [Scottish winter climbing] teaches virtues which are the essence of successful Alpine and Himalayan climbing – speed, resourcefulness and, above all, accurate route finding. Nevertheless I would recoil from describing Scottish winter climbing merely in terms of training for (so-called) Greater Mountaineering. That would be heresy: the Scottish brand of winter mountaineering is unique!

Scottish winter climbing had consolidated, and the stage was set for a great leap upwards.

132

When he was not climbing, Hamish MacInnes, cosy in his Glencoe cottage, had been thinking and scheming. A brilliant engineer, by the mid-1960s MacInnes was already a mountaineer of international stature. One day he appeared with a secret weapon which was soon to become known throughout the climbing world as 'the message'. It was an all-steel ice tool, short and heavy with a hammer-head and a vicious pick. It was a wicked implement but it worked, and eventually a production version reached the market. Indestructible and finely tempered, the new tool appeared similar to the traditional axe except that the mechanics were different; for instance, the angle of the pick was finely calculated to one degree, and the shaft, unlike the traditional wood, was unbreakable. MacInnes assembled these tools in his own Glencoe workshop.

Back in 1953 MacInnes had attempted to climb Mount Everest with fellow Glaswegian and Creag Dhu climber Johnny Cunningham, an audacious project which ran out of upward momentum, not because Hilary and Tenzing got there first, but because the English expedition had eaten the food abandoned on the previous Swiss attempt and on which the Scots had depended. After many adventures Cunningham went to Antarctica where he passed the time experimenting with his crampons and working out new techniques for climbing the ice that surrounded him. He pushed the teutonic 'dagger' method to its limit but was unhappy with it. It was difficult to stop or to rest, and very easy to fall off – and while (unless rival climbers should attack!) the daggers were of limited use, the picks of the ice axes then current were the wrong shape.

He returned to Scotland, where, working as an instructor at Glenmore Lodge, the S.C.P.R.'s national mountain centre in the Cairngorms, he discovered the answer – the Chouinard hammer. This is an American tool, developed from the piton hammer of the Yosemite rock climbers, with the head elongated into a thin six-inch beak-like pick gracefully curved to a far steeper angle than the normal axe. It was just right for Cunningham's requirements. Using the new tools and climbing with fellow instructor Bill March, a Londoner, he developed a new method. With 'lobster-claws' honed to a chisel edge, and with Chouinard hammers razor-sharp in each hand, they learned to climb plumb vertical ice in twenty- to thirty-foot stages. After each stage, and hanging on to one hammer, an ice screw was fixed and the climber rested on it before proceeding. Never a step was cut. It is a bold technique and very exacting on both man and equipment. Sometimes hammer picks were known to break in awkward situations. But it is a direct and very swift means of mastering steep or vertical ice, and on a snowy mountain speed is safety.

Bill March explains that on the steepest ice, margin for error is minimal, that such things as the exact angle of the ankle are crucial, and he admits that he has taken many falls perfecting the technique. 'You should keep a file in your pocket to keep things really sharp,'

he says, 'and if the ground is really steep it's the only thing liable to hurt you should you come off . . . always assuming you've obeyed the usual rules for belay and protection!' He points out that on ground less than vertical the method is very safe; it involves a natural movement.

Over the last four years Cunningham and March have exploded into the limelight with a series of exceptionally fast and effortless ascents of many of the hardest and longest Scottish winter climbs. The methods have been tried and accepted now by all the hard 'ice men' – both the older established ones and the young and aspiring – and at Glenmore Lodge the 'method' is now official teaching for students of winter mountaineering. Abroad too there is considerable interest, and

Above left: A typical short Scottish ice climb, the Left Fork of Y Gully on Cairn Lochan of Cairngorm: Johnny Cunningham brings up Tom Patey

Above centre: Using Chouinard hammers Bill March makes a difficult move during the first ascent of Window Gully on the Lurchers Crag above the Lairig Ghru in the Cairngorms

Above right: Bill March demonstrates the use of terrordactyls and front-points on vertical ice

Yvon Chouinard himself is a regular winter visitor to Scottish ice. In the Alps thc British have always seemed reluctant to venture on to the great ice faces, but Scottish lads who recently climbed the direct route on the north flank of Les Droites in the Mont Blanc Range, which until recently was considered perhaps the hardest ice route in the Alps, reported that technically its difficulty rated only a Scottish winter III. Point Five Gully is considered a hard Grade V! While, of course, there is far more to great alpine routes than mere technical difficulty, the future augers well for experienced Scottish ice men.

Meanwhile, with several manufacturers now producing curved or 'dropped-pick' axes in the new style, and some climbers actually

The North-East Buttress of Ben Nevis falls 1000 feet into the corrie beneath. The lines of Zero and Point Five Gullies – the two modern classic gully climbs – are labelled. Between them is the Observatory Ridge, a fine but easy route first climbed by Harold Raeburn in 1901. Raeburn also made the first winter ascent in 1920

Opposite: Cairngorms – looking south from Braeriach (4248 feet) across the Garbh Coire to Cairntoul (4241 feet). To the left is the deep defile of the Lairig Ghru. The relative lack of snow is unusual for winter but ice crystals coat the foreground granite boulders

curving their own picks with a blow lamp and retempering them, MacInnes has unveiled his latest 'message' – the Terrordactyl. This all-metal weapon is revolutionary in concept. Not only is it light and perfectly balanced, but its head is bent entirely from a special sheet steel and the talon-like pick is straight, but angled very steeply downwards, giving the silhouette that inspired the late Ian Clough, while helping MacInnes with the initial development work, to coin its name. As revolutionary too is a new crampon that is already taking shape in MacInnes's workshop.

The Terrordactyl is not easy to use correctly and it takes time, patience and bruised knuckles to learn the peculiar downward 'swipe' that places it in steep ice. But once this is perfected it is easy to use and feels enormously safe. In contrast to curved-pick tools it is easy to remove when necessary, a most important point when strength is ebbing. Because of its mechanical configuration the climber can clip into the hole at the end of the short shaft and, supported solely by his lobster-claws and the pick of the Terrordactyl in the ice above, can lean back, drop his arms to his side and rest. As winter lines move on to steeper and more blank rock, still more applications appear for the tool. I have seen MacInnes climb a rock wall in Glencoe, steep, smooth and glazed, where the tiny incut holds would have been useless wearing gloves, using two Terrordactyls as steel fingers. It is bold. It is revolutionary. It is fast.

The winter of 1972–73 was an unremarkable one. Ice conditions were not good but eventually in March they became fair on Ben Nevis. 'Big Ian' Nicholson, one of the best of the younger generation of Scottish climbers, was working at the time for MacInnes's ice climbing school in Glencoe. On a rest day he visited 'The Ben' and using in one hand a Chouinard hammer and in the other a Terrordactyl he soloed both Zero and Point Five Gullies in a morning! The former, 1200 feet of extremely steep ice rated at Grade V, took him all of sixty minutes, about the same time as the latter – perhaps harder, but only 900 feet. By lunchtime 'Big Ian' was drowning his thirst in a public house in Fort William. As he said, '. . . steepness presented no problems . . . the tools were going in beautifully . . . my confidence was greater than ever before. . . .' But he adds, '. . . we're no better climbers than the lads of ten years ago – we've just got better equipment and that makes the climbs easier . . .'

In February 1974, using techniques similar to the modern Scottish ones, the young French guide Walter Cechinnel, who has since made a fact-finding visit to Scotland, made the first ascent of the viciously steep ice *couloir* between the Grand and the Petit Dru in the Mont Blanc Range. It was a climb very much in the Scottish style as distinct from what has been done before in the Alps, and of it 'Wee Brian' Robertson, who attempted it in February 1967, said: '. . . it's for the next generation of men – but Scotsmen'. The climbers are ready. The equipment is waiting. The revolution is upon us!

Top left: Beinn Alligin
(3232 feet) — rises across
Loch Torridon, a beautiful
sea loch in Wester Ross. The
traverse of the four tops and
several pinnacles of this
sandstone mountain is an
entertaining expedition

Top right: Suilven (2399 feet)
— an autumn storm breaks
over the long but narrow
ridge of this fine little
mountain in the Assynt
region of Sutherland. There
is rock climbing on Caisteal
Liath — the Grey Castle — the
left-hand top

Below: Cairngorms — January
dawn in Coire an t-Sneachda.
Just to the right of the
climber is Aladdin's Couloir
from where crags lead round
to Fiacaill Buttress on the far
right

Top: Creag Meaghaidh — perfect winter conditions in late March on this fine 1500-foot cliff in the Central Highlands. Left to right: Raeburns Gully, Pinnacle Buttress, Easy Gully and the Post Face with its three great gullies. To the right the crags of the Inner Coire disappear out of the picture

Lower left: On the Direct start to South Post — a difficult 1500-foot ice climb. Jim McArtney is belayed by Alan Fyffe

Lower right: On the Girdle Traverse of Creag Meaghaidh — the first section — 'The Scene' — of this superb expedition. A concept of Tom Patey's, the Girdle gives some 8000 feet of sustained, but never really hard, winter climbing. The steps in front of the lead climber are Patey's as he moved on ahead to make the first complete traverse in five hours solo

Right: Tom Patey

The incredible Joss

Top centre: Joss Naylor in
his Wasdale farmyard.
Bottom: Breaking the Welsh
Fourteen Peaks record — Joss
descends fast down Cwm
Glas. Below is Nant Peris and
the Llanberis Pass, and
opposite the next mountain
he must climb, Elidir Fawr.
Far right: Joss at speed in the
Nant Ffrancon Valley near
Lake Ogwen.

At exactly 2.46 p.m. on Sunday, 17 June 1973, two figures in bare legs and flapping cagoules trotted out of the west mist to the summit of Foel Fras – most northerly of the 3000-foot Carneddau summits. Their arrival seemed unremarkable to the three cold soldiers with their crackling radios who had been huddled by the cairn for several hours while they checked the Army teams on their own annual Fourteen Peaks exercise. Unbeknown, they had witnessed sporting history, for Joss Naylor, the Wasdale shepherd, had just arrived from Snowdon summit, via all fourteen 3000-footers, in the incredible time of 4 hours 46 minutes.

The Welsh 'Fourteen Peaks' is one of the classic mountain runs of Britain: from the Snowdon summit at 3561 feet to Foel Fras at 3092 feet is almost exactly twenty-two miles – not in a straight line, but the quickest way taking in the summits of the other twelve 3000-foot tops. Between the three summits of the Snowdon group and the Glyders – the next range – the deep trough of the Nant Peris must be crossed with a descent to 350 feet, and later, between the last of the five Glyders and the Carnedds, the runner must go down to Llyn Ogwen at 985 feet. From top to top, not counting the climb up Snowdon in the first place, there is nearly 11,000 feet of ascent and a little more of descent. To get round the course at all, at a steady walk, is a fine and gruelling expedition, and over the last century many well-known names have clipped hours from the ambling progress of Eustace Thomas and his Rucksack Club party who walked it in 20 hours in 1919. In the thirties W. W. Stallybrass managed 13 hours 20 minutes, Showell Styles 12 hours 44 minutes and Frank Shuttleworth 10 hours 29 minutes. In 1938, after considerable planning and training, Thomas Firbank, a gentleman turned sheep farmer, cut the record to 8 hours 25 minutes – quite a feat, and well recorded in his classic book *I Bought a Mountain*.

Just after the Second World War two instructors from the Army's Mountain Warfare School in Llanberis, Jack Haines and E. A. Hamson, broke Firbank's record by exactly one hour. In the *Climber's*

Club Journal Hamson noted: 'It was hot for the time of year so we wore only shorts and boots: half way round Jack Haines discarded his shorts and went on just in boots. Someone clothed him to go through Nant Peris but at Blaen-y-Nant he stripped again and sent a runner ahead to the top of Snowdon with his trousers. He arrived, however, before the runner. There were several ladies, including his wife, waiting at the top and I heard later how his wife welcomed him with open arms while the others discovered a new beauty in the view over the Lleyn Peninsula.' But John Barford, editor of the *Journal,* commented: 'It is to be hoped that these times are so good as to discourage others from racing over our hills with a stopwatch.'

Certainly it was not until the advent of mountaineers who are also top-class athletes that the seven-hour barrier was broken. In 1953 and 1954 John Disley, John Mawe, Chris Brasher and Eric Herbert, after careful reconnaissances and strategic changes of footwear for different sections, all clocked excellent times. None of them, however, were within a distance of the incredible new record of 6 hours exactly set up by Bertie Robertson, a Gloucestershire schoolmaster, in September 1954. Nobody could get inside this time for ten years; but in 1965 the great Eric Beard, past president of the Rock & Ice, committed mountaineer and fell-runner extraordinary, added the 'Fourteen Peaks' to his growing list of record fell runs. His time was 5 hours 13 minutes. Just before 'Beardie's' tragic death on the M6 in November 1969 he had been on a training run with his friend Joss Naylor and he told Joss that: 'if you want my records Pal – they're yours'.

And so it has been. Joss Naylor (to whom his father said, when he took up running thirteen years ago, '. . . forget about it lad, you'll never compete with them fellows') is without doubt the best fell-runner in Britain today. And at the age of thirty-eight he is at his prime. He says that he needs a race of over three hours' duration, preferably with at least 5000 feet of climbing and plenty of rough ground, to be at his best. Certainly in these sort of conditions he is an athlete fit to be ranked with men like David Bedford and Tony Jacklin in the annals of sport.

Along with Cumberland Wrestling, rum butter and mint cake, fell-running is a speciality in the English Lake District. A popular local sport, it has become in the last decade something of a national sport attracting competitors from the cities, especially in the North and Midlands. But it wasn't until he had been invalided out of wrestling with an old schoolboy back injury and spent eight weeks in a strait jacket that Joss decided to give fell-running a try.

Wasdale is a narrow valley which cuts north-east deep into the knot of high mountains that is the heart of Cumbria. Wastwater, a dark and profound lake, blocks the valley beneath a forbidding line of crags and steep screes. But isolated, as it were, beyond the head of the lake, the valley widens into a green sanctuary of pastures and farms and little stone-walled fields round which rises a wall of mighty hillsides –

Fast going on steep scree descending from the North Ridge of Crib Goch

Yewbarrow, Kirkfell, Great Gable and mighty Scafell himself – 3210 feet and England's highest mountain.

Wasdale is Joss Naylor's home. His father farmed at Raw Head, one of the 'sanctuary' farms, and his mother was a 'Wilson of Wasdale'. And so it was appropriate that his first race was a Wasdale Mountain Trial, a gruelling fell-race over the surrounding peaks. Wearing big hobnail boots and spending half an hour twisted with cramp, Joss finished sixteenth. It was two years before he raced again, but in the meantime he had moved to his own farm beside Wastwater, got married and, having met up with Eric Beard, learned about the necessity of training. Again he entered the Wasdale Mountain Trial and this time was first home by an unprecedented twenty-five minutes, only to be disqualified on a technical point. As if to prove that this was not just 'local lad's luck', Joss entered the highly spectacular Ben Nevis Race in 1962 and placed fifth. As he says, 'if I'd really trained . . . I'd have shown them . . .'.

And since then he has 'shown them' – often in company with his friend Alan Walker, a building society manager from Whitehaven (the nearest town), with whom Joss trains or partners for such team events as the Two-Day Mountain Marathon, and who in fact paced him for the final section of the 'Fourteen Peaks' over the Carneddau.

The 'Fourteen Peaks' attempt was only Joss's third trip to Wales (or fourth if you count his honeymoon) and his unfamiliarity with the route did present some problems. For a few minutes he was, as he put it 'crag-fast' on Crib-y-Ddysgl; he got cramp on Dafydd and was lost in thick wet mist on Llywelyn. Given good luck, he feels that there is still some ten minutes to knock off his own new record.

What of the future? Joss will admit that he does have certain ambitions. First there is the Pennine Way in under four days – the record standing in 1973 was four days five hours for the 270 miles by Alan Heaton.

Then there is the 'Skye Ridge', the traverse of the main ridge of the Black Cuillin, a rocky arête some eight miles long, with another four miles of approach at either end, never falling below 2500 feet and involving some 10,000 feet of ascent and descent. This would be a new departure, as it involves actual rock-climbing, some quite exposed. Not that Joss is a stranger to steep rock – it's all in the shepherd's job.

Alan Walker is trying to persuade him to try the four Cairngorm tops, and with a far-away look in his eyes he talks of the Kilimanjaro–Mount Kenya record: a descent of over 14,000 feet, a drive over bush roads of over 400 miles, followed by a climb of some 12,000 feet – and all on the equator. Rusty Baillie and Barry Cliff's time is twenty-three hours.

But meantime there is Mary and the three children at home, some sixty-five cattle down the dale and a thousand Herdwicks and Swaledales on the fell. Even if he is the best fell-runner in Britain, a shepherd's work is never done.

How we climbed Am Buachaille

There is no land between Cape Wrath and the North Pole. It is the ultimate north-westerly tip of main-land Britain. The name is taken from the Norse *Hvarf* – a turning point – for here the long-ships turned south towards the Hebrides, Ireland and the rich plunder of more populous coasts. In the Gaelic, the wild and empty moors of Torridonian Sandstone behind the Cape are known as 'The Parbh', a corruption of the Norse, and they are haunted, it is said, by the legendary Cu-Saeng. Those who have glimpsed its shadow say that this terrible monster has two heads – but all who have actually seen it have died.

The cliffs run south from Cape Wrath for five miles until they relax into the wide dunes of Sandwood Bay, one of the finest beaches in the whole of Britain and perhaps the most remote. Mermaids have been seen here. The Bay too is haunted, but by a more likely ghost, the spectral figure of a pirate wearing a tricorn hat. Off the cliff-girt southern point of the Bay, and from a rocky plinth over which the tides swirl back and forth, rises a 200-foot column of red sandstone. It is slab-sided and undercut, its faces wrinkled with the typical horizontal bedding of this ancient and ironhard rock. This is Am Buachaille – 'the herdsman' – a notable landmark for the trawlermen working the Minches into the tiny fishing village of Kinlochbervie five miles to the south.

Tom Patey was the doctor in Ullapool, a fishing village and the largest habitation on the north-west coast – just across the Sutherland border into Wester Ross. Now Tom happened to be the finest mountaineer in Scotland. Conqueror of the Mustagh Tower and Rakaposhi and alpinist extraordinary, he was an inveterate explorer. Where better to dwell than in the wild country of the north-west where fine upstanding mountains rise from a tangle of remote sea lochs and empty glens? Despite the great potential of the mountains around him Tom was not blind to the possibilities of his local sea cliffs. He had served as a doctor in the Royal Marine Commandos at Plymouth and made routes on many of the high and virgin crags on the savage northern coasts of Cornwall and Devon – routes not repeated for fifteen years and then marvelled at by mind-blown youngsters of a new generation. When he first arrived in Ullapool in 1961 Tom started a systematic exploration of the local coastline.

I had accompanied Tom on several of these trips and when one day he telephoned me in London, mentioning Am Buachaille, I knew something exciting was afoot. I dropped everything – rang the Observer newspaper to line up a possible story – and caught the next plane to Inverness. Here Ian Clough, a kindly Yorkshireman – and top alpinist – who worked as a guide in Glencoe, and his raven-haired wife, Nikki, collected me in their old Volkswagen and we buzzed seventy miles over the Dirrie More to the west coast, and down to Ullapool on the sheltered waters of Loch Broom.

That evening we visited a certain pub in Ullapool. When we left

Tom Patey is proud of his new discovery – the virgin stack of Am Buachaille

sometime later, we were carrying two long sections of aluminium ladder borrowed from the friendly innkeeper, who seemed not in the least surprised at the request – as he took our empty glasses he wished us good luck with a knowing wink. Tom assured us that the ladders were essential for the coming day's programme, and after all who were we to dispute the good Doctor's requirements? But next morning as we tripped out over the wide moors beyond Kinlochbervie where not a rock is in sight, wearing, yoke-wise, 18-foot aluminium ladders, we passed crofters working at the peat cuttings. They wished us a cheery good-day, but as we passed they looked at each other and shook their heads. At least, unlike the Cu-Saeng, we were harmless enough! Cloughy and I felt very foolish.

The day was bright and sweet. Curlews cried overhead and the blue sky was reflected in every moorland pool. The white heads of the bog cotton rippled in a gentle breeze. Three miles from the peat cuttings we looked down on Sandwood Bay. Beyond the white surf, the white sand and the brilliant green of the marram, craggy headlands marched towards the distant white thumb of the Cape Wrath lighthouse. We carried on round the cliff edge, and looked down to our stack. It stood several hundred yards back from the cliff bottom, its plinth separated from a large area of pool-dotted and weed-covered ledges and boulders by a channel of deep water. The sea was calm and ruffled only by the breeze: it was nearly low tide and the clear green waters were darkened with kelp where they heaved languidly against the rocks.

We fixed an abseil rope on to a large boulder, manhandled the ladders and ourselves down the 300-foot cliffs and struggled out across the slippery ledges to the deep water channel. If you have ever abseiled carrying an 18-foot aluminium ladder you will know what fun it is! At its narrowest point the channel was about thirty feet wide and thick beds of brown kelp swirled in the powerful current which swept through it. I am a good swimmer but the weed looked uninviting and the water cold and powerful, and Tom muttered blood-curdling tales of man-eating seals and the dangerous currents and carnivorous seaweed of this coast. So now the ladders came into their own: lashed end to end they just reached across the narrows. The far end was lodged precariously on a tiny ledge on the steep wall of the plinth while the near end rested awash on a kelp covered boulder. Hands and feet on the ladder Tom started gingerly across. The ladders flexed badly; by the time he had reached the middle Tom's feet were well under water but he eventually made the far side safely. It was obvious the ladders would soon be submerged by the incoming tide so Cloughy and I rescued them and fixed up a tyrolean traverse rope way above the water to reach Tom and to safeguard our return.

The landward face of the stack was just as steep as it had looked – plumb vertical in fact – and the bottom overhanging. Torridonian Red Sandstone, however, is a surprising climbing rock and often

148

Top: 'Tom started gingerly across'. Left: Ian Clough on the first pitch 'climbing easily through the bulging overhangs'. Bottom: 'He tried traversing out left and tried to pull over some fragile looking flutings — there was one dicey moment'.

149

provides hidden holds in the most unexpected places. Tom led easily up through the bulging overhangs, the climbing strenuous but the rock solid. Above the overhangs he reached a sort of prow, crossed a series of horizontal faults and, traversing to the leftward arête, found himself on a good ledge some 80 feet above the ground where there was a large and rusty piton. Someone had been here first! It seemed, however, from the strands of rotting line tied through the eye of the peg that it had been used for escape, and some months later we found that this had indeed been the case. The peg was at the limit of the previous party's upward exploration. Tom placed a running belay and hurried on. From his lofty viewpoint he was aware of the incoming tide. And only he was aware of its implications for him! The next few moves were hard: a strenuous V.S., out right onto the wall of an overhanging beak, across, up, and a mantleshelf on to the top of it. Above this was a line of cracks, but the rock had become very brittle and coated with a fine film of sand. Every other hold was loose and the climbing became harrowing. But a traverse led to another good ledge on the leftward arête. And Tom was two-thirds up Am Buachaille.

When he had belayed and taken in the rope, Cloughy and I followed him up. On every little ledge and cranny sat a young Fulmar. Now Fulmars have a peculiar method of welcoming visitors: when they are really close they fire at them a powerful gush of oily yellow puke. The throw is accurate and the range as much as four feet. It seems Fulmars have a multiple stomach and they can operate in machine-gun fashion. Tom – from long experience – had evolved a technique of dodging the first salvo and quickly walling the poor bird round with small blocks of loose rock. He was then at liberty to look for the next holds and continue the route upwards unhindered by enemy bombardment. The second man, however, arriving in turn at every ledge, was obliged to liberate the walled-in and now irate Fulmar. For his pains he received, not just a salvo, but a saturation barrage of evil smelling muck. By the time we reached Tom we were liberally coated and smelling like two fish-wives.

Nikki, who had left us early on to visit Sandwood Bay, had now scrambled down the cliff and set up the gear for a brew among the boulders. She came over the ledges to the channel and called across that the rope was now awash; the tide was coming in very fast and the thirty foot channel had become sixty.

Tom led off again but the wall above was vertical and broken by a series of wafer-like overhangs. First he tried an obvious crack-line to the right but it was steeper than it appeared and he came back. He tried again traversing out leftward and managed to pull over some of the fragile-looking flutings. There was one dicey moment when, mantle-shelfing precariously on one wafer, his climbing harness caught on another, and we had to watch powerless while he fought to untangle himself. He eventually succeeded and disappeared upwards with a stream of oaths.

150

The landward face of Am Buachaille. Tom Patey, high at the top left, is still some fifty feet below the summit. Ian Clough is on the face nearly 100 feet below him

Cloughy was not feeling well that day and he decided to come no further. He arranged the spare rope as an abseil and went down to rejoin Nikki and start the tea. At last the rope went tight and it was my turn to climb. The pitch was intimidating and I too snarled up in the flutings: my pullover, my belt, my slings, my hammer and the straps of my camera – they all caught! Leaning out of balance, every biscuit-like hold threatened to snap off in my hand. Then I found myself kicking steps up a headwall of slimy guano – P.A.'s are not the best footwear for this sort of climbing – and there I was on easy ledges leading to the summit, a pile of shattered blocks just above.

But there were coils of rope lying everywhere. Far from taking it in, Tom was in the act of hurling it into space and starting his abseil descent. 'Have ye seen the sea', he shouted at me. 'The tide's right in and we're cut off!', adding as an afterthought as he went sliding off into space – '. . . and I canna swim'.

Despite the worrying peg below there was no sign that anyone had been here before, and I built a small cairn. Then I searched for a more stable-looking abseil point and, making sure that the rope would pull down after me, started my own descent. The channel was now 120 feet of seething water; Nikki was in the process of hauling Tom across the submarine tyrolean rope. He was shouting and splashing and kept disappearing beneath the incoming waves. He struggled out on the far side, shaking off the water and laughing. Cloughy and I stripped off and sent our clothes, gear and cameras across in a polythene bag. Then we plunged in ourselves, aided by a quick haul on the rope to stop getting washed down the channel. The sun had gone by now and the water was cold: Nikki's hot cup of tea was just what we needed.

There is always a thrill climbing a virgin summit. And anyway the Observer liked the story which they ran, picture and copy, on the sports-page the following Sunday. So it was worth the flight to Inverness after all!

The tide has come in! Nikki Clough coils the rope while her husband, trouserless, tries to keep warm

Sea-cliff climbing
in Britain

The year was dying and the heavy Atlantic swell heaved and swirled ten feet below us, every few moments soaking us in the welter of spray. The grey limestone arched out above our heads into an even greyer winter sky. 'It goes free', said Biven reassuringly. 'But it's hard V.S. and it's all on the fingers.' I looked at Rusty. He frowned. 'It's not my scene today', he grunted. 'Not after a week of Christmas!' 'Nor mine', I replied. 'What's round the corner?'

We were below 'Moonraker' – the sole, and then still unrepeated, route on the 300 foot wall of the Old Redoubt cliff at Berry Head in South Devon. We had approached through a great sea-cave, a difficult traverse only possible at low tide. The cliffs fall into deep water; to escape now would mean a long and dangerous swim, loaded with gear. There was nothing to lose by looking. While Biven and Frank swung on aching arms through the overhangs above, Rusty and I swung round the corner into the unknown.

We found ourselves on a line of horizontal strata – a natural traverse line – between the sea and the jutting roofs. It was night-time and half-a-mile further on before we emerged at the next break in the cliffs, where a scrambly ridge leads through to the grassy sward of the Redoubt itself, a ruined Napoleonic Wars fort. We were exhausted and soaked to the skin. We had passed problem after problem, hard sections linked by easy but strenuous climbing, and never more than thirty feet above the waves. Once we had pegged down a great over-hung prow before tensioning across to a line of holds at sea-level. We had swum the mouth of a fresh-water grotto going deep into the limestone, and finally tyroleaned a natural arch through which the winter sea pounded in vicious foam. And so 'Magical Mystery Tour' was born; it was destined to become a classic and a milestone in a new form of rock-climbing.

Rock-climbing on sea-cliffs has come of age as an integral part of the British climbing scene. On a typical weekend climbers will be at work on sea-cliffs from Aberdeen to Anglesey, from Lundy to Land's End. Even in North Wales, that cradle of British rock-climbing, the 'hard-men' seem to have deserted the crags of Snowdonia. Instead they head for Craig Gogarth, the huge Holyhead sea-cliff, where (in common with most other sea-cliffs) the sun always seems to shine while the mountain crags are shrouded in mist and rain.

Probably the first climber to take advantage of our coast was Mummery, the Alpine pioneer who disappeared on the Diamir Flank of Nanga Parbat in 1895. Armed with axe and crampons he climbed on the White Cliffs of Dover, treating the crumbling chalk as if it were alpine ice. He made what was perhaps the first 'Sea-Traverse' when he linked Dover Harbour to St. Margaret's Bay by a sea-level girdle, where the tide-washed chalk offered reasonably safe climbing.

Another pioneer was Dr. Tom Longstaff, later to climb and explore in the Caucasus, the Himalaya and the Arctic. He scrambled and traversed on the coasts of his native Devon and made possibly the

The first pitch of Moonraker, overhanging straight out over deep water, on Berry Head near Brixham in Devon. Magical Mystery Tour works round the corner between the sea and the bulges above

153

first ascent of Gannet's Rock, a large stack off Lundy Island. But he was not happy climbing over the sea. He wrote: 'Climbing on the sea-cliffs does not grant us that freedom of spirit which we find on mountain tops. The surf confines us with elemental restraint: thus far and no further.'

The notorious black-magician, Aleister Crowley, was another early climber on chalk. There is a photograph of him in 1894, alpenstock across his knees, on the summit of Etheldreda's Pinnacle, an impressive *gendarme* high on the wall of Beachy Head in Sussex. The Pinnacle is still there and so is Crowley's cairn. In 1969 Tom Patey and I

Magical Mystery Tour – Odd Eliassen has swum the final cave and is struggling out of the calm dark sea

Right: Perdonlie Edge rises above the wild North Sea at Longhaven near Aberdeen

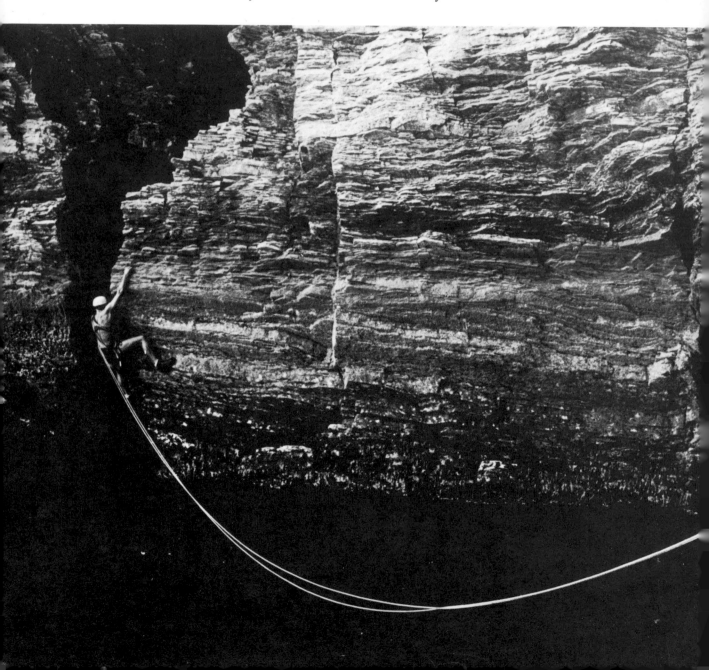

attempted to repeat his climb, but – like others before us – we failed: perhaps Crowley had supernatural assistance that is not available today?

But these were isolated instances; there were few climbers in Britain and hundreds of virgin mountain crags. It was not until the years before the Great War, when A. W. Andrews, instrumental in the exploration of Lliwedd – in those days THE cliff in Snowdonia – inherited a house in Cornwall near Land's End, that sea-cliff climbing as we know it today was born. Andrews naturally turned his attention to the rough red granite of the rocky coast below his new home. His

early explorations were often horizontal for, like others since, the pioneers were discouraged by the earthy and vegetationous steep ground usually found on the cliff tops. He was to anticipate developments of fifty years later.

His friends, men like Mallory and Winthrop Young and Odell, joined the fun. In 1912, describing the first ascent of the ridge of Carn Lês Boel with Mallory, Young wrote:

It was a rock surface of volatile changes, from chimney or column, crystallized, friable and prickly, to the sea and the time-smoothed perpendicular or overhang. The slow waves as we climbed into the sun muttered and yawned round the bases of the ridge, and the echoes whispering up the hollows in the walls met the ceaseless sibilant recession of broken water off the rocks . . .

He had realized, as Longstaff had not, that it was that very intimacy with the sea that is the unique fascination of sea-cliff climbing. There were innovations too: it was Andrews, in Cornwall, who first used the rubber-soled tennis shoe on difficult rock, the forerunner of the now ubiquitous P.A. While on Sark, Leslie Shadbolt was experimenting with carefully selected limpets as portable footholds. (He was unsuccessful!)

After the Great War the granite cliffs of Land's End grew in popularity. In 1938 Andrews leased to his club – the Climbers Club – an old mine building at Bosigran, the best climbing area, for use as a hut. But Cornwall was still not taken seriously; there was a holiday atmosphere distinct from the 'real sport' taking place in Snowdonia or the Lake District. It was the Second War that changed all that. The Cliff Assault Wing of the Royal Marine Commandos was established near Land's End; their exploits gave a fresh momentum to Cornish climbing which has lasted to this day. Nowadays there are climbs in Cornwall as hard as any in Wales, perhaps harder.

But it was not until the late fifties that climbers turned any serious attention to sea-cliffs outside Cornwall. Many of these cliffs were limestone and previously considered unjustifiably dangerous. But the limestone 'renaissance' in Yorkshire, the Peak and especially in the Avon Gorge at Bristol had shown that if traditional attitudes to loose rock were abandoned and new protection techniques developed, these vertical cliffs would yield safe and excellent climbs. Besides which, virgin rock in the usual mountain areas was getting scarcer weekend by weekend. Many climbers living in the south and west found the regular Friday night drive to Snowdonia or Langdale tiresome and gruelling. They discovered that there were over 500 miles of almost unexplored coastline – much of it crag-dirt – in the opposite direction. And what Englishman is not beguiled by the sea?

There were new problems to overcome on sea-cliffs. Potential lines are difficult to spot, for it is often impossible to get back more than a few feet from the base of a crag unless a boat is available. The finishes of many climbs are dangerous where the transition from steep rock to easy angled grass is a zone of shattered blocks and vertical

Joss Naylor — champion
fell-runner, at his Wastdale
farm in the Lake District on
a damp June day

Top: Looking down the gloomy defile of the Llanberis Pass in Snowdonia from Pen-y-Pass. The crags of Dinas Mot and Dinas Cromlech can be seen on the left and right

Below: Peter Crew, one of the leading figures on Welsh rock in the 1960s, leads the crux of 'M.P.P.' — an airy and extremely difficult climb on Dinas Mot in the Llanberis Pass. This was the second ascent — Peter Crew had made the first some months earlier

earth. Communication between leader and second may well be impossible above the roar of the surf. Many climbers also found the environment unnerving and distracting. At this stage two different approaches to the development of sea-cliffs became discernable. In the south-west particularly there were climbers, living remote from the mountains, who grew to specialize in sea cliffs and their problems, out of preference for the atmosphere and loneliness they found; they treated the nautical difficulties as an interesting new challenge. Northern and Snowdonia-oriented climbers however tended to develop their new discoveries as mountain crags; they tried to ignore the sea beneath them and the horizontal potentials. This new approach was vividly demonstrated in the late sixties when Little Orme, a high limestone sea-cliff rising from deep water, was discovered on the coast of North Wales. An obvious line could be spotted through glasses from the opposite headland a mile across the bay, but the Snowdonia climbers were unable to locate the bottom of it by abseil because the cliff was so overhanging and the topography very complex. They were beaten at the game by a party of south-west sea-cliff 'specialists' on a lightning visit, who – floating their gear with them in polythene bags – swam to the bottom of the line and bagged the route. This was a technique already well established to approach similar cliffs in Devon.

The first limestone area to receive much attention was the four miles of south-facing cliffs near Swanage in Dorset. These crags are but 115 miles from London – whereas Snowdonia is over 220. The cliffs are only 120 feet in height; they are often overhanging and bottom into the sea. But the rock – to almost full height – is as solid as limestone can be. The dangerous transition zone from rock to grass was eventually overcome here using ice-hammers and cutting earthy holds. But early on, leaders were discouraged by it and developed the lines where there were natural features such as chimneys or towers which provided living rock right to the top. Bold lines weaving through the impressive overhangs can give four-pitch routes of 200 feet or so.

It was perhaps a sneaking fear of these cliff-tops that led to the birth of the modern 'sea-traverse'. In 1963, when Rusty Baillie was fresh from his success with Haston on the Eigerwand, he and I completed 'Traverse of the Gods' at Swanage. We tried to link two places nearly a quarter-mile apart on the map, where descent to the sea is easy, by a traverse through a virgin area where access from above was impossible – owing to lack of abseil points in the steep grass. The object was to use all means at our disposal and to take to the water only as a last resort, since a strong current and tide rip made swimming dangerous. The first traverse took us seven hours and we crossed ground that was always new and exciting. Our line above the seas was continually split by caves and zawns and overhung by massive roofs barring any escape upwards. It was the sort of lonely place where you expect to find the body of a long-dead sailorman lashed to a spar, rising and falling in the sucking green tide in a dark zawn. We used every rope-

The Old Man of Hoy – Rusty Baillie climbing on jumars during a reconnaissance on this incredible 450-foot sea-stack in the Orkney Islands off the North of Scotland. The Old Man became nationally famous when the climb was televised live by the BBC in 1967. The easiest route follows a fierce crack line through the overhangs above Rusty and is a very serious climb. Other climbs have been made on the 1000-foot walls of St. John's Head in the distance

161

Top left: 'The slow waves as we climbed into the sun muttered and yawned...' Gill Cannon on Ochre Slab at Bosigran in Cornwall

Bottom left: Peter Biven climbing the Devils Slide, with the twin towers of St James Stone beyond

Below: Looking up the classic Devils Slide on Lundy Island – 400 feet of rich curling granite

trick we knew – the very first pitch required a tension rapelle – and we climbed and lassoed and tyroleaned our way until a 70-foot wide zawn, deep with swirling black water, stopped us dead. We swum this, roped together, one at a time, to land on easy ground only a few yards from hot tea and dry clothes.

'Traverse of the Gods' led to the concept that the natural line on most sea-cliffs is horizontal – with notable exceptions. On a normal mountain crag, safe ground is at the bottom and easy ground at the top. But the climber at the bottom of a sea-cliff is out in the cold – he may well be completely cut off from safety. The 'line' will be one joining easy ground to left and right. It was soon discovered that even on crags impossible to climb – impressive headlands of slate, shale, new red sandstone and other appallingly loose rocks – the lower twenty or thirty feet near the tide-line can be relied upon to provide solid rock suitable for traverses. This discovery opened up whole new stretches of the coast. Unlikely areas such as the slates of Cornwall's Bedruthan Steps and the conglomerates of Devon's Teignmouth have yielded novel traverses of great character.

The coast from Sharkham Point to the famous yachting centre of Dartmouth provides some eight miles of traverse – the 'Bluebell Line'. Eight days were spent working on this scenic expedition, across walls and through caves and arches of flaky shales below lush hillsides covered in impenetrable vegetation. By contrast a party attempting a continuation on the west side of Dartmouth in winter were forced to swim out, defeated by verglassed rock at sea-level! The aesthetics of sea-traversing are more alpine than those of traditional rock-climbing. A knowledge of the tides and the weather is essential. Speed, stamina and fitness will keep you alive and you must be a strong swimmer. Cannyness and drive are more important than sheer technical ability. The 'Master' – Joe Brown himself – who has girdled much of the rocky coast of Anglesey, the large island off his local North Wales, has claimed that sea-traversing is the most potentially serious form of rock-climbing he has encountered.

Apart from Swanage there is limestone at Torbay, where besides 'Magical Mystery Tour' and some superb vertical lines like 'Moonraker' and 'Last Exit to Torquay' – Torquay is the Monte Carlo of the English Riviera – there is the entertaining 'Five Star Traverse' passing across deserted and secret walls a few feet below the plush and unsuspecting Imperial Hotel! There is plenty more limestone in South Wales.

Lundy is one of the most interesting areas; it is a narrow granite island some three miles long lying twelve miles off the North Devon coast. It supports a farm and two lighthouses and an interesting population of seals, rare sea-birds and wild sheep, goats and deer. It has a long and varied history. It was the stronghold of a robber baron, the lair of Turkish pirates and a convict settlement. It is the grave of countless ships including the first-rate Dreadnaught H.M.S.

163

Montague which ran ashore in 1906. Lundy is ringed by 350-foot cliffs of the Cornish pattern, individual crags rather than continuous traversable walls, but the vertical-type climbing is second to none in Britain and there are three superb sea-stacks for those who like the unusual. A unique route, one of the truly great sea-cliff climbs, is the Devils Lime Kiln. The Kiln is a huge blow-hole taking its name from the clouds of froth and foam that blow from it over the island during westerly gales. Its 400-foot depth is inescapable and the route is a serious one, including darkness, loose rock and grass overhangs, although only technically a mild V.S. The bottom of the 'Lime Kiln' is reached at low tide through a long and narrow cave below a huge cliff. Two pitches in a difficult wet chimney lead out of the darkness onto a succession of bottomless and overhung slabs that weave their way through the upper funnel towards the sky.

The centre of development is now the long and wild north coast of Devon and Cornwall. Tom Longstaff traversed parts of this coast in the 1880s and '90s and he wrote: '. . . The cliffs are only slate but finely fretted by tumultuous seas.' Tumultuous seas there are indeed on this coast open to the full force of the Atlantic. Sea-cliff climbers have learned that one wave in twenty-three is twice average height and scientific research has shown that one in 1175 is thrice and one in 300,000 over four times normal height. Statistics worth remembering on this lee shore. Longstaff was wrong about the slate however; much of the rock is good, if unusual. Tom Patey made the first great routes on this coast, his finest being 'Wrecker's Slab', a bold 350-foot lead on remote Cornakey Cliff. Since it was first climbed in 1959 it has been repeated only a handful of times; but the delightful climbing and incredible situations warrant a mention in any list of sea-cliff classics.

'Pink Void' on Baggy Point is a similar but more recent route. A thin slab of good rock rises through a chaotic cliff face of terrifying rubble. The hardest route in the area is perhaps Pat Littlejohn's 'Il Duce' on Tintagel Head, taking a magnificent overhanging line up metamorphosed shales that look terrible but are remarkably solid. Retreat would be impossible; when Littlejohn's second, Keith Darbyshire, fell during the first ascent he was unable to regain the rock and was forced to climb up the rope using jumars. There are other fine routes at Pentire, Sharpnose and Blackchurch and development is proceeding apace at Carn Gowla near St. Agnes.

The Pembroke coast in South Wales is also an interesting area – the topography is complex and it is a maze of different rock types. St. David's Head is a small area of exceptionally rough gabbro-like granite on the far tip of Wales. Opposite is Ramsey Island, reputed to contain 400-foot granite walls; but access to it is almost impossible. The island is private and a bird sanctuary. The Head gives good routes of all standards but no traverses, although nearby the mile-long 'Eldorado' traverses through an area of yellow igneous intrusions, through shadowed canyon-like zawns where white rock-doves breed,

Above: Tom Longstaff's route from the last century – Scrattling Crack on Baggy Point in North Devon

Right: Keith Darbyshire attempts Alpine Groyne – later climbed by the author's party – at Lower Sharpnose Point in North Cornwall

and through a series of fabulous natural arches. The climb has been
completed only once, and we used six lasso-tyroleans. The continuous
short swims gave us exposure problems even in high summer, for the
water temperature round the British Isles is never very high. We have
now evolved special neoprene 'wet suit' type clothing for this sort of
expedition.

Castle Martin in Pembrokeshire is a limestone area similar to
Swanage but more broken and eroded. Here are two beautiful stacks,
both around 100 feet high and accessible only for a few moments at

low spring tides without a swim – the Elugug Tower and the Elugug Spire. These were first climbed by south-west 'specialists' in the autumn of 1970 (with military permission, for unfortunately the whole of this particular limestone area is a NATO tank range and closed to the public).

North Wales has several areas of sea-cliff but none more impressive than Craig Gogarth, the sea-cliff where Holyhead Mountain drops into the sea on Anglesey, facing across towards Ireland. The climbs are long, steep and spectacular and rise from deep water. None is easier than hard V.S. – and most are harder. This is the current playground of the Welsh 'tigers', and because of its good weather, even in midwinter, its continual use has led to a new breakthrough in the already high standard of Welsh rock-climbing.

The most spectacular route is 'Spiders Web', where a huge natural arch links the back of the 300 foot deep Wen Zawn with the open sea. The first pitch is slightly overhanging and far from easy and leads up the left wall to the apparent roof of the arch – which is found to be hollow, a deep and bottomless chimney. You bridge this until it closes in the darkness high up out over the sea. A peg is placed and you abseil down from it into space level with the curtain-like lip of the arch. You start swinging and eventually manage to grab the lip and from a sort of upside-down bridging position you place a peg in the lip and transfer onto it. Several awkward movements and you are free-climbing up the outside of the arch. As one might expect, 'Spiders Web' is a product of Joe Brown's fertile mind.

Further north in Britain development has been only sporadic, for the mountains are always easily accessible and there has been little reason for radical departures from traditional concepts. The exception is at Aberdeen, where the granite cliffs are seamed with long-abandoned quarry workings and the city is the home of many keen climbers schooled in the harsh world of Scottish winter climbing. Here the coast-line is unlike Cornwall; the cliffs, although seamed with little inlets, offer a wall to the turbulent North Sea, and the cliff-top is a dour landscape of small farms and bleak tree-less fields. The climbs tend to be long and easy or short and vicious, but are a popular venue for an Aberdonian afternoon.

Tom Patey might be said to have invented the sport of sea-stack climbing. The coasts of Ross and Sutherland and Caithness and the northern islands are liberally studded with sea-stacks. Besides Am Buachaille, whose first ascent is described elsewhere, Tom also discovered the Old Man of Stoer. This 250-foot spire of Torridonian Sandstone was considered to be impossible to climb, but in 1966 Tom made the ascent and discovered that the technical difficulties of this splendid stack were merely hard-severe. Ladders were used, as on Am Buachai'le, to reach the base of the pinnacle.

Further north is the Great Stack of Handa, which rises 350 feet from a deep zawn on a small island. Tom crossed to its summit along

An angry winter sea breaks round the Elugug Towers on the Pembrokeshire Coast. Climbers are descending the Tower after its first ascent

a fantastic tyrolean, a trip of over 150 feet along a 600 foot rope drawn outwards on either side of the zawn until the middle was across the top of the stack. But this was not a first ascent, for a similar trip had been made in 1876 by an islander from Lewis in the Outer Hebrides, while gathering sea-birds for food – and not on a nylon rope in those days!

Perhaps Tom Patey's greatest stack climb was the first ascent of The Old Man of Hoy, the great 450-foot monolith in the Orkneys. This is well described elsewhere. Near it, however, is St. John's Head, at 1140 feet the second highest sea-cliff in Britain. Tom had picked out a route on it but he never lived to make a serious attempt for he was killed abseiling off The Maiden, a really beautiful sea-stack not far east of Cape Wrath, having just completed its first ascent in 1970. Two routes, in 'big wall' style, have since been made on St. John's Head.

Many of the Hebridean islands are crag-girt, and there is a strong tradition of climbing, largely for economic reasons. Sea-fowl and their eggs were a staple part of island diet in days gone by. Nowhere was this more so than on the tiny islands of St. Kilda, isolated fifty miles out into the grey Atlantic beyond the Outer Islands – the last speck of land between Scotland and America. The cliffs here rise to over 1200 feet and remarkable feats of cragmanship were performed using bare feet and horsehair rope, both to gather food and as tests of manhood for the young men. In the spring of 1970 Tom Patey, Joe Brown, Pete Crew and I carried out a reconnaissance of the cliffs for a BBC climbing broadcast project, and what we saw – the very scale of things – put the idea out of the question. We planned to stay for three days but were marooned for nearly three weeks: there is no harbour on the island and all landings are across an open beach. The islands are now deserted except for a small army garrison.

It is off St. Kilda that the highest stacks in the British Isles rise from the sea. Stac Lee is 544 feet high and Stac an Armin is 627 feet: both were climbed by the native St. Kildans to harvest the gannets, over six thousand of which nest on Stac Lee alone. The climbs are not very difficult; the major problem is the landing from a small boat tossing in the perpetual heavy swell onto steep rock rising from deep water, and of course the hostile birds. There are several lower but very difficult stacks in the archipelago.

Inland in Britain there is now little scope for climbing on virgin rock except in the far north-west of Scotland. But miles of sea-cliffs remain untouched particularly in the Isles of Shetland and on the coasts of Ireland. Rock climbers from other countries too are showing interest in sea-cliffs – the Germans are climbing on the coasts of Crete and the Tasmanians are showing great interest in the fine stacks round their own island. Maybe sea-cliff climbing will become a popular new trend, but it must always be of particular relevance to an island people like the British.

167

Left: The south face of the 450 foot sandstone pillar of the Old Man of Hoy. The South Face route lies up the left edge of the Face and the South-East Arête up the edge of the shadow to its right. The *voie-normale* — the East Face — moves from the Pulpit some 80 feet up the Arête round the corner and out of sight

Right: Joe Brown in action on Spiders Web at Craig Gogarth on Anglesey, North Wales. Joe has abseiled from the roof of the hollow arch into space, he starts swinging and eventually reaches the curtain-like outer lip of the arch

Blizzard on the Ben

It all started when I fell through the ice on the River Coe. It was dawn on New Year's Eve. The ice was thin enough, the water cold enough and my clothes wet enough to send me shivering back to our camp at Jacksonville below the Buachaille, for dry clothes and a hot brew. By the time I had recovered it was too late to attempt a major climb in Glencoe so, just for the hell of it, Tony and I decided that we would go to Ben Nevis and see the New Year in from a bivouac on the summit. It was a long time ago and in those days it sounded very romantic.

That night was an incredible experience. The snow was iron hard and we scooped out a hollow in a drift close by the tumbled walls of the Observatory ruins, and propped our tent – a small, flimsy hiker's model – into it. The frost held all Scotland in a steel grip. The moon was near full and it hung low over Loch Linnhe as the old year died, a silver pathway shimmering to Mull with Colonsay and Islay floating black against the sea 70 miles away. Westward were the crystal teeth of Skye and the Cuillin of Rhum hanging icy above the shadowed cornices and the black abyss of Tower Gully. And floating between them – neither sea nor sky – a hint that was perhaps the Outer Isles? Or Tir-nan-Og maybe?

Northward mountain after mountain white in the moonlight disappeared behind a northern horizon beyond which massed artillery thundered in silence. Great flashes of blue and red and green stabbing into the black dome above us. Half the sky blazing with the flames of the Aurora. But the only sound was the creaking frost, the pulsing stars and our beating hearts. It was a night I shall remember as I die.

The following year we thought to repeat the experience, but on the Ben the New Year was blasted in on the wings of the blizzard and luckily we were well equipped this time with a proper mountain tent and survival gear. We battled through sixteen hours of darkness to prevent the tent collapsing under the weight of driven snow. It was just another of those squalid nights that is an adventure only in retrospect.

As one grows older and wiser masochism for its own sake becomes less attractive, and the next autumn we were able to book two places in the Scottish Montaineering Club's C.I.C. Hut below the great Northern Cliffs of the Ben. In those days the hut was a mere rectangular stone refuge, but its bunk-lined interior was wood panelled and cosily dark and a famous cast-iron stove stood in the middle of its one room. Stoked with the coke which lay piled beneath a snow drift against the wall outside, the stove could be adjusted by skilled hands until it glowed red hot. Our Christmas dinner that year was eaten sitting in our underpants, the ruddy glow of the stove glimpsed but distantly through the clouds of steam rising from our drying clothes.

We climbed happily for several days in fair weather and then decided to go for Glovers Chimney, still considered in the mid-fifties to be the best of the classic generation of ice-climbs on the Ben. Our comfortingly out-of-date guide book even suggested that it was perhaps the hardest winter route on the mountain.

The climb itself did not seem particularly difficult technically and Tony led the steep initial 120 feet ice-fall with apparent ease. We had no ice pegs or 12-point crampons, but with his 3-foot axe Tony simply hewed a zigzag ladder of small nicks, with the grace for which his late father – Frank Smythe, perhaps the greatest British alpinist of the thirties – had been justly famous. Things became rather different, however, in the slabsided runnel of the narrow gully above. We soon realized that we had left far below the tranquil silence of Coire na Ciste and that we were now climbing high on the steep flanks of Tower Ridge itself. Spindrift poured constantly down the chimney, a stifling torrent of stinging crystals, and the wind shrieked through the Tower Gap where the chimney ended high above our heads. The spindrift poured down our necks and up our sleeves. Somehow the cold bit through our gloves and our balaclavas and into our boots. Each time I belayed, the sweat froze on the small of my back and I was forced to stuff my spectacles into a pocket, their lenses verglassed inside and out. The top pitch was my lead and I remember bridging wide, crampons scrabbling for tiny holds in the vertical verglas on the chimney walls, and looking down myopically between my legs. There was Tony, huddled against his belay a hundred feet below, patiently braving the cold, the lashing spume and the torrent of ice chips from my axe. Uncomfortable as I was there was no denying that the situation was splendid and the climbing superb.

Suddenly I was there. Head bent and eyes screwed up against the stinging punch of the gale, I pulled out of the chimney and onto the narrow arête that is the bottom of the Tower Gap. Clinging on with difficulty I somehow found a belay. Tony came up fast and while I crouched grimly holding his rope he grappled with the gale and the short ice-covered upper wall of the Gap. He disappeared from view. A few frozen minutes and I followed. Now we were on easy ground, the final ridge leading onto the summit plateau, but so strong was the wind that we remained roped and crawled upwards on hands and knees. Visibility was nil. We moved in a white tunnel of tearing spume and rushing cloud. When the ground no longer rose in our faces we knew that we were on the summit of Ben Nevis.

But there was no cause for alarm. We knew the summit plateau well – indeed we had crossed it daily, in varying conditions of visibility, for the week past. We knew exactly our location and exactly our compass course for Number Three Gully – the easy way down into the back of Coire na Ciste and the return route to the Hut. Number Three Gully itself is unmistakeable; there is a conspicuous rock pinnacle in the gully top. We had no fears of missing our route and plunging down any of the adjacent gullies whose hidden recesses harbour vertical ice and difficult climbing.

With the gale behind us and bent double so as not to get swept away, we set off in the direction the compass pointed, but something went wrong – or perhaps we sailed past our rock pinnacle without seeing it, for all ideas of distance or gradient were lost, swept away in the blowing maelstrom of whiteness. Sometime later we were descending steeply but still on course. It was obvious we had overshot our gully but we knew we were on safe ground. A compass cannot lie in skilled hands. The wind eased and we could stand upright and then suddenly we broke through the cloud into that incredible darkness that is still daylight but where the white of a snowstorm ends and the dun of the moor and the black bog begins. Below us wreathes of cloud hung lifelessly over the leaden surface of Lochan Meall an t-Suidhe. We had descended 2400 feet, over one and a half miles, hardly realizing it. But at least here was the usual track from Fort William to the C.I.C. Hut, and by following it – and not very steeply uphill either – we would be home and dry. A long way round perhaps but an easy way out of the inferno on the summit plateau!

But even here it was snowing – big white flakes drifting from the grey ceiling, though the featureless moorland was too wet for it to settle. We set off in the gathering dusk across the hillside, following the well-defined path that contours into the narrow glen of the Allt a'Mhuilinn, the valley below the great north-east face of Ben Nevis.

The gale hit us as we rounded the shoulder of Carn Dearg, and as the path dropped towards the invisible burn we lost it. Despite our head-torches it was obvious that we would never find it again, for we were in a maze of drifts and boulders and bog holes. We were still not worried. We knew that the Hut stood on a rocky bluff a few feet above the junction of the Coire na Ciste stream and the main burn, so we decided to cut down the hillside to the burn and follow it up for a mile or so until we found the hut. It would be a simple exercise, it wouldn't even require navigation.

It was heavy going in the darkness beside the burn, and no wonder the path kept high on the hillside. As we gained altitude the drifts got deeper and the driving snow fiercer, until we were moving into its very teeth. And then at last the burn divided – it was frozen up here but when we scrambled down into its gorge we could hear the rumble of the water beneath the ice and there in the torchlight, stuck in the ice and half buried in snow, was a large red shape. We recognized it as the empty 40-gallon kerosene drum which must have been blown from beside the Hut door earlier in the winter. Less than a hundred yards away was the warmth and shelter of the Hut. We were very tired and very thirsty. But we were nearly home and dry. Thankfully we scrambled up the steep bluff above the oil drum and back into the fury of the storm. But where was the hut? Nothing was recognizable in the flickering white cones of our torch beams. We crossed the bluff and found ourselves above the main burn again. Back we went and there was the oil drum. But no Hut. For half an hour we struggled back and forth, sometimes on wind-scoured rock, sometimes through knee-deep drifts. But always in the white darkness there was nothing. It was impossible. It was a nightmare.

Tony and I crouched in the lee of a boulder and unpacked our emergency rations of biscuits and chocolate. The situation was serious. We were cold and tired and wet and we shuddered at the idea of a bivouac. The Hut was hard-by, for certain. But we realized we could never find it now unless we actually stumbled into it. There were no decisions to make. Our course was obvious.

And so we turned our backs to the wind and started the interminable drag back down the Glen. Follow the burn. Drifts and boulders and mud and boulders and darkness. Downhill. Thank God for downhill! The wet bog was warm and spicy and the wind and snow were above and behind. After three stumbling miles there were twinkling lights below and the sweat was warm again on our backs. We slithered down an unseen bank and elder bushes whipped our faces. We clambered awkwardly through a fence, tripped through the sleepers and cold steel of a railway track and then we were blinking beneath the lights of the Inverlochy distillery. No-one dies of exposure here! But the road was hard and it was not yet midnight and there was bed and breakfast with lights aglow beyond the tall dour door. And the land-lady said welcome and the tea was hot. And then there was sleep.

Next morning the weather was brighter as we plodded back up the path beside the Allt a'Mhuilinn, and as each great white-sheathed cloud-topped buttress succeeded the last we marvelled at the calm of the new day and the snow buttressing every twig of heather and fluting every rock.

Could it be just a few hours since we had fought along this very way? There above us, on its little bluff, was the Hut. We scrambled down to the oil drum, but the wind and the blowing snow had obliterated all trace of our search. The walls were piled high with drifts but there in the lee behind the Hut were half-filled steps in the snow. They were ours. They were four feet from the wall. We kicked away the drift outside the door and went in.

Above: A rare grouping of top British climbers on the occasion of the BBC's Old Man of Hoy television programme. Left to right: Joe Brown, Dougal Haston, Chris Bonington, Ian MacNaught-Davis, Tom Patey and Peter Crew

173

5 Africa

Africa, the second largest continent, spans 5000 miles divided almost equally north and south of the Equator. Yet of its eleven and a half million square miles, the area above 10,000 feet is tiny: its highlands hold far less glacier than any of the other five continents, and enigmatically, the three small areas of ice lie virtually astride the Equator. Africa's mountains hold much for the cragsman and explorer but relatively little for the alpinist. But the quality of this small offering is unique and splendid.

The most northerly of Africa's mountains are the Atlas, running east-west for some 1200 miles behind the Mediterranean coasts of Algeria and Morocco. Although other areas rise over 11,000 feet, the best mountaineering area is the High Atlas, immediately south of Marrakech in western Morocco, from where in winter the glittering snows present one of the most famous of all mountain prospects. The High Atlas is a complex 200 mile chain of jagged ridges and buttresses; it is subject to great seasonal variations, in summer harsh and waterless beneath a hot sun, in winter crisp and white and icy. Spring and autumn are the seasons for climbing; recently there has been some winter mountaineering as well. Skiing is well developed and there is good scope for ski touring. The highest peak is Toubkal, 13,666 feet, a popular tourist summit, and this massif does offer the only really developed climbing in the whole range, much of it on good granite. Most major summits are easily reached, but there is considerable scope for long rock climbs of high standard and in winter good snow-and-ice routes of Scottish style. In the foothills routes have been made on some huge limestone crags.

Unlike the plains of Morocco the High Atlas are inhabited by Hamitic Berbers, an aloof, independent people; the highest summit was not located until the twenties. Much development took place over the next twenty years, especially by the de Lépiney brothers; a CAF section was started and several huts were built in the Toubkal Massif. Despite the political upheavals since the war there has been more activity by the French, including a productive visit by the guides Charlet and Contamine, and more recently many visits by British parties, notably those led by Hamish Brown, who have made many excellent new climbs in the range – some in winter. With such easy access from Europe the Atlas hold much promise for the exploratory mountaineer escaping from the 'rat-race' of the high Alps.

Egypt's mountains are interesting: much of the Sinai peninsula is raw desert, and since the late forties the battle ground of successive Israeli-Arab wars. Its southern apex, however, is a tangled mass of tortured peaks rising above deep ravines. The highest, Jebel Katerina, rises to 8535 feet above the famous Convent of St. Katherine. From here the nearby holy mountain, Jebel Musa (Moses's Peak), is easily reached by a magnificent flight of 2000 steps carved by the monks in ancient times. The scenery is magnificent and the heat intense. Sinai has been dubbed the 'Red Dolomites', so fine are its colours. Some-

Dawn at the Kami Tarn. On the far side of the Tarn is the little Kami Hut and beyond rise the twin peaks of Tereri (15,467 feet) and Sendeyo (15,433 feet) – two distant outlyers of Mt Kenya

times snow falls in the winter and great torrents flood the ravines. Some climbing has been done in the area, notably by Lord Hunt during his army days. He found some superb granite, and rock climbing similar to that in the Cairngorms but up to 2000 feet high.

Fourteen hundred miles of desert, the Sahara, divides the Mediterranean coastline from the heart of Africa, and in the middle of this once fertile vastness lie two major mountain groups. Near the southern border of Algeria are the Hoggar, a chaotic group of isolated volcanic spires rising from a dead world, almost devoid of vegetation and inhabited by fierce Ahaggar Toureg tribesmen. Not until 1906 did Europeans first penetrate the Hoggar, and although French climbers first visited the region in 1935, little was achieved until the fifties when several French expeditions and a British one – Sutton, Fraser and Wrangham – managed a series of fine and difficult ascents. Since then there have been numerous expeditions. The highest peak is Tahat (9870 feet) not far from Tamanrasset, a desert town on the Trans-Sahara route. Tahat is not a difficult peak and camels have reached the summit, but close by is Ilamane (9050 feet), a magnificent aiguille and the most famous peak in the area. The strange structure of the basaltic rock offers smooth rounded holds and few piton cracks; Hoggar climbing is steep and sensational and often requires aid techniques.

Four hundred miles south of the Hoggar, in the Republic of Niger, lies the massif of Air, a similar but smaller group of desert mountains – the highest peak only rises to 5910 feet. The massif was first visited by climbers in 1943 and there have been only a handful of expeditions since, although recently some 1000 foot routes of Grade VI have been put up by visiting French and Italian climbers.

Seven hundred miles to the west in Chad lies the other major Saharan range – the Tibesti. It contains several impressive mountain

Left: Twenty-three miles away from Naro Moro Mt Kenya rises from the surrounding high moorland and forest. Point John stands out to the right; to its left is the Darwin Glacier, and under the summit of Batian the Forel and Heim Glaciers are visible. Lower and to the left, close to the small spire of Point Peter, is the ice of the Cesar and Josef Glaciers

Above: Snow on the Equator. Plastered with new snow, Batian rises beyond the lake at Two-Tarn. High on the left is the Tyndall Glacier complex and to the right, between Batian's South-West Ridge and Point John, lies the Darwin Glacier

groups – all extinct volcanoes. Access is more difficult and the region is less explored than the Hoggar; but the mountains have little to offer the rock climber, for the rock is poor, a sort of volcanic conglomerate. Several British expeditions have visited the area but usually with more geological than mountaineering interest.

Elsewhere in the desert, climbs have been made on spectacular 7000 foot granite peaks on the Egyptian Red Sea coast and on the peculiar spires of the Aiguilles Sisse near the Chad–Sudan border.

By contrast to the vast Sahara the mystic kingdom of Ethiopia is almost completely mountainous. Little of the country falls below 3000 feet and its summits rise above 14,000 feet. Ethiopia contains the largest area of high country in Africa, and probably still some virgin tops. Although there are historical records of heavy snowfalls, there are now no permanent snows; but hail is frequent and often lies of several days. There are nine major mountain groups including the Simien Range – an extraordinary group in the north containing the highest peak, Ras Dashan, whose most recently surveyed height is 15,159 feet, although claimed by the Italians during their occupation to be in excess of 16,000 feet. Most of the higher summits are accessible by mules; like the other mountain groups, the Simien is of more interest to the mountain explorer than to the climber, although there is a profusion of huge basalt cliffs and lofty isolated pinnacles surrounding the group, probably of great interest to the cragsman. The first climbing visit was by the ubiquitous Duke of Abruzzi in 1928 and 1929, but little was known of the mountains until after the Second World War. With its history of early Christianity and its wild and inhospitable terrain, Ethiopia has much to offer seekers of the unusual.

A mere twenty miles north of the Equator lie the legendary 'Mountains of the Moon', the Ruwenzori. These were known to Herodotus in 450 BC, when he claimed them to be the source of the mighty Nile. The Ruwenzori were forgotten for centuries, until the famous explorer Sir Henry Stanley took note of them in 1876. The mountains lie astride the Uganda/Congo border between lakes Albert and Edward in the great Western Rift Valley. They cover some sixty miles and contain six major massifs, all liberally plastered with small glaciers. The local people call them Runssoro, 'the rainmaker', for they are notoriously mist-shrouded and rarely visible – hence perhaps their twenty-three centuries of mystery.

Ruwenzori is, geologically, a 'block mountain', unlike Africa's other highest peaks which are volcanic. The rocks are gneiss and quartzite and all six massifs rise above 15,000 feet; the highest, Mt Stanley, has nine summits above 16,000 feet, rising to 16,763 feet. Permanent snow lies to 15,000 feet and some glaciers flow below this; in the past they flowed far below.

Despite their wet reputation they give some good climbing weather in January and February and again in July and August – but even then there may be little let-up in the mist, and this is what hinders climbing.

177

Access is not easy: even the shortest approaches involve a two- or three-day march through dense and boggy forest and over muddy peat hags. There are seven huts among the peaks belonging to the Mountain Club of Uganda and several fine rock shelters. Ruwenzori is a naturalist's paradise: vegetation ranges from montane forest draped in wierd moss to an alpine zone dominated by fantastic giant groundsel, heather and lobelia.

This mysterious range has always attracted mountaineers. The glaciers were first reached in 1900; an Alpine Club party, Freshfield and Mumm with their guide, Inderbinnen, attempted to go higher in 1905, but with little success. The following year the Duke of Abruzzi – the famous Italian mountaineer and explorer – arrived with a powerful and well-equipped expedition and made the first ascents of Margherita, the highest point of Mt Stanley, and other major peaks. Many other expeditions followed, notably Eric Shipton and Bill Tilman who made the third ascent of Margherita and several difficult first ascents in 1932. Before the political troubles of 1972 Ruwenzori was much frequented and many fine climbs have been done, some of them mixed routes of great difficulty. There is still scope, weather permitting, for hard first ascents and high ridge traverses, in this unique and beautiful mountain range.

The Virunga are a group of active volcanoes on the Uganda–Congo–Ruanda border immediately south of Lake Edward; the highest is Karisimbi (14,783 feet). The high forests of these mountains are the home of the rare mountain gorilla. The peaks are of little interest to climbers, although ascents to witness the astounding spectacle of an active volcano at close range are well worth making.

Mt Kenya rises in regal isolation 12,000 feet above the Kenya plateau, right on the Equator. The peak is the eroded plug of an ancient volcano; its twin summits, Batian (17,058 feet) and Nelion (36 feet lower), which are separated by the icy gash of the Gate of the Mists, are surrounded by a cluster of satellite aiguilles on which hang no fewer than fifteen tiny glaciers. The rock is syenite, firm, coarse and granite-like, and Mt Kenya provides some of the finest alpine-style mountaineering in the world.

Because of its position the southern side of the mountain has a summer season in January and February, while in August and September the northern side is 'in condition'. Meanwhile the opposite flank is plastered in snow and ice and offers excellent and only recently realized winter potential.

Over the last decade many long and hard rock and mixed routes, often requiring bivouacs, have been put up, mostly by British climbers working in Kenya for whom weekend access from Nairobi is possible, or by visiting Austrians. The Diamond Couloir, an ice runnel leading to the Gate of the Mists, is the greatest ice climb in Africa. The easiest route to the summit of Nelion is Shipton and Wyn Harris's 'normal route', a serious rock climb graded IV Inferior. Batian is harder;

Left: Kami Hut is almost due north of Mt Kenya, and the Northey Glacier hangs at the head of the cwm — a picture taken during the northern summer season. On the right is Point Dutton and on the left the Firmin Tower

Below: Point Dutton (16,025 feet) is a peak on the North Ridge of Mt Kenya. Frank Cannings is climbing close to its knife-edge summit arête

most tourists, of whom there are now many, are content with the easy snow-plod up Point Lenana, an outlying minor summit nearly 1000 feet lower.

Mt Kenya is sometimes visible from a hundred miles away; the distant snows were glimpsed early by Europeans, but it was not until 1899 that Sir Halford MacKinder's large expedition reached above the glacier line. After several unsuccessful attempts he finally reached the summit of Batian with his two Courmayeur guides, Ollier and Brocherel, via a complex and difficult route on ice and rock. There were no more successful attempts until 1929 when the 'normal' route on Nelion was added; but the following decade saw several other routes, notably by Shipton and Tilman. Climbing in the forties was dominated by Arthur Firmin who made many fine routes until the Mau Mau emergency closed the area.

The Kenya Government is well aware of the attractions of the mountain. It now lies within a well-run National Park and the active M.C.K. maintain eight huts and two bivouacs in strategic positions. Vehicular access on modern tracks is easy almost to the forest line at 10,000 feet; above this attractive moorland valleys with tinkling streams and groves of giant groundsel lead to beautiful green tarns high among the peaks.

There is much excellent rock climbing in Kenya, both in the arid Northern Frontier District on isolated inselbergs and on a huge variety of 'bush crags', some over 1000 feet high, further south, many of them still virgin. Mention should be made also of the two famous and difficult inselbergs of eastern Uganda – Amiel and Rwot. There is a nucleus of fine expatriate rock-climbers based in Nairobi and working away at these problems.

Legend has it that Queen Victoria presented Kilimanjaro to her nephew – Kaiser Wilhelm II – for his birthday. Hence the fact that the highest mountain in Africa lifts its mighty cone to 19,340 feet from a kink in the border just twelve miles inside Tanzania.

Access to the summit of Kibo, as the ice-covered cone of this huge dormant volcano is known, is not difficult. Many 'tourists' make the long, gruelling scree-slog to Uhuru Point on the crater rim every year. But Kilimanjaro, with its immense bulk and icy brow, guards secrets worthy of its height – both unique and unexpected. The crater is choked with ice, often in weird and unique formations and from it great streams of ice pour down, particularly on the south-west and northern sides. There are so far half a dozen major routes on these ice-falls; the vast gash of the Great Western Breach promises rock and mixed climbing of the highest standards for the future.

Separated by a high moorland saddle to the east of Kibo are the jagged rock pinnacles of Mawenzi, rising to almost 17,000 feet. There is serious rock climbing here: the east face is an immense mountain wall whose base can only be reached by complicated approaches through forested gorges; it has only recently had a direct ascent.

Hanging mysteriously in the dusk above the mists of the giant heather forest, Kibo, the highest peak of Kilimanjaro, 'guards secrets worthy of its height'

The history of difficult climbing on Kilimanjaro is very recent, and is largely due to visiting climbers from Nairobi, although the highest point of Kibo was reached in 1889 by Hans Meyer and L. Purtscheller. Mawenzi was climbed in 1912. The Tanzania-based Kilimanjaro Mountain Club maintain some eight bivouac shelters at various places on the mountain.

Mount Kenya displays conventional – indeed classic – mountain form; but Kilimanjaro is different. The well-travelled mountaineer will find its atmosphere and beauty and its secret ice climbs unlike anything he has experienced before.

Close by is Mount Meru, a beautifully proportioned dormant volcano, not quite 15,000 feet high. There are large crags inside its crater and an ascent through the montane forests and high moorlands of its flanks is a worthwhile experience. There are tales that somewhere on the mountain are huge caverns of salt where elephants come to lick. . . .

Most of southern Africa is above 3000 feet, for the great continental plateau rises towards the Cape. Although there are hundreds of isolated inselbergs and outcrops, the mountains themselves border the plateau where it falls eastwards. Climbs have been made on Mlanje (9840 feet) in southern Malawi, while the Chimanimani Mountains near Rhodesia's Mozambique border are more akin to Scotland than the Alps; they have been well developed by active Rhodesian rock climbers. Inyangani, their highest point, rises to just over 8500 feet.

South-west Africa contains chains of arid and little-known mountains of no great stature; among them, however, is the Great Spitzkop – the 'Matterhorn of Namibia'. This spectacular and difficult spire of pink granite rises 2300 feet above the surrounding plains; it was eventually climbed by a difficult route in 1946. There seems great potential for this sort of problem in the territory.

In South Africa itself mountaineering is highly developed; there is a flourishing Mountain Club founded in 1891. Mountaineering became popular early in the century and South African climbers have been active among the greater ranges of the world. They have a reputation for hard free climbing, and plenty of opportunities to practice their craft.

There are the Drakensberg of Natal and Basutoland rising to such summits as The Sentinel, Champagne Castle and Cathedral Peak, over 11,000 feet high. These splendid scarp mountains with their sculptured ridges and deep *kloofs* contain some fine pinnacles and huge walls. Many difficult climbs have been made, although the rock is said to be poor; the area fostered the development of the 'grass piton'. In winter there is often considerable snowfall and winter climbs have been made on these beautiful mountains.

Further south range after range of lower, but impressive mountains, lead round the Cape towards Table Mountain. Groups, such as the Cedarberg, the Hex River Mountains and du Toit's Kloof Mountains,

Map legend:
peaks ▲
lakes
ranges

High Atlas
Toubkal
ATLAS
HOGGAR
TIBESTI
AIR
Lake Chad
SINAI MTS
Tropic of Cancer
Ras Dashan
Lake Tana
ETHIOPIAN MTS
MT CAMEROON
Lake Albert
Lake Rudolf
RUWENZORI
Equator
VIRUNGA
Lake Victoria
MT KENYA
KILIMANJARO
MT MERU
Lake Tanganyika
Lake Nyasa
MT MLANJE
CHIMANIMANI MTS
Tropic of Capricorn
DRAKENSBERG
N
1000 miles
Table Mt.

Right: The impressive Champagne Castle in the South African Drakensberg Mountains is over 11,000 feet high

Far right: Groundsel grow over ten feet high on Mt Kenya: Batian and Nelion are seen over two miles away from Mackinder's Camp in the Teleki Valley

Below: A typical 'bush' crag in East Africa. Climbing in the Kedong Valley below the Ngong Hills close to Nairobi. John Temple leads Shannon Firmin

contain miles of steep cliffs, usually of sandstone or quartzite. The rock, usually vertical and horizontally bedded, gives excellent and spectacular climbing on good holds. Table Mountain itself (3582 feet), where the climbing is only a few minutes from the centre of Cape Town, is laced with first-class rock routes. The climber in South Africa is fortunate. What his mountains lack in height they make up for in quantity and quality.

Thus Africa – alone of the continents – embraces every kind of mountaineering. There are weird desert needles, high and eerie ice peaks rising above tangled forest, remote cliffs probably still unseen by Europeans and the beautiful quartzite crags of the Cape rising steep above the blue Southern Ocean. It is certainly a continent of contrasts.

The Roof of Africa

It was a long time before I fell asleep. Beneath me the scree was hard and angular and the blowing mist was damp on my face. I thought back over the past three days.

It seemed weeks ago that we had driven out of Nairobi at dusk in John's battered Landrover. The hundred long miles to the Tanzanian border at Namanga had been livened only by the animals which leapt through the bright cone of our headlights and our arguments about their identity. Once across the border in the early hours we had turned down a side track and dossed below the 15,000 foot cone of Mount Meru towering black against the stars.

We had never glimpsed Kilimanjaro, only the steep forest rising into cloud. Then, as the road had started its long climb through the coffee and banana shambas there had been that nasty metallic grating sound from the rear differential. We'd limped into the Umbwe Mission

Tangled glaciers and great shattered rock walls — the western flanks of Kibo rise above the Barranco. The Breach Wall seen from the lava deserts at about 13,500 feet high on the Umbwe route

where the brothers had allowed us to brew up while we stripped the half-shafts and removed the rear prop' shaft. John and Frank were good mechanics: I would never have thought of engaging four-wheel drive and using just the front wheels till we got home to Nairobi! The wide track cut through the forest had been steep and slippery and with two bald tyres we hadn't got far up it before we stuck. It was dusk anyway, so we kipped down there and then. It must have been about 5000 feet.

In the damp and misty dawn we'd locked the Landrover and started off up into the forest. Among the tall trees it was eerie and cool. Our rucksacks were heavy and at times the faint trace of track had been difficult to follow in the diffused green light. At 9500 feet there was a cave beside a tiny stream – the usual 'first bivouac' – but we'd brewed up and continued, soon finding ourselves on a wooded ridge from which vertical forest plunged into a deep valley resonant with waterfalls, where wreaths of mist clung round craggy outcrops rising through the green. Gradually the trees gave way to the moss-draped skeletons of giant heather, forty and fifty feet high. The mists closed in round our ridge, which had narrowed in places to a rocky arête.

At 'One-point-five bivvy', another 2000 feet up, there was a tiny pool of fresh water and we'd brewed up again. It was evening. Shortly afterwards in a beautiful glade of giant heather, floored with clumps of the rare grey and yellow everlasting flowers, the mist had suddenly opened. A huge icy dome hung above us, pink in the alpenglow. It had been our first sight of Kibo, our goal. We could see the huge cliffs of the Great Breach Wall and the tumbling ice tongues of the south-western glaciers. Kibo was aloof and mysterious and unlike any mountain I had seen before. In the dusk we emerged from the last of the heather forest: a crag, like the bows of a great ship, blocked the ridge ahead. We dossed down beneath it, lying round a roaring fire of heather logs drinking tea, and yet more tea, until we drifted into deep sleep.

A cloudless morning of stupendous views had taken us into the deep cwm of the Barranco. The whole western side of the mountain was deep in blue shadow and we'd made out little detail of our proposed route. The Great Breach Wall was supposed to be Africa's outstanding mountaineering problem and we'd hoped to have a close look at it, maybe forcing a route up its southern side. It was certainly vast and intimidating. But the sky soon clouded and as we'd wound through a maze of moraines below the Breach Glacier the mist swept down on us again. The going was steep and gruelling and the unaccustomed altitude was telling. Uncertain of our exact whereabouts, we'd stopped for a brew and caught glimpses of evil-looking snow patches, ugly icicles and rotting walls through rents in the mist. It had not looked encouraging. Occasionally a rumble of rock fall echoed through the mist; it sounded very unhealthy. And when we had caught a glimpse of our key couloir with a rock avalanche actually thundering

185

L

Above: 'It was a damp and misty dawn when we left the Landrover high on the forest track at about 5,000 feet and started off into the forest'

Below: On Kilimanjaro's Umbwe Ridge – passing through a weird area where the moss-hung giant heather is dead

Below right: 'A cloudless morning had taken us into the deep cwm of the Barranco. The whole western side of the mountain was deep in blue shadow . . .'

down it, we'd decided that discretion was the better part of valour. After all, the scale of the mountain was Himalayan, and to attempt a major new route without seeing it, well – it had seemed futile. We'd decided to try the Heim Glacier instead. It was the longest ice-climb on the mountain and had had very few ascents; it would be a worthy objective as well as giving fine views across the Breach Wall.

Back down the hard-won screes we'd gone, and, unable to see more than ten yards, we'd found the Barranco Shelter Stone by a fluke. Up the rock wall behind it we'd scrambled. The guide book suggested that this would lead to a traverse line below the southern glaciers. We'd scrambled and traversed and scrambled again until the ground dropped in front of us and then we'd struck north-east in what seemed the direction of the glacier, steadily gaining height through an eerie desert of wild lava cliffs, knife-edged ridges and tumbled moraine. We had kept our eyes open for water and eventually as night fell we'd found a snow patch and settled down for the night in a hollow scooped in the fine scree.

We'd come a long way and seen a lot in the past three days. As I lay considering them, I eventually drifted into deep sleep.

The sun hit me and I woke. I rolled over and looked up. Towering over us, the sun on its shoulder, was a great blue shadowed mountain-side of tangled ice split by seracs and rockbands. I had no difficulty in recognizing the Kersten Glacier.

'Fabulous – eh?' said John, who was already awake and stirring the porridge. 'They say it's been climbed only once,' he added. 'Incredible!' I agreed. 'But we've come too far round for the Heim haven't we?' 'Yes, I think that's the end of it', he said, pointing left. 'But we're not far out!'

The porridge was glue-like but this was our last chance to eat, for what we couldn't carry we'd abandon; we could no longer afford heavy sacks. The moraines above us were tiresome, and it was further to the ice than we thought. Once John stooped and held up a long white bone. 'What's that?' asked Frank, suspiciously. 'Human', said John. 'Thigh bone, wonder if the rest's about?' We found nothing and it was already late morning when we reached the ice.

By Alpine standards it seems a ridiculous time to embark on a major ice climb, but, John insisted, this was Africa and things were different. Not that I could see why, but at least he'd lived in Africa for years and had been on 'Killi' before. John is a cheerful Yorkshireman and it was comforting to have an old 'Africa hand' around.

Almost at once we had to rope up to climb a steep and gritty runnel to gain the obvious corridor up the middle of the ice. Mist was already swirling round us and now that we were in a position to plot our route through the ice-fall we could no longer see it. But we pushed ahead hoping for the best and turning each obstacle as we came to it. Frank and I led alternate pitches with John in poor crampons carrying the larger load in the middle; often we were able to move together. Only

The Heim Glacier rises behind Window Buttress towards the summit of Kibo — a thousand feet below the summit and close by the far right-hand end of the Breach Wall's upper tier can be seen the tiny rognon on which we bivouacked

once did we meet difficult climbing; a short, vertical serac wall which I led easily with terrordactyls. Then we heard the heart-chilling crump of collapsing ice from somewhere above and sometimes stones came spinning through the mist. We determined to keep left out of the line of fire.

Then the ice reared up and, as it often does when it steepens, it became bare and hard. Each pitch was a full run-out, usually just reaching an ice-cave or perhaps a small crevasse in which to belay. There were no technical difficulties, just those of route finding through thick mist on ice steep enough, hard enough and exposed enough to require careful cramponing and three-point contact. Once we reached a dead-end below a high green wall and had to retreat for two pitches to try elsewhere. Always the issue was in doubt, so it was always rather exciting.

Eventually a high and distinctive serac towered above through a hole in the mist and we thought we recognized it as the inside of the 'elbow' where the glacier bent sharply and the ice-fall eased. I led a long delicate pitch rightwards until I could cross the wall above me, slashed a quick step to stand on and belayed to a couple of screws. 'I guess you'll make it in one run out', I said when Frank arrived. 'It's an awkward stance here. John can come when you've got there.' But it was further than I thought and it was three pitches before Frank cramponed through a curtain of icicles into a long blue cave below the serac.

'Great place to bivvy!' exclaimed John as he arrived. 'You're joking,' said Frank. 'Let's have a brew, I'm thirsty.' We soon had a hot cup of tea going, which as everybody knows prepares an Englishman for great deeds. Refreshed and hopeful we scrambled to the end of the cave and I led round the corner, the ice steep at first but soon easing into gentler slopes. The mists kept parting and we caught glimpses of tangled ice and rock towers below us and occasionally distant sunshine. We still met lines of huge seracs and in one place a series of elephantine crevasses, but we gained height steadily and suddenly the mist dropped below us and we were in bright sunshine.

We were level with the upper tier of the Great Breach Wall itself – tall red buttresses falling into a snowfield before plunging into the mists of the Barranco. The Wall was draped with fantastic icicles; one, a slim pillar linking the snow band to the tiny Diamond Glacier overhanging the Wall, was 500 feet long! That was the line! But it would wait for the next generation.

Confident now that we had passed all the major difficulties we took off the rope and cramponed slowly up the easing slopes. The sun was low now, dropping fast towards the horizon, and we were alone – three tiny specks crawling over a huge sphere spinning through space. In every direction the finite curved out of sight and distance ceased to exist. The vast convex slopes were thrown into extraordinary texture. The ice was an intricate maze of wafer-thin flutings, maybe a foot deep and like nothing so much as giant tripe. It made heavy going, each step crunching down the ice. I was very tired, but outlined against the sky on the great golden dome was a tiny *rognon*. We'd bivouac there.

It was another uncomfortable night. We watched the sun fall behind the rim of Africa; then the stars came out and unfamiliar constellations circled overhead. We brewed up, but despite our duvets and full sleeping bags the cold was intense. Frank was sick. The rock was steep and uncomfortable, and the Zardsky sack tight and restricting. You don't expect luxury at 18,000 feet.

Nights are long on the Equator but eventually the sky lightened and the cloud sea below took shape. Then the sun hit us again and we were up and away, up the final slopes towards the summit. Suddenly we were on rock, cindery scree and boulders, and looking down into the huge snowfields of the crater. Could this be a mountain top? It was more like the moon; a stark, primeval landscape. An insane dream world. The roof of Africa.

It was John's turn to be sick, and while he curled up in the sun to

THE TANGANYIKA FLAG
AND THE TORCH OF UNITY
WERE FIRST RAISED HERE ON THE
9TH. DECEMBER 1961
BY LIEUTENANT A.G. NYIRENDA
TANGANYIKA RIFLES

"WE, THE PEOPLE OF TANGANYIKA, WOULD LIKE
TO LIGHT A CANDLE AND PUT IT ON TOP OF
MOUNT KILIMANJARO WHICH WOULD SHINE
BEYOND OUR BORDERS GIVING HOPE WHERE
THERE WAS DESPAIR, LOVE WHERE THERE WAS
HATE, AND DIGNITY WHERE BEFORE THERE
WAS ONLY HUMILIATION."
JULIUS K. NYERERE.

Kilimanjaro. Top: High above Africa on the Heim Glacier John Temple toils upwards. Right: Evening clouds swirl round the top tier of the Breach Wall and the central ice field below it. Above: There is a bronze plaque on Uhuru Peak, the highest point in Africa

sleep, Frank and I plodded a few hundred yards round the crater rim to the obvious summit, Uhuru Point. A few stones, a tattered flag, a metal cross and a bronze plaque – it was an anti-climax. Our names we wrote in the summit book before collecting a few interesting lava crystals among the cinders and rejoining John. Then we all dozed. A superb scree run dropped us 500 feet to the snowfields of the crater and we threaded our way through ice pinnacles towards the Breach, the great western notch in the crater rim. Eventually the ice curled away beneath us and we had to don crampons again to reach the rock of the Notch itself.

The Western Breach is the standard 'mountaineers' route up – or down – the mountain. It is easy for experienced climbers but it is rather harder and considerably more interesting than the tourist route from the eastern side. The rock scenery is splendid and the initial descent, down a steep pinnacled ridge, entertaining. All around are towers and walls, rotting and covered in yellow lichen, or draped with icicles. Then comes 1500 feet of unpleasant and unrunnable scree, a tiresome descent to the ice-filled aluminium bivvy hut beside the fossilized remnants of the Arrow Glacier.

There we brewed; then, while the afternoon mists blew round us we plunged down through the lava deserts, across strange fields of ever-lasting flowers where we saw leopard footprints, and down into the forest again. At last it rained, big cool drops like nectar while we made our forth bivouac in the excellent cave at One-Point-Five. We had no food but it was delicious to hear the raindrops through the velvet dark and to smell the wet forest.

It was still early when we reached the Landrover again, but the door was ajar and the inside was rifled. We had hidden anything of real value but some things were gone.

'The bastard's had my manky old sleeping bag,' cried John. 'He's welcome!' Frank too had lost something. 'My underpants,' he gasped. All I'd lost was a pair of very smelly dirty socks. 'Come on,' said John. 'Let's get the hell out of here. Rotting clothes are a fair swap for a fabulous climb. There's bound to be some food at Moshi.'

And there was, but it wasn't the end of the story. It seems that agri-culture in Tanzania is nationalized and that cattle therefore are Government servants. That was the only reason I could find for my arrest on the road back towards the Kenya border, where we had stopped so that I could photograph distant Masai herding cattle. I was charged with photographing government servants and after several tense hours in the wayside police station I was released 'on bail'. At least that's what they called it – but no doubt it went towards 'running expenses'. Despite the tenseness of the situation and the uncertainty of achieving a hot bath that night, it was difficult to remain straightfaced, so it wasn't until we were safely over the Kenya border and the hot bath looked like reality that we allowed ourselves to laugh. And laugh we did all the way back to Nairobi.

Hell's Gate

Lake Naivasha lies about forty miles north-west of Nairobi, at an altitude of 6000 feet yet still at the bottom of the Rift Valley, cradled by the high blue hills of the Mau Escarpment on the west and the Aberdares to the east. On the southern shore of the lake low hills hide a secret: a wide gorge runs through their heart. It's a lonely echoing place, floored in August with dry yellow grass and thorn bushes and walled by lines of vertical fluted cliffs, tawny coloured in the high African sun. This is Hell's Gate.

The cliffs rise some 500 feet at their highest, and the miles of walls offer few major features, just a maze of shattered columns and over-hung cracks like a nightmare Fingal's Cave formation kicked in by giants.

Pin drove the Saab fast down the dust track on the gorge floor with a contempt for the springs bred of undue familiarity. The cliffs were impressive, and this was Africa – bold, raw and colourful. But they looked mean and uncompromising, and the flat bush covered hill-top above was guarded by a line of earthy-looking overhangs. I could find little enthusiasm for climbing.

'You just walk off round the back', Pin was saying encouragingly. 'Someone saw lions up there once you know.' 'Where does Olympian go?', asked Frank when the car stopped. 'See the rockfall scar', Pin pointed, 'and the pile of blocks behind it? Starts just to the left, up for three pitches, then leftish on to that obvious ledge line, then back right above the dark patch, very loose, then the crux – it's an aid pitch – and some incredible climbing up under the tatty roofs at the top with a really exciting and unexpected finish!'

I knew what Pin meant by exciting and unexpected. So did Frank because he grunted and said 'I can't see what's holding the face together meself.' Neither could I. As we unpacked the climbing gear we could hear baboons howling on the cliffs across the gorge. 'They'll climb up to hard VS,' Pin explained. 'Then what?,' asked Sugar. 'Well, they don't use ropes you see, and sometimes they push themselves a bit too far.' 'Oh!' said Sugar. 'Yes, we did a route on that crag once,' Pin went on. 'Quite hard it was because all the holds were polished where they'd used them for centuries – then we found the remains of one who'd wound his neck too far out . . .' he laughed. 'I don't want to know,' retorted Sugar firmly.

Pin pounded up the short steep slope below the crag, his bare brown legs oblivious of the prickly grass. Frank and I picked our way carefully round the newly-fallen blocks and a few largish trees. We had both been in Africa only a few days and we were sure, both of us, that we must soon confront the snakes with which we knew the dark continent abounded.

Thankfully we reached the rock alive; we decided that Pin should lead the climb. After all he had made the only previous ascent – and it was Hell's Gate's biggest wall! The first pitch was long, and about 80 feet up the crack line was barred by a roof where he struggled a bit

Mount Kenya – its twin summits, Batian (left, 17,085 feet), and Nelion (17,022 feet), rising either side of the Gate of the Mists below which hangs the tiny Diamond Glacier and the white slit of the Diamond Couloir. This is the south-west flank of the mountain, seen during its 'winter' season from the Teleki Valley near Mackinders Camp. The left skyline is the classic West Ridge, by Shipton and Tilman, while the route Mackinder took on his first ascent of the mountain in 1899 appears over the right-hand ridge (the south ridge of Nelion) below its steep upper part, and traverses to the Diamond Glacier which it crosses to reach the final rocks of Batian

Left: On Kilimanjaro's Heim Glacier: steep slopes near the start are threatened by rock-fall

Below: Frank Cannings leads-through past a stance in an ice cave in the confused middle section

Lower left: Heavy going for John Temple at nearly 18,000 feet as the setting sun drops towards the rim of Africa

to place an aid-sling on a chockstone above it. It looked hard but he was soon up. My turn next. The rock was compact and very smooth, the crack edges were sharp and even for PA's, there was so little friction that I had to look for incut holds every move. 'Could do with some good honest frost erosion here!' I thought. The climbing was disconcerting and fingery. I reached the chockstone move but the sling was a long way above me. Pin had made a wide bridge here and he was good at that sort of thing; but when I tried it my groin cramped up and in the hot sun I felt awkward and lethargic. I was in no mood for fighting.

'I'm going to chicken,' I called up. 'Keep the rope tight.' And I clipped on a jumar and swung out into space. There was no satisfaction in the pitch after that but there was a fine stance and I tried to photograph Frank while Pin took in his rope. With a lot of puffing and panting he got Pin's sling off and then managed to hand-jam past the chockstone without aid. It looked terribly strenuous and he arrived on the ledge with his hands raw and bleeding. 'Hell's teeth Pin', he panted. 'That was hard but the rock's so smooth. It's very off-putting. I'm not on form!'

Pin led the next pitch in fine style. There was a difficult wide bridging move from one crack into another and then a scramble up a sort of chimney. Once again it seemed too much effort to climb it properly. I was feeling rather depressed and particularly hot and sweaty. I kept thinking of frosty air and a low sun glinting on blue ice.

Eventually we reached the ledge line and plumped ourselves down on a big block while I got out some sweets. Frank played with his descendeur: I could guess his thoughts. 'Is there any point in going on?' I asked. 'We could look for those hot springs Pin said were down the gorge', added Frank hopefully. Pin said nothing. I could tell he was disappointed.

But it was a fantastic viewpoint. Girdled by the great walls of cliff the floor of sun-scorched grass far below was dappled with moving shadow. Little white clouds floated across a sky as June-blue as English summer, while a hot breeze sent waves rippling across the yellow sea to where a huge pinnacle stood at the gorge mouth like a proud stack off an iron-bound coast, and the ocean faded into purple distance beyond it.

I watched two giraffes with their peculiar stiff-legged dipping stride making their way along the opposite side of the gorge. Far out into space a huge black bird hung on the breeze in lazy circles. Pin had said Lamergier nested here. I wanted to go neither up nor down. I wanted to stay and watch Africa below me.

'Right then – all set?' I started out of my reverie as Pin rose and picked up the coils of rope. 'We move back rightwards here and I want a good belay because it's rather loose.' Frank jerked awake. 'Christ,' he muttered and then, 'Do we have to?' but Pin was already on his way. I resigned myself to my fate. After all they reckoned Pin

Above: Kilimanjaro — dusk near the upper limit of the heather forest on the Umbwe Route. In the foreground are clumps of Everlastings (Helichrysum)

Below: Uhuru Peak (19,340 feet) — the summit of Kibo, Kilimanjaro's major top — is the highest point in Africa. Frank Cannings looks out across the moonscape of the ice-filled crater

was the best climber in Africa, and Frank was one of the best in Britain, even if he was off-form. I was in good hands and I had got a couple of jumars!

The traverse was a long one, a series of difficult and thin walls linking tiny rubble-covered ledges. The protection looked adequate until one reached each nut only to discover that the crack could be eased apart to remove it! The face below was concave and the exposure mind-boggling. The final forty feet was a shattered vertical wall held together it seemed by faith and split by a vertical crack. Everything was so loose that one was forced to ignore the plentiful and tempting holds which obviously keyed together the whole disintegrating mass, and use painful and untrustworthy jams in the crack. I reached the top with a dry mouth and quivering with fear. Pin was grinning. 'Christ,' I said. 'That was a good lead' – I didn't add that I felt we shouldn't have been there. But it was too late to turn back now.

We were on a small, square-cut platform piled with bat guano and above us the rock appeared newly carved and jutted outwards into the sky. Three monolithic and angular pillars held a pair of fiercely over-hanging cracks. 'This is the crux,' said Pin. 'Do you want to try it, Frank?' 'Which crack did you climb?' he asked. 'Oh, the nearer one – it's much longer and we used aid.'

'Well, I'll look at the other.' Frank nodded towards the second crack – it was much shorter and even meaner looking. He climbed

Top left: One of the five-hundred-foot walls of Hell's Gate, near Lake Naivasha. The line of Olympian (HVS A1; 800 feet) is marked, but there are several yet more recent routes on the surrounding wall

Top right: 'About 80 feet up the crack was barred by a roof where he struggled a bit'

Below left: 'I want a good belay here because it's rather loose.' A series of difficult and thin walls linking the rubble-covered ledges

Below right: 'Three monolithic and angular pillars held a pair of fiercely overhanging cracks.' Frank Cannings in action

across to the bottom of it and fighting for balance against the bulging rock struggled to place a jam of some kind. Eventually he climbed back. 'It's a bastard size – too wide for an arm, too narrow for a shoulder,' he panted. 'Whillans would manage it okay, but not me today!' 'Try the other one?' Pin suggested. But Frank was firm. 'No thank you.'

Pin collected all the big pegs and nuts from us and set off. He jammed up to a small chockstone, placed a sling on it and stepped in – he was hanging right out in space. Another jam, a bong and more slings. It looked desperate and uncompromising and was obviously extremely tiring. At long last he disappeared over the top of the pillar. Frank went next, so I could take more pictures, and then I went up with the strenuous task of removing the gear. I used my jumars on the rope for with every blow of the hammer I felt the whole pillar might fall away.

Another guano covered ledge. A brief pause for refreshment. In the distance a peculiar hum like a speedboat far out to sea swelled on the breeze. I looked enquiringly at Pin. 'Watch it,' he said urgently. 'They're wild bees swarming – they may not come this way but if they do for Christsake don't move or say anything – just freeze till they're past. We'll probably be okay if we don't alarm them.' He crouched back on the ledge, arms round his knees and tried to blend into the rock. 'Here they come.'

The humming grew louder and a small cloud closed in on us. It swept by only a few feet away and it must have been ten seconds before it passed. Frank and I held our breath. Then they were gone. Just a buzz fading into the distance. I heaved a sigh of relief and straightened my legs. 'They can be very dangerous,' said Pin reassuringly. 'It'd be a question of waiting till they stung you to death or leaping out into space to escape them!' He went on to explain that on one crag he had discovered a wild bees' nest and leading to it a bold ladder of wooden pegs up a fierce crack line. 'The Masai developed pegging on their own,' he laughed.

We were close in under the roofs now and any way through them looked so improbable that had we been on a first ascent I would have counselled retreat. But for the next hundred feet the way seemed clear. A large pinnacle like Cleopatra's Needle was stuck to the face, its base a square overhang. Nothing could be holding it there, but we had to squeeze into the chimney behind it and jam up – back and foot – to its sharp top. I was certain my feet would ease a thousand tons of rock into the void, but the pinnacle was still in place when I stepped off its summit onto the steep wall behind. It was solid and there were holds – in fact it was excellent climbing but wherever next?

We were on a tiny eyrie right under the great roofs. We could see now how tottery they were – just loose rocks cemented together with earth it seemed. The ledge was tight and we sat there dangling our legs over the edge, our arms behind each other's shoulders. Below us the wall overhung: exposure no longer had meaning. We were in that crazy, illusory world where the horizontal in the distant depth is a

'The exposure no longer had meaning but sure enough there was a steeply sloping foothold on the blank wall.' Ian Howell leads off on the crux pitch of Olympian

figment of the imagination and bears no relationship to the vertical present. It is a feeling I've never had in Britain but only on major overhanging Alpine rock climbs like the Grand Capucin or in the Dolomites.

We watched a feather of dust crawl across the gorge floor and a safari car drew up beside the toy Saab below us. A tiny dot – Sugar – got out and faint voices drifted up to us.

'Where the hell does it go now?' asked Frank. 'I'm not going up there,' he nodded upwards. 'Out right,' said Pin and he stepped off into space. Sure enough there was a steeply sloping foothold on the blank wall. Pin balanced there. I was sure his PAs would just slide off, but he reached gingerly up and placed a nut in the cracked roof above his head. I noticed him relax and then he stepped on round the corner out of sight. The rope went out steadily but it seemed ages before it stopped. 'Now watch me,' I said to Frank. 'Keep the rope fairly tight. I don't want to come off here and it looks bloody impossible,' and I lowered myself slowly over the edge of the ledge. My heart was in my mouth. I felt for holds, fingers flat on the rock and slippery sweat on the tips. But there were none. I felt powerless. I reached the sling and grabbed it. Suddenly a loud mid-western voice reached up from below. 'Say, Elmer, are they goin' hup er comin' down?' 'You may well ask madam!' I muttered as I let go the sling, and still balancing with my fingertips made three impossible strides and found myself in a bottom-less chimney. I wedged across it and relaxed. It hadn't been that hard, just extremely intimidating. I felt very happy. Between my feet I could see nothing but the white tumble of the fallen rock below the cliff. What a situation! As I wedged up the chimney, blocks broke out of their earthy matrix and went crashing down but I enjoyed it. I reached the top and there was Pin grinning down at me. I wiped the dusty sweat off my forehead.

'How d'you like it, man?' he said. 'Jesus, that was incredible. What a pitch. You led it on the first ascent?' He nodded. 'You must have blown your mind,' I gasped. 'Too true!' he replied.

Pin shouted to Frank but we could hear no reply. He took in the rope and it came slowly and jerkily. Then there was the rumble of falling rock and muffled oaths. Eventually Frank struggled into sight. 'Bloody hard and bloody loose,' he shouted up. I felt a glow of satisfaction inside – I was pleased I hadn't chickened out now.

The vast flake that formed the chimney led out in a long ledge to an open gully choked with vines and undergrowth of all sorts. It was getting late and we were in the shade at last – a blessed relief. Careless now of snakes and lions and all the other fearful natural hazards I pulled over the last bulges of loose tot and onto the level ground once more. Pin was coiling the rope.

'That's quite a route,' I said. 'There's plenty more like that in Kenya,' he replied as we set off through the African dusk across the hill-top.

201

The glass wall game

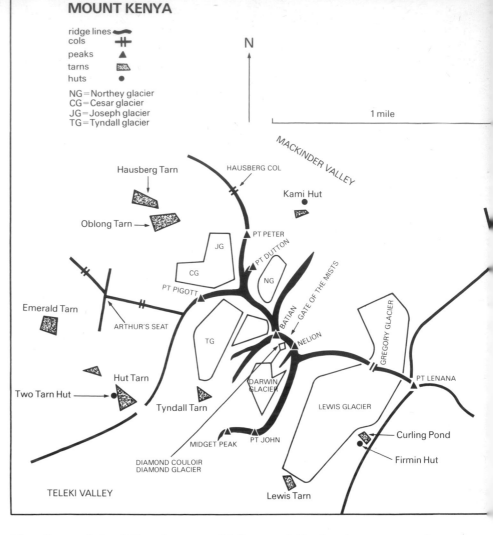

MOUNT KENYA

ridge lines	∽
cols	✚
peaks	▲
tarns	▨
huts	●

NG = Northey glacier
CG = Cesar glacier
JG = Joseph glacier
TG = Tyndall glacier

N

1 mile

MACKINDER VALLEY

Hausberg Tarn

HAUSBERG COL

Kami Hut

Oblong Tarn →

PT PETER

JG

PT DUTTON

CG

NG

PT PIGOTT

GATE OF THE MISTS

Emerald Tarn

ARTHUR'S SEAT

BATIAN

NELION

GREGORY GLACIER

TG

DARWIN GLACIER

PT LENANA

Hut Tarn

Two Tarn Hut →

Tyndall Tarn

LEWIS GLACIER

Curling Pond

Firmin Hut

MIDGET PEAK

PT JOHN

DIAMOND COULOIR
DIAMOND GLACIER

TELEKI VALLEY

Lewis Tarn

The Gate of the Mists between Nelion and Batian is a narrow ice arête, and from it on the southern side hangs the steep little icefield of the Diamond Glacier. The snout of the Diamond curls out into space in a fearsome overhang and from the icy jaws beneath, toothed with huge icicles, is born the Diamond Couloir – a 1200-foot ice channel dividing the southwestern buttress of Batian and Nelion.

In the season of southern summer the Couloir, its ice blackened and stone-scarred, drops into the upper névé of the Darwin Glacier over a gaping 'schrund of polished rock and rotting ice. Winter snow fills this vast hole and the Couloir spills through its rocky throat into the Darwin as a steep ice pillar, sometimes vertical and up to 250 feet high.

The aesthetic beauty and simplicity of its line is enough to make the Diamond Couloir the most obvious ice climb in Africa, and because of its difficulty, probably the greatest too. But climbs of this nature are often dangerous, and the Couloir is no exception. Any pebble or ice-

chip falling in the south-western cirque of Mt Kenya will end up
spinning down the Couloir, and every so often the Diamond curling
over it will spew forth a mass of ice to thunder down destroying anything in its path. Indeed, in the mid-sixties an RAF party innocently
crossing the Lewis Glacier were annihilated by an avalanche from the
Couloir above them. I once asked Barry Cliff, a very experienced
Kenya mountaineer, why such an obvious line was still virgin. 'Hell
man – it's a death trap!' he replied. 'You'd have to be insane to go near
it.' But those were the days before climbers ventured onto the out-of-
season flanks of Mt Kenya and the Diamond Couloir was unknown
in winter. No one had yet had a close look.

Then in November 1971 there was a rumour that the Couloir had
been climbed the previous month. The audacious climbers were said
to be Ian Howell (my friend Pin) and Phil Snyder, the American
climber who runs the Mt Kenya National Park. But Pin sent me a
long letter, he wrote: '. . . the Couloir was hard but it went OK. There

was one steep ice pitch at the bottom, a 150-foot run-out, and then easier going to another major ice pitch leading onto the Diamond Glacier at the top. It seems to be fairly safe in winter and nothing came down it while we were there . . . We had to get back to Nairobi that night so we didn't actually get to the top. But I think we'd almost cracked it before we abseiled down . . . Why not come out here next summer instead of the Alps and we'll burn it off properly?'

It is the pitch darkness of that hour before the dawn. The only sound: boots on rock, muffled curses and the occasional metallic jangle of crampons and karabiners. By the light of our head-torches the going is slow as we slither and scramble our awkward way across the steep rocks below Two-Tarn towards the Tyndall Glacier. We reach the moraine below Tyndall Tarn and the going is easier for a few minutes; but then begins the sweaty scramble up rock slabs and rubble towards the Darwin Glacier.

Dawn in Africa comes up fast and it is suddenly light as we strap on our crampons and start up the steepening ice of the Darwin towards the dark gash of the Couloir above. But today the light is dead. The mountain ahead and the sharp summit of Point John behind rise into a leaden cloud ceiling. Beneath it the morning is flat and grey, and the great cirque just a primeval chaos of black-streaked rock and dying snow. I am reminded more of Ben Nevis on a bad November day than the Equator in August. Who's for a holiday in purgatory?

The final snow cone, before the walls of the Couloir close round us, is pretty steep; but Frank locates the end of the fixed rope from yester-day and, grateful for its security, we drag ourselves over the bergsch-rund and across to the stance under the right wall that we cut during our reconnaissance last afternoon. Pin ties into the two rock pegs. 'You can carry on where you left off, J.' he says meaningfully.

I strain my head back and look up the bulging blue ice to where the rope – the rope from my waist – passes through a runner round a tiny rock spike thirty feet up. It had been very unpleasant up there yester-day afternoon when we had tried to get the climb started. It had begun to snow and small powder avalanches had poured continuously down the Couloir. Every few minutes someone had shouted a warning and I'd had to brace myself on front points and terrordactyl picks to wait for the white surge to hit and pour over me. Each time the danger had passed I was surprised still to be there, but progress was slow and after thirty feet we had pulled out.

But today I am not very determined. I am stiff and cold and my stomach is hollow. Half an hour later I am back at the stance with only a few extra feet to show for it. 'Someone else have a go,' I suggest, and add unconvincingly 'I'm not with it yet this morning.' Pin leads off. He is soon on front points on 80 degree ice. 'It's a bloody sight harder than last year,' he shouts down as he passes my high point. 'It's much steeper and all hard ice!' He reaches the smooth rock of the right wall. I'd hoped the junction of rock and ice would ease the upward

way. 'No chance. Smooth as a baby's arse! I'm coming down a bit and I'll try leftward.'

Half an hour later Pin too is back at the stance. His rope runs through an ice screw almost in the middle of the Couloir. 'You see where I was making for,' he explains breathlessly. 'There's a slight kink beyond the screw where the ice isn't quite vertical. I think if we can follow it to the left-hand side there'll be odd holds on the rock wall. Certainly the angle eases sooner that side – it's quite obvious from where I was.'

And so it's Frank's turn. Slowly he inches across that faint ripple in the ice. It looks very precarious. Every couple of moves he cuts a small step and rests. Once he places another ice screw. Eventually he reaches the far side of the Couloir and balancing precariously on his front points and hammer pick he places another ice screw one handed. He clips in and relaxes. So do we. 'It's plumb bloody vertical but I think it's the right way,' he shouts down. 'There's a couple of rock holds and I think the ledge is about thirty feet up. But I'm shattered. Can I come down?' 'Okay', yells Pin and turns to me, grinning. 'It's your turn now, J. You can bloody finish it.'

As Frank tensions gingerly back on the rope I look far out and down beyond the clinging cloud to the sun-speckled green of the Teleki Valley three thousand feet below. I shiver and my stomach rumbles – after five nights on the mountain I need a good meal. I think of steaks and beer in the balmy warmth of Nairobi. Confidence and boldness evaporate so easily when the crunch comes.

But now I am on the sharp end of the rope and I'm a long way out from the stance. There's no problem with route-finding; it's just straight up. Leaning back on the screw I cut a couple of nicks in front of my face and mantleshelf into them. Another couple of moves and I can stick my foot out onto that little snow-covered nick on the rock wall. I bridge wide and lean forward with relief. Between my legs the ice falls a sheer 150 feet into the 'schrund. I place another ice screw, why not? It's a long way down. Another few moves, my forearms ache, my ankles ache and then again a leg out on the left wall, crampon points scratched into a tiny hold, and relax. Totally engrossed in the technical problem of surmounting my glass wall there is no longer room in my mind for fear. Now I'm warm and confident and enjoying myself. More aching movement, precarious but deeply satisfying and then above my head the ice leans back. One last screw, a scraping of front points and there is a sloping ledge of deep powder in front of my face. I hammer in a terrordactyl shaft and muscle up.

'That's the end of the rope.' The shout snaps my concentration. Hells teeth, 150 feet! Just made it! But can't stop here – it's steep and narrow but the bulging rock that pushes you out has a good crack in it. Slam in a peg. 'Undo your belay – give me ten more feet.' Clip in a sling – lean out – wide bridge – good hand jam – and I'm there, crouched on a comfortable snow-covered rock ledge on the left wall big enough for a

M

bivi! Wheeee – I'm up! A shout drifts up from below, 'Well done, J. Bloody good.'

Frank comes up next. He arrives panting and crawls in beside me. 'Here's some chocolate, man,' he gasps and drags a bar out of his pocket. 'Jeez – that wasn't easy!' Then Pin arrives, the ice screws jangling at his waist. 'Time's getting by,' he pants. 'Better push on. I think you ought to lead.' Nothing ventured, nothing gained, and I relish the thought of getting warm. I swing down to my peg again, and standing just in balance I size up the ice above.

The lowest point of the next bulge is a few feet right, and then it's straight up over the bulge before it leans back again. But it's aid climbing this time, ice splitting round the screws, crampons catching in the tapes and hell on the arms. But only twenty feet and then another sloping mantleshelf and I stand gingerly up. Above me a powdery runnel runs up beside the rock wall thirty feet into a narrow cave. Feeling very insecure I plough up towards it looking for nut or peg cracks in the wall, but they're all blind. I reach the cave and there to the right, beyond another bulge of ice are the easy slopes of the upper couloir!

'We've cracked it,' I call down. 'Just a short traverse to make.' Everywhere the rock is loose; but there's a fair nut placing that might hold. On front points I move carefully outwards. I've got to swing on that loose flake – but it holds. I lean across and cut a handhold. Fingers slot into it. Crampons kick in. Two swift moves and I'm on easy ground. Below me my glass wall curls downward into the mist and I realize quite suddenly that it's snowing.

White flakes swirl down through the mist and ahead the Couloir disappears into the murk, its surface a hissing stream of spindrift. And I'm right out in the middle of it. I crampon up and across to the rock wall where there's a safe looking cave. I whack in a peg, and as I clip in the first powder avalanche roars by, a waist-deep torrent of billowing white powder. I'm aware of fear again. Pin and Frank are safe but I could be in trouble up here.

'I don't like this,' I shout down. 'This Couloir's dangerous.' 'There's only three hours of daylight left,' returns Pin and a terse conversation follows, interrupted occasionally by the whoosh of powder avalanches. The final decision is to retreat. We are not equipped to bivouac and there are considerable difficulties above. 'Can we come back in a few days time?' I yell down. 'Why not,' shouts Pin. 'Tie off the ropes and we can just jumar back up them.'

Arranging an abseil I swing back round the corner out of the main runnel and slide down to Pin, removing the ice screws en route. Frank is already half-way down the ice-wall below. Every now and then a swishing torrent of powder completely covers him. Soon he disappears into the mist. I'm last one down. It's lonely up here. I eye the small wedge of steel and the stretched nylon, my only link with warmth and safety and future. And then it's over the edge for me, sliding down through the gushing powder still amazed at the angle of it all. My disappointment is overwhelmed by relief but the tension must stay until the ground is flat.

It is four weeks later and another dawn. Crouching on a rock below the Darwin Glacier, Pin and I await the first light to lead us back towards the Couloir. The sweat is cold on my back and already we feel sleepy. For two hours we have struggled upwards through the darkness, from our bivouac site beneath a giant groundsel plant among the rocks below Midget Peak. Twenty-four hours ago we were leaving Nairobi, bleary-eyed after a party, to start the 150-mile drive to the mountain. Each time we stopped during the tedious 4000-foot slog up the moors from the road-head we had fallen asleep. I am still trying to reconcile the urbane bonhomie of the party with the equatorial darkness here at 15,000 feet.

The sky lightens and dawn sweeps over the ridge. We struggle to our feet, pleased to leave behind our thoughts and start the serious business. Although tired we are very fit and the going to the bergschrund is swift. But where is the rope? The ice has claimed it and its outline is barely visible, a dark line leading upwards through the translucent blue. 'Hell, that's going to be an effort,' I grunt.

'I'll take first go on this, J.' says Pin. And he starts laboriously to hack the rope end from its blue sheath. He cuts out six feet, clips on his jumars and slowly cuts his way upwards. I tie myself to an icicle and shiver. Has the rope beneath the ice been damaged by stonefall? I wonder. It's hardly quicker than climbing at this rate. Eventually I doze. 'Come on up, J.' I jerk awake, gather my senses and clip on my own jumars. As I work slowly up the still slippery rope I am amazed that we managed to climb this glass wall at all. The second pitch is mine to clear, but because of the overhang most of the rope is free of the ice. Soon we reach the upper cave and stop for food. Already the time is late, we'd reckoned an hour to here – not four! And the day is another dull one, dead and murky, the mountain above us disappearing into grey clag. The huge jutting snout of the Diamond is just visible hanging over us. Wow! If that came down . . . But the going now is easy; it's not steep and we can make full run-outs. The only problems are keeping out of the centre of the Couloir, the fall line for stones and ice, and finding belays on the rocky walls. Polished by centuries of moving ice, they offer few cracks for pegs or nuts.

Three pitches up, or is it four? – The rope goes tight. Ahead, perhaps six feet, is a hopeful looking crack for a belay. 'Pin,' I call, 'Can you give me six more feet?' Nothing. 'Hey, Pin!' 'What? – Hell, sorry man – I dozed off. What's up?' I get the rope and the crack is good. But then it's my turn to wait and I too fight the oppressive grey weight of sleep.

The angle steepens again. A steep ice-fall rears above leading into a huge ice cave – the jaws of the Diamond. Enormous icicles seem to hang right over us. We are terribly vulnerable. If Damocles' hell had been ice it could have been here!

'It's changed completely since last year,' growls Pin. 'This was a short easy-angled pitch and look at it now. I'll bet it's a hundred feet and it's bloody vertical!' 'How about the right flank?' I suggest, pointing hopefully to a ramp line of rock with icy bands leading out of the Couloir. 'We'd reach that big rock wall and then traverse back along its base into the cave. Then we're almost through.' 'Okay,' says Pin, without enthusiasm. 'Off you go.'

I lead one pitch; it's awkward but not too difficult although the next one looks hard. I belay on a poorly placed nut and Pin takes over. It's a continual battle with sleep as I watch him fight his way up the rocky band above me. He has no protection and he is climbing difficult glazed rock. The scrape of his crampons searching for rock holds is horrible. I breathe a sigh of relief when he makes the top but there is still no runner. He moves across steep ice and reaches the bottom of the big rock wall. He finds a peg crack and I relax and slip momentarily into sleep. I find the pitch frightening; crampon points on tiny rock crystals and the ice thin and brittle. I'm thankful for a tight rope from above. I reach the ice but the rope is slack. 'Take it in,' I call. No reply. I shout again and Pin grunts, 'Sorry, man.' I reach him, and stand on crampon points below his tiny ledge.

'God!' he says. 'It's bad, I dozed off again.' 'I did too,' I admit. 'It's not very funny is it? That pitch was hard – well done!' 'But look at the next one – rather you than me.' I move off leftwards towards the gaping mouth of the Diamond. The ice is steep and the traverse far from easy. Usually there is an easy line at the junction of rock and ice but not here! It's a long way before I can place a nut and rest on it. Suddenly I jerk awake. Hell! I'm asleep leading! This is terrible – really dangerous! 'I keep falling asleep,' I shout back to Pin. No reply. 'Pin are you awake?' 'Eh? Uh, what's that? Yes man!'

As I look at my watch I feel the first flurry of snow and the cave ahead is looming dark through the descending cloud. It's very late. At 150 feet, I find a good peg crack. I belay and cut a small step. 'J, are you awake?' Pin calls. I jerk to, I've been asleep again! There is no discussion. We both know the score.

It's a crazy descent through the falling snow. Snatches of sleep alternating with dream-like abseils from pitons and ice bollards while the snow avalanches hiss by. We doze together briefly in the cave before plucking up the courage to slide over the edge and down the great glass wall.

The sky cleared at dusk and the pinnacles of Mt Kenya stood black above the frozen tussocks of the Teleki Valley. Glinting in the last light between the twin summits was the narrow slash of the Diamond Couloir. 'We should never have gone to that party,' said Pin.

A hyrax shrieked from the boulders behind us and the stream tinkled its crystal way towards the distant Indian Ocean. 'It deserves to stay virgin,' I said softly.

208

6 Himalaya

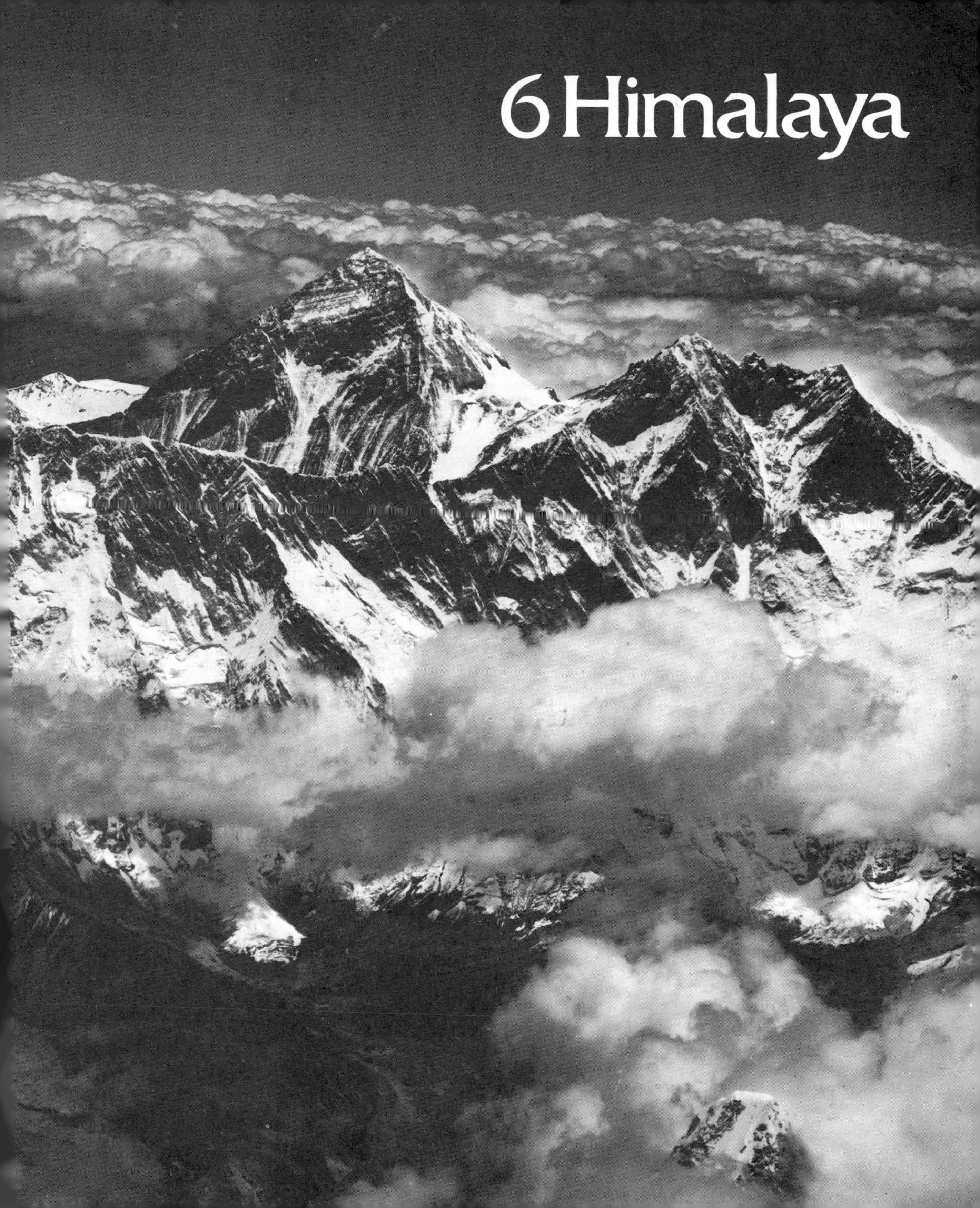

Which way up Everest?

One day in 1852 the head of the Calculating Office of the Survey of India in Dehra Dun, a Bengali, Radhanath Sikhdar, burst excitedly into the office of Sir Andrew Waugh, the Surveyor General, and cried: 'Sahib, I have discovered the highest mountain in the world.'

That at least is the story, for it was that year that the height of Peak 15, hitherto just another high summit in forbidden Nepal, was calculated to be 29,002 feet, nearly 900 feet higher than Peak 9 – Kangchenjunga – long considered the world's highest.

Immediate enquiries were made as to the peak's name; but when these proved fruitless the Indian Government approved the suggestion made by the Surveyor General and the R.G.S., that Peak 15 be known as Mt Everest, in honour of Sir George Everest, the late Surveyor-General of India and a man who made memorable contributions both to India and to science. Several names had in fact been discovered. One was Chomo Kangar – 'White Snow of the Mother Queen'. Others were Chomo Lungma – 'Goddess Mother of the Land or Goddess of the Wind' – a very appropriate name, and Sagamatha. Yet another was translated as 'you cannot see the summit from nearby but you can see the summit from nine directions and a bird which flies that high goes blind'. But all these names were of the massif itself, and so the big black cone rising above remained as Mt Everest.

Early attempts to reach Everest were frustrated by its position on the border between the closed Kingdoms of Nepal and Tibet. Charles Bruce, a Gurkha officer and great pioneer of Himalayan climbing, planned an expedition as early as 1893 and again – together with Longstaff and Mumm – in 1907, but with no avail. In 1909 permission was granted for a joint Anglo-Nepalese expedition but the Indian Government turned down the idea, much to Bruce's disgust. Then came the Great War.

After the war the Everest Committee, jointly formed by the Alpine Club and the R.G.S., tried the Tibetan approach and finally obtained permission from the Dalai Lama for an expedition to the mountain. The permission was for two years: first a reconnaissance and then an assault. Bruce was not available, but Colonel Howard-Bury, who had been responsible for the negotiations, was selected as leader and £10,000 was raised to support a team of Himalayan explorers and surveyors stiffened by four experienced mountaineers – the veterans Raeburn and Kellas, and the younger alpinists Bullock and Mallory. The expedition left Darjeeling for Tibet in May 1921; committed to the northern approaches to the mountain.

In Darjeeling, Sherpas had been recruited as expedition porters. These natives of Khumbu, the Nepalese region immediately south of

Previous pages: 'The South-West Face of Everest is a huge triangle of dark rock some 7000 feet high.' An aerial picture of Everest from the south, with the upper 5000 feet of the Face appearing over the summit ridge of Nuptse, and Lhotse on the right. The route of all South-West Face attempts has been up the great central couloir and then right along the snowy ramp below the Great Rock Band. The left skyline is the West Ridge and the right is the South-East Ridge rising from the South Col. The 'south facet' which confronted Whillans at Camp VI in 1971 is clearly seen between the Face and the South-East Ridge

Opposite: Sherpa sirdar, Kancha, with his wife and family at the door of his home in Namche Bazar

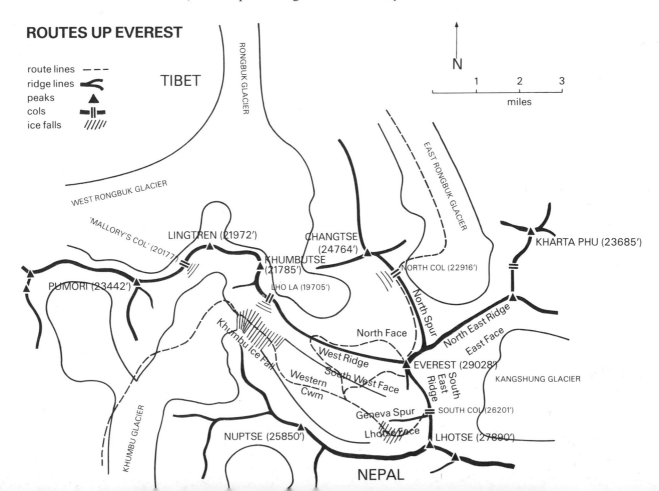

ROUTES UP EVEREST

The twin peaks of Kangtaiga
(left, 22,235 feet and right,
21,926 feet) rise over 8000
feet above the yak pastures
at Pheriche across the valley
of the Imja Khola

Everest, had first come to Darjeeling at the turn of the century, looking for work and good wages. They had already worked as high altitude porters for Kellas, and their performance on these early Everest expeditions established their place and high reputation in world mountaineering.

Once in the Everest region, the survey and climbing parties split up. The former ranged over a wide area and did much valuable work to the north of the watershed, which is still unsurpassed. The climbing team was reduced to two; Kellas had died of a heart attack and Raeburn was ill, but Mallory and Bullock ascended the Rongbuk Glacier flowing from the north flank of Everest. They saw that the feasible-looking upper section of the long N.E. Ridge could be joined at a shoulder some 1500 feet below the summit by an easy-angled northern spur rising from an icy col. This they named the North Col (Chang La; 22,916 feet).

From the head of the Rongbuk they climbed easily to the Lho La from where they noted that the western flanks of the North Col looked dangerous and difficult, but possible. They could look down a steep ice wall into Nepal. Again by easy slopes they gained 'Mallory's Col' (20,177 feet). It lies between Lingtren and Pumori, the peak Mallory had called 'Daughter Peak' after his infant Clare. From there they looked across the tangled Khumbu ice fall below and into the shadowed sanctuary of a high and deep valley they dubbed the 'Western Cwm'. They were unable to see the South Col itself, but the route up the Cwm seemed feasible, although Bullock wrote in his diary:

... it was guarded by a steep and broken glacier so that any attack from this side would need very elaborate organisation for a lengthy expedition. Practically out of the question ...

Then the whole expedition moved to the east side of Everest. The huge East Face above the Kangchung Glacier they declared quite impossible, although the South-East Ridge looked feasible above the South Col (which was inaccessible from their side). There was no approach either to the N.E. Ridge; but when they crossed an easy pass to the head of the previously unnoticed East Rongbuk glacier they found easy slopes leading 2000 feet up to the North Col. A few days later Mallory, Bullock and Wheeler reached the Col. The spur above it was merely moderate snow slopes and easy slabby rock. Their mission had been fulfilled: a way had been found, and the expedition returned to Darjeeling well satisfied.

The 1922 expedition was led by Bruce himself; it must have seemed, when Camp IV was established on the North Col, that success would not be long delayed. But it was not to be. Camp V was established just above 25,000 feet, but the Shoulder was never reached. After bad weather Finch and Bruce Jr. reached some 27,300 feet, having left the crest of the spur because of the high wind and struck across the northern slopes on seemingly easier ground. It was here that they first encountered the awkward calcareous slabs of the Yellow Band sloping

Everest is still 36 miles away and 20,000 feet above – its huge black pyramid apparently dwarfed by the nearer peaks of Tramserku (21,647 feet) and Kangtaiga. This is the first sight of Everest on the approach march from the Salung Ridge above Junbesi

Opposite below: John Evans crosses a crevasse in the Khumbu Ice-Fall

Breakfast at Camp II in the Western Cwm. Clockwise from 12.0 — Murray Sayle, Arthur Chesterman, Dave Peterson, John Cleare (at 6.0), Ian Stewart, Wolfgang Axt, Ned Kelly and Leo Schlommer

Right: Colourful wayside Chorten on a ridge above the Sun Kosi provides a foreground for distant Dorjei Lakpa (22,240 feet)

Below: The route into the Western Cwm enters the dangerous Khumbu Ice-Fall. Above, seracs hang menacingly from the massive south-west shoulder of Everest

downward like slates on a roof, which seemed to protect the whole northern side of the mountain. They are not steep – a mere 35 degrees – but dangerous when covered in new snow and difficult to protect. The expedition ended tragically when an avalanche below the North Col killed seven Sherpas.

The Mount Everest Committee sent out a further expedition in 1924. Norton and Somervell established Camp VI near the highest point they had reached the previous year just 700 feet below the Shoulder and then, following the line of least resistance, made a gradually ascending traverse across the face and the overlapping snow-powdered slabs of the Yellow Band. Eventually Norton, alone and without oxygen, reached the Great Couloir, the wide gully separating the N.E. Ridge from the final pyramid. He crossed it in thigh-deep powder snow and climbed a short distance beyond to about 28,124 feet, before retreating. Mallory, accompanied by the inexperienced Irvine and using oxygen, made the next attempt. From Camp VI, instead of traversing across the face, they pushed up to the Ridge, and Noel Odell who was in support saw two tiny figures below a rock step through a rent in the mist. Mallory and Irvine were never seen again. Did they reach the summit? Did they die on the descent? Maybe we shall never be sure.

By now it was evident that there were two possible lines from the North Col to the summit. Norton had preferred the rising traverse across the easy but treacherous rocks of the northern face, towards the Great Couloir. Quite how he – or others – proposed to continue is uncertain, but it would probably have been up the rocks on the far side, towards the base of the final pyramid at about 28,200 feet. Then here are two alternatives: either traverse back to join the final snow arête of the N.E. Ridge proper, or climb the pyramid direct where a line of linked snow patches indicates a weakness. A third possibility, a long rightward traverse over snow slopes towards the upper rocks of the West Ridge, is probably the least practical.

Mallory, however, had favoured joining the N.E. Ridge near the Shoulder and taking it direct. It is a better line, shorter and perhaps easier, except at two points. The First Step at about 27,800 feet offers little problem. Beyond it a thin broken ridge leads to the Second Step at 28,130 feet. This is a major obstacle, a steep wall about 100 feet high completely barring the narrow arête. It was later described by Ruttledge as: '. . . like the bows of a battle cruiser'. Above it the snow arête of the N.E. Ridge continues to the summit (?).

Further permission was not forthcoming until 1933, when a powerful young team led by Ruttledge established Camp VI just below the crest of the N.E. Ridge at 27,400 feet, considerably higher than before. Wyn-Harris and Wager, attempting Mallory's Ridge Route, found an easy traverse just below the ridge crest which by-passed the First Step. They reached the Second Step which they considered impossible, and Wyn-Harris attempted to by-pass it by a chimney 200 yards

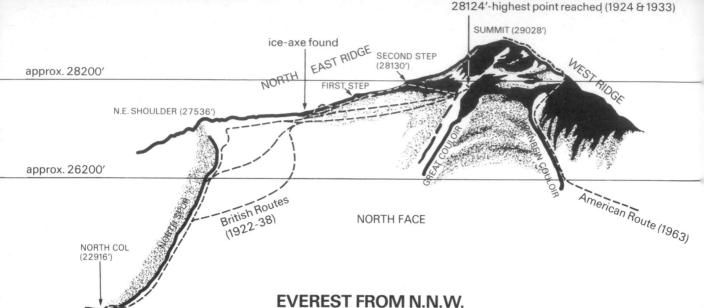

28124'-highest point reached (1924 & 1933)

SUMMIT (29028')

ice-axe found

NORTH   EAST RIDGE

SECOND STEP
(28130')

WEST RIDGE

approx. 28200'

FIRST STEP

N.E. SHOULDER (27536')

GREAT COULOIR

NORBEN COULOIR

approx. 26200'

American Route (1963)

NORTH SPUR

British Routes
(1922-38)

NORTH FACE

NORTH COL
(22916')

EVEREST FROM N.N.W.

further on but without success. So they continued the traverse right across to the Great Couloir and reached the same point as Norton in 1924. Near the First Step they had found an ice axe, probably Mallory's. It was the last trace of the two climbers. A few days later Smythe, climbing solo, also managed to reach the same point via Norton's traverse but could climb no higher.

The 1935 expedition led by Shipton was again a reconnaissance to examine the mountain under monsoon and post-monsoon conditions, and to re-examine the Western Cwm and West Ridge. Shipton reported: 'As far as we could see the route up (the Western Cwm) did not look impossible and I should very much like to have the opportunity one day of exploring it . . .' But Nepal was to remain closed for another fifteen years.

The following expeditions of '36 and '38, led by Ruttledge and Tilman achieved little in the face of impossible weather and early monsoons. The 1938 ascent of the North Col from the west was of little note. And then another war shook the world.

In the light of subsequent happenings it is interesting to speculate on the potential of the northern route. Hillary, after his successful 1953 climb told Ruttledge that, seen from the summit, the final 900 feet looked unclimbable. The terrain above and beyond the Great Couloir is obviously far more difficult than the comparatively easy ground below, and is at the practical limit – about 28,000 feet – of climbing without oxygen. Small wonder that this was where all attempts ended. But to avoid the Couloir means surmounting the Second Step. Smythe suggested that it might be turned on its eastern side – the Kangchung flank – by moderate ice slopes, and from post-war aerial pictures this does appear to be the case. That last thousand feet is the most intriguing in the Himalaya.

218

Since the post-war occupation of Tibet by China, occasional news from the northern side of Everest, often unreliable and fragmentary, has reached the west. Apparently a Soviet post-monsoon expedition in 1952 reached 27,000 feet via the North Col. Then six climbers disappeared without trace. More important however, is the claim by the Chinese pre-monsoon expedition of 1960 to have reached the summit. Somewhere they found and buried the body of an English climber clad in a green suit; unfortunately they gave no location. From a top camp at 27,900 feet a team ascended the Ridge to the Second Step which they described as: 'A sheer and slippery wall . . . of rotten rock.' They climbed it with difficulty and bivouacked in a snowhole above before turning back.

A second party, none with more than two years' mountaineering experience, climbed the Second Step, taking five hours for the hundred feet and using combined tactics. Three members of the party continued and eventually reached the summit in the middle of the night, having held a 'party meeting' and run out of oxygen en route. In the darkness no photographs were taken but a plaster bust of Chairman Mao was set up and a glove containing a written note buried in the snow. On the descent a further night was spent in the open due to faulty navigation. Despite two days without food or drink they were none the worse for their ordeal. They attributed success to 'the party's general political line showing how to dare to think and act' and described the climb as 'the most arduous and dangerous trek in mankind's history'.

Himalayan scholars have naturally queried the authenticity of the ascent. There are several inconsistencies in the descriptions, and photographs claimed to have been taken at 28,500 feet have been shown by comparison with pre-war pictures to have been taken at approximately 27,890 feet near the First Step. The Indians camped above the South Col on the day of the ascent were unable to proceed because of storm conditions. Many experts, however, prefer to keep an open mind about the Chinese claims, and a further ascent claimed by a survey party in 1969.

Two years later a highly irresponsible effort was made by an American, Woodrow Wilson Sayre, with three companions, on the Northern Flank. Having illegally crossed the Nup La from Nepal they reached a short distance above the North Col and were lucky to return to Nepal without being either killed or arrested. This foolish escapade contributed much to the decision of the Nepalese authorities to close their country to mountaineers for five years soon afterwards.

Now that the 'ping-pong diplomacy' of Chairman Mao has extended the hand of friendship, permission for an expedition from the north does not seem impossible, operating out of Nepal perhaps via the easy Nangpa La. A tantalising thought!

We should consider now the south side of Everest. Tibet was closed, but Nepal opened its borders to mountaineers in 1950 and the following year a small British reconnaissance party led by Eric Shipton

'. . . Could the Western Cwm be reached via the Khumbu Ice Fall?' A party starts off into the Ice Fall a few hundred yards above Base Camp

Right: 'The Ice Fall is a terrible obstacle . . .' Near the top of the Ice Fall, fallen blocks of ice strew the route ahead. Above is the great North Face of Nuptse rising from the Western Cwm

'. . . and entered the Western Cwm — the mysterious valley of silence . . .'

arrived. There were several questions to answer. Could the Western Cwm be reached via the Khumbu Ice Fall? Could the South Col be reached from the Cwm? Did the South-East Ridge between the Col and the summit appear feasible?

From the flanks of Pumori opposite the Ice Fall Shipton could see into the Cwm; he concluded that once above the Fall there were no apparent difficulties all the way to the South Col. The Ice Fall is a terrible obstacle, a mile and a half of moving ice tumbling nearly 2000 feet, but the expedition penetrated to the top and were prevented from entering the white sanctuary of the Cwm itself only by the enormous crevasse which extends from wall to wall at its very lip. But they had seen enough to justify a full scale assault.

The Swiss however had booked the mountain for 1952, and a powerful expedition led by Dr. Edward Wyss-Dunant climbed the Ice Fall, crossed the great crevasse with difficulty and entered the Cwm – the mysterious three-mile glacier basin, all above 19,500 feet, which they named 'The Valley of Silence'. The South Col rises 3600 feet above the head of the Cwm; they reached it by a short open couloir between the serac-barred ice wall of Lhotse to the right and the rocky rib they called the 'Geneva Spur' to the left. The Col is possibly the highest in the world, at a height of 26,201 feet; here they placed Camp VI. The South-East Ridge was approached by its southern flank above the Col, and a tent erected at 27,230 feet where Raymond Lambert and Tenzing, the Sherpa Sirdar, spent the night. Next day, exhausted and in worsening weather, they climbed another 800 feet before retreating.

After the monsoon a further attempt was mounted by a reconstituted team. Tragedy struck when a Sherpa was killed by an ice avalanche in the couloir below the South Col, and consequently a new route was worked out further right, through the contorted seracs of the Lhotse Face with a final traverse leftward onto the Col. Cold and wind stopped all progress above the Col. The brave Swiss had proved that the South-East Ridge was climbable to at least 28,000 feet, but that to climb higher powerful logistic support was necessary above the South Col. This route was very different from the northern one: there the difficulties had been high up. But here the major problem it seemed was the Khumbu Ice Fall.

Colonel John Hunt was chosen by the Everest Committee to lead the British 1953 team. He planned his expedition with the systematic expertise expected of a soldier, and three members of his team, Hillary, Bourdillon and the doctor, Ward, had been with Shipton's 1950 reconnaissance. All were fully acclimatized and oxygen was planned as a major factor in the assault. Everything went like clockwork, and despite the usual run of poor weather the Col was reached by the Lhotse Face route and Camp VIII established on it.

The first assault team, Tom Bourdillon and Charles Evans, using oxygen, reached the South Summit at 28,722 feet in just over six hours from the Col. It is a small point on the ridge some half mile from the

221

top; they were able to study the final arête closely. Having fulfilled their mission they returned to the South Col.

After a day of storm a second assault team, the New Zealander, Hillary, and Tenzing the Sherpa, well supported by other climbers, established Camp IX at about 27,900 feet on the west flanks of the Ridge. They reached the South Summit early the next morning and dropped 30 feet down to the final arête. There were large cornices on the eastern side and rocks on the west. After an hour, a forty-foot rock step barred the way; they turned it by a chimney between the rock and the ice. Then they cut steps up snowy humps on the ridge. Two and a half hours after leaving the South Summit they arrived on the top of Everest.

The summit is a small snow plateau big enough, said the Swiss later, 'for a teacher to gather his class around him'. Mighty cornices overhang the Kangchung face, while to the west the summit falls away to rocks.

Interest in Everest did not diminish with the successful ascent. Indeed it led to a succession of other expeditions attempting to repeat the South Col route, now considered the *voie normale*. By the end of 1973 it had been successfully attempted by seven expeditions who had put thirty-five climbers onto the summit. Certain venturesome mountaineers started dreaming of new routes up the mountain. Among these was Norman Dyhrenfurth, a Swiss-American and son of G. O. Dyhrenfurth, probably the world's foremost Himalayan scholar. He had been on Everest with the Swiss during their 1952 post-monsoon attempt and had been in the Western Cwm again with the 1955 Lhotse expedition. His enquiring eye had noted the potential lines of both the West Ridge and the South West Face. Jimmy Roberts, one of the most experienced British Himalayan explorers wrote: 'The West Ridge gives rise to interesting thoughts – it would take one close to the old pre-war North Face route . . .' It was intriguing indeed, and aesthetically still perhaps the finest line on the mountain.

In the spring of 1963, Dyhrenfurth arrived in Nepal at the head of the large and powerful American Everest Expedition, with Roberts as Transport Officer. But the final decision to make a reconnaissance in force on to the West Ridge was not taken until the expedition was nearing Base Camp.

The Americans were as well organized and led as had been Hunt's party ten years before. From Camp II – advanced base – half way up the Western Cwm at 21,350 feet, the West Ridge party left the main team and, traversing upwards and leftwards over complex ice slopes, reached the Ridge at 23,640 and pushed some 1500 feet above. Although a route up the rocky summit pyramid ahead looked possible, campsites were difficult to find and logistics seemed problematic. Prompted among other things by consideration for the expedition's sponsors, the Americans postponed further attempts until the South Col team had reached the summit. Willi Unsoeld, of the West Ridge

Above: In the Western Cwm, en route for Camp II. On the left is the huge South-West Face of Everest, ahead is Lhotse, and between them the South Col, the highest col in the world at 26,201 feet. The Geneva Spur is the rocky rib falling from it

Below: A view of Everest looking eastwards. North Peak, North Col, North Face and South-West Face, South Col, Western Cwm, Ice Fall Khumbu Glacier are visible. Behind Everest is Kangchenjunga, 70 miles away. Pumori is visible in the foreground

team, wrote in his diary with a sentiment common to great climbers: 'Surely mountaineering is more than a matter of summits – even when the summit is that of Everest'.

Everything went smoothly and 'Big Jim' Whittaker and Sherpa Gombu reached the summit on the early date of 1 May. There they left the American flag, but discovered no traces of the controversial 1960 Chinese ascent. And then the West Ridge team swung into action, while a second team returned to the assault via the South Col. There were problems. Camp IV West, just below the first difficult rocks at 25,100, was virtually destroyed by wind during the night and had to be temporarily abandoned; the monsoon was now rapidly approaching.

The Ridge crest itself appeared difficult and the climbers thought aid-climbing might become necessary; but they managed to avoid it by the 'Diagonal Ditch', a long ramp slanting leftwards up and into the North Face. Here the climbing was on packed snow but there were occasional outcrops of the notorious North Face rock slabs. Then at 26,200 they reached the base of a snowy gully, which they named the Hornbein Couloir, only a few hundred yards west of the famous Great Couloir of pre-war days. They cut steps up it to the Yellow Band and here on a tiny platform at 27,250 they established the one tent of Camp V West.

While their supporting companions went down, Tom Hornbein and Willi Unsoeld spent a fair night. Next day they continued cutting up the steep couloir. At one point it narrowed right down almost to a chimney and when finally it degenerated into a mere narrow crack, a break in the right wall led them to a broad shelf leading back towards the crest of the West Ridge. But the shelf was still not easy, it was steep and on a short rock wall two pitons had to be used for progress. Technical rock climbing at 28,200 is not easy! At this point a crucial decision had to be made. To continue would mean cutting off retreat and relying on traversing the summit to descend by the South Col route. A marvellous goal at which to aim – but should the South Col team not reach the summit that same day, almost certainly disasterous for already exhausted men. Unsoeld and Hornbein decided to push on. Now above the Yellow Band, they traversed back across open slabs to regain the crest of the Ridge.

Again the climbing became difficult, as the Ridge narrowed to a steep knife-edge. But the rock was good and taking off their crampons and overboots they enjoyed an exhilarating 400 feet of exposed rock climbing. And suddenly they arrived on the top. Jerstad and Bishop had reached the summit two and a half hours before. In the dusk they were grateful to find their steps leading downwards to the South-East Ridge. Below the South Summit they caught up with their friends and all four bivouacked at about 28,000 feet. Luckily the weather was still so they survived the night and reached the South Col in the morning. It was a magnificent effort.

With Everest traversed and the South-East and West Ridges now climbed, attention focused on the face between them. The South-West Face of Everest is a huge triangle of dark rock some 7000 feet high. Above the ice fields rising about 1500 feet from the Cwm, the Face is split into a maze of ribs and gullies until, at about 26,000 feet, it rears into a band of almost vertical cliff. Below the cliff is a sort of snowy ramp, from the centre of which a huge icy couloir falls straight to the Cwm. Above the Rock Band the Face leans back again, into the slabby rocks of the Yellow Band. At the level of the South Summit more broken rocks narrow to the top itself.

The first team to enter the lists in the quest of a route up the Face were the Japanese who, when Nepal was re-opened to climbers in 1969, sent out a strong reconnaissance. The technical problems up the flanks of the huge couloir were not extreme, but they had difficulty finding campsites; eventually they reached the base of the Rock Band. The next spring they were able to push no higher, so they transferred their efforts to the South Col, where they succeeded in placing four climbers on the summit. One of them was able to descend a little way onto the Face from near the South Summit. He reported that the climbing looked far from easy.

In 1971 it was the turn of Norman Dyhrenfurth and Jimmy Roberts, joint leaders of what appeared to be an extremely powerful international expedition, well conceived and planned. Its major objective was the 'Direttissima' on the South-West Face; but the expedition also planned to attempt a direct line up the West Ridge.

Originally conceived as a mammoth effort all the way from the 19,705 foot Lho La (reached from the Nepalese side by American climbers in 1963), the International Expedition planned to cut out the long traverse off the West Ridge made by the Americans and tackle the Ridge crest the whole way. It transpired that the Americans had preferred to call their '63 route the 'West Buttress', but strictly speaking they had entered Tibet at extreme altitude and so for political reasons the climb remained 'West Ridge'. This direct line is in itself a very worthy goal, but from the Lho La it proved an impossible ambition. For a start the climb would be nearly four miles long and the initial 4000 foot slopes of the west shoulder are tedious-looking and most unpleasant.

The story of the 1971 International Expedition and the controversy that it generated has been well aired. Suffice to say that due primarily to the worst weather for some 70 years and an associated abnormal incidence of sickness, the West Ridge attempt was aborted after the Ridge shoulder had been reached, while the Face attempt continued but without its planned physical and material support. Camps III, IV and V were established on the Face, the latter below the Rock Band above the Couloir. Despite Japanese claims, campsites were found. Camp IV was the only problem; it was occasionally struck by rock fall down the Couloir. Like Camp III it utilized alloy 'bedstead' frames specially developed to hold a tent on a steep slope and aban-

doned by the Japanese. The lead climbing fell almost entirely to the British pair, Don Whillans and Dougal Haston, and the two powerful Japanese, Naomi Uemura and Reizo Ito.

The direct line up the Rock Band looked extremely intimidating. Any ideas of breaking out left high onto the West Ridge by a series of steep icy chimneys were dismissed when seen close-up. Holed-up at Advanced Base in the Western Cwm during a ten-day storm, Don Whillans, John Evans (the American team co-ordinator) and myself calculated that a minimum of a ton of equipment would need to be carried to Camp V to support two men to the summit via the Rock Band. This was plainly out of the question. When the storm finally subsided the four climbers pushed rightwards up the snowy ramps at the base of the Band. Here the height and angle of the wall lessened and they hoped to find a weakness leading through it. No longer were they on the 'direttissima', but searching instead for the easiest line up the Face. They placed a Camp VI at 27,200 feet on the far eastern edge of the Face, and Whillans looked round the corner to discover in front of him the true south flank, a small easy-angled facet separating the South-West Face from the South-East Ridge. The line across to the Ridge not far below the South Summit looked simple and Whillans

South-West Face, showing camps set up by the 1971 International Expedition. The Great Rock Band is clearly seen above Camp V, and the slabby rocks of the Yellow Band above it. The South Summit is on the skyline just above and to the right of the Yellow Band

reckoned it would not even require a rope. Should Whillans and Haston make for the Summit by the easiest way? Or should they stick to the Face they had come to climb – even though success on it now seemed doubtful? It was a dilemma. Echoing Unsoeld's sentiments, they discovered an icy gully in the Rock Band above Camp VI and started to fix ropes up it. They climbed 300 feet and realized they could go no further. The top was still 1470 feet above them with the rest of the Rock Band and the nasty slabs of the Yellow Band. Below them the Expedition had run out of man-power and supplies. They started down.

In 1972 a 'European' Expedition arrived to attempt the Face. It was composed mainly of Germans and Austrians, but included Whillans and two other Britons, Hamish MacInnes and Doug Scott, led by Dr. Karl Herrligkoffer, the well-known German expedition impresario. Despite perfect weather, Camp VI was the highest point reached, and the Expedition dissolved into petty squabbling and personal rivalries. That autumn, when an Italian expedition surrendered its permission for the mountain, Chris Bonington stepped into the breach and led a hastily organized but extremely powerful small British expedition to the Face. It aroused much controversy, for Whillans who knew the Face better than anyone was not invited and many Himalayan experts felt it would have been enough to have attempted the *voie normale* in the bitter cold of the post-monsoon season. The climbers did well to reach Camp VI, which was occupied by Haston and Mac-Innes. But the extreme cold and terrible winds precluded further progress, and it was left to the Japanese the following autumn of 1973, when they too had reached their limit at Camp VI on the Face, to make the first post-monsoon ascent of Everest by the South Col.

Many climbers consider the route being attempted on the South-West Face to be a poor line. Aesthetically there is no doubt that the only good line on the Face must take the Rock Band direct at its highest point at the head of the Couloir. The 'Direttissima' in fact. While an ascent by the route already attempted would be a fine achievement, the fact that escape can be made easily to the right must make it almost an alternative start to the South-East Ridge. A jaundiced view perhaps but not without some accuracy!

And so Everest remains the goal of almost every nation which can field a team in the Himalaya. While eyes are still on the South-West Face, mountaineers are talking avidly about a return to the North Ridge – Chairman Mao permitting. There are even ideas of an attempt on the huge East Face above the Kangchung Glacier. Although probably dangerous and rather dull, it rises 10,000 feet in a little over two miles and its average angle is only just under 45 degrees. Depending on the Chinese of course, there is no doubt it will be attempted sooner or later. The highest mountain in the world will always hold its attraction for somebody, if only, in the now hackneyed words of George Mallory, 'because it is there'.

Loaded climbers and sherpa cross the dangerous couloir below the Nuptse Face on the long slog up the Western Cwm

Agony in the Western Cwm

Don Whillans, John Evans and I lay on a pile of sleeping bags and down gear. There was a faint hiss of snow on the taut orange nylon of the tent, and sometimes the rattle of wind. Don sucked at his cigar. 'Aye', he said. 'So that'll be four oxygen bottles at top-minus-one, right?' 'Okay', said John, scribbling hard. 'Makes sense. Now what about the ropes?'

It was Thursday 22 April, at Camp II in the Western Cwm of Mount Everest – height, about 21,000 feet. It had been snowing for nearly five days, denying us the opportunity to appreciate the incredible, yet claustrophobic, scenery of the highest mountain valley in the world, and the huge mountain sides which surround it. Whenever the snow clouds blew aside, there was the 8000-foot South West Face of Everest looming vast and white over us. This was what we had come to climb.

I have the highest regard for Don Whillans. His doings on British rock are legendary and his alpine achievements – on the Dru, the Blaitière, and the Frêney Pillar, his epic on the Bonatti Pillar, and his run of bad luck, culminating in Nally's rescue, on the Eiger – have marked him out as a very special alpinist; not just a 'doer' but a survivor. In the greater ranges Don has added to that reputation. He has not always been lucky, but in Patagonia and the Andes, on Masherbrum, Trivor, Gauri Sankar and Annapurna he has demonstrated his sound judgement and extremely powerful climbing ability. One day Don and I were talking of that crucial period on any high expedition when the chips are down and the decision has to be made whether to push for the top. 'It's softly, softly catchee monkey', Don said. 'No point in going for top till everything's right. Yer won't get Grandpa Whillans going oop a mountain he can't coom down agin. Yer get medals that way but yer die yoong'. Sometimes Don can be right mean, but he's good company and one of the very best mountaineers in the world. Life at Camp II would have been more difficult without him.

Looking back in my diary, I find the bare story of those traumatic days at Camp II: days that were among the most miserable in my life, yet when the warmth of friendship somehow beat the cold, the damp frustration and the bitter sorrow.

Wednesday, 14 April 'Camp I – about 19,500 feet. Up early to pack gear for carrying to Camp II – the dawn light is weird and a peculiar spectrum hangs in the clouds blowing down the Cwm. Pin still feels sick and is to stay behind as one of the doctors is coming up today. Leave about 9.30, carrying a movie camera and heavy pack. Going like a steam engine at first so must be quite fit, and soon catch up Norman, Duane and Toni, but then a long purgatory begins in new snow often calf-deep. Not very funny with two-and-a-half miles and 1500 feet to go! As we cross the couloir below the Nuptse Face, the sun disappears. The wind rises and soon spume is howling down the Cwm and we have to move into its very teeth. The track up the last slope to Camp II has been obliterated and the going is real hell.

227

Despite my triple boots and thick gloves my feet and hands are completely numb. John Evans comes charging down to help us up the final few hundred yards into camp. He's a great fellow! It's about 2.30 and I'm absolutely whacked: the wind finished me. I move in to share John's tent – it's flapping like hell and wants to take off – but I soon thaw out with a brew and some nosh. When the Sherpas dish out the meal at about 6.0, the evening is clear and very, very cold. In the dusk the Cwm is hauntingly beautiful and, despite the stillness down here, snow plumes are blowing vertically upwards from the ice-fields above us. Up on the Face I can just make out the tiny red dot of Camp III, which Don and Dougal established yesterday. It's very encouraging, and I sleep like a log.'

15 April Camp II – about 21,000 feet. 'A still warm morning and we breakfast in the sun. I have been worrying about my feet after the cold yesterday, but so far they seem okay. On the morning radio call from Camp III, Dougal complains they have no fuel left and the breakfast was miserable – he and Don will be working up towards IV today. I need to recce III and the route up to it for filming, so I volunteer to carry up a re-supply for them. Three Sherpas are going up too, with ropes and another tent, and they leave before me: everyone else is going down to Camp I for a mass carry-up. It's an appalling slog to the bergschrund in deep new snow; it's about a mile, and not steep, but it takes two hours. Crossing the 'schrund is entertaining – it's almost climbing! But the slope above is a big monotonous ice-field, about 45 degrees and unbroken, with snow on top of ice. Jumaring the 1200 feet or so of fixed ropes takes two hours; as I reach Camp III the Sherpas start their descent. It's been quite an effort and there's a dull ache in my shoulders.'

'It's an impressive and airy situation: an overhanging buttress rises straight out of the ice-slope – all twisted yellow and grey strata – and the one Whillans Box is pitched right beneath it on one of the tubular alloy platforms the Japanese abandoned last year: cantilevered out

228

into space. Saves the effort of cutting a platform! The buttress gives good protection from the falling rock and ice that plagued the Japanese. There's a lot of their colourful old fixed ropes in the ice here. Having unloaded the supplies into the tent I watch several goraks gliding round the camp. What the hell can they find to eat up here? The view down is incredible – cloud is boiling up the Ice-Fall, choking the mouth of the Cwm, while remote above it all rides the summit cone of Pumori. I'm excited and happy, it's a privilege to be in this remarkable place. Doze for an hour. Before starting down I heap some more snow onto the Box roof to melt in the sun for when the lads return. A few hundred feet down I hear a shout as Don and Dougal arrive back at the camp. We exchange greetings. Duane comes out from II to greet me with a cup of tea – I'm quite tired now . . . great lads these Americans! On the evening radio call Don reports that they have pushed another thousand feet up the couloir beyond III.'

16 April My diary records little of interest: 'A warm morning; I did maintenance on the film cameras, lying on my sleeping bag stripped naked – the first time for many days. Very pleasant! It started to snow at lunchtime; in the afternoon Don and Dougal came down for a rest: Dougal planned to go on to Base next day, but Don preferred to stay up high. It was clear again at dusk, with a fine alpenglow on Lhotse and Everest.'

17 April 'Sunny morning and I accompany Leo who is going up to Camp III to fix the winch: I plan to film the operation. Good time to the 'schrund – one-and-a-half hours – but already the wind is high and spume is pouring down the Face. I manage to shoot 200 feet around the 'schrund, but conditions are rapidly worsening. The cold is intense and the air soon full of blowing spindrift: cameras and faces ice up rapidly and soon both filming and climbing are impossible. We retreat to Camp II, very frustrated, but the mail has arrived and I have two letters. The mess tent has been blown down during the day and the evening meal is cold. Harsh and Wolfgang report by radio that they have established Camp III West en route to the West Ridge.'

Sunday, 18 April 'Snowing gently at breakfast. Harsh and Wolfgang report on the radio that they plan to re-site Camp III West, some 500 feet higher, before they come down today. Norman suggests they descend at once, but these lads are keen! We film a complex sequence with Naomi and Ito setting out for Camp III, but the wind is rising and the job becomes a frigid epic. Attempting to film at midday, a tripod is blown over and one of the Eclairs badly damaged. Wolfgang staggers in alone about 4.30. It's an emergency. Apparently Harsh is stuck on a fixed rope across an ice-wall not very far up. Visibility is nil, it's blowing a storm; but we can hear him shouting above the wind.'

'A rescue team is hurriedly organized and sets off into the driving snow – Odd, Michel, Carlo, Pierre and Peter. Pin and I follow with camera and sound gear, accompanied by Don, who has grabbed every ski-pole he can find to leave as markers as we cross the glacier. "It'll be bloody dark when we get back", he says. On the first steep ground my crampon strap breaks. It's very difficult to fix again. The storm is terrible and the light is failing fast. By the start of the fixed ropes, it is too dark to film at all. There is no point in hanging around getting frost-bite, so we fight down in the darkness, blessing Don for those ski-poles. John Evans comes out across the glacier with a torch to guide us in. Hands and feet are completely numb; in the mess tent, our boots are removed and our feet massaged and we're pumped hot tea. Then Odd crawls in, he is weeping. Harsh is dead! Peter crawls in – in tears – followed by the other boys on the rescue . . . all are completely broken. Only Don seems under control. There is nothing we can do now. Tea, whisky and sobbing exhausted men.'

19 April 'It is still snowing. In the mess tent, Norman holds an enquiry into Harsh's death. Apparently Don did some fine unroped climbing, trying to get Harsh off the steep ice, but it was no use and he was already unconscious. Don had to make the terrible decision to leave him – still alive – and save the rescue team itself from a probably fatal bivouac in the blizzard. Peter confirms that Harsh had no hope. Some of the "Latins" tried to blame Wolfgang, but as far as I can see, like most mountaineering accidents, it was the culmination of a long series of unlucky incidents. Pierre suggests the expedition abandons all its objectives and attempts to climb the mountain via the South Col. This sounds a bit hysterical to me and results in a long, sensible harangue by Don. Naturally everybody is extremely depressed. It seems that we have food left for only one more day.'

20 April 'It is still snowing hard. Naomi and Ito come down from Camp III. Their descent down the fixed ropes was unpleasant. They are very upset to hear about Harsh. A team attempts to break out down to Camp I to bring up more food and fuel – action is good for morale – but they return empty handed. Big powder avalanches are pouring off Nuptse all the afternoon. I am sleeping badly.'

21 April 'Still snowing and the Sherpas predict the early advent of the monsoon! All India Radio claims we are to have two more days bad weather and then two days slowly clearing: the blitz spirit is evident – "it might be worse". Don is full of droll humour. He is a pillar for us all. Gary and Michel, with four Sherpas, leave in an attempt to link up with a supply party from Camp I while Don, John and I spend most of the morning planning the Face logistics. In the late afternoon Gary, Michel and team arrive back in driving snow. They met the Camp I boys and have returned with some food – a really brave effort, and we film them ploughing home through crutch-deep drifts. Morale is considerably higher tonight.'

22 April 'It snows hard all day. Don, John and I work again on the plans for the Face assault. Don has the bright idea of working backwards from the minimum requirements of two men on the summit, and we discover that we'll need at least 2000 lb of gear at the foot of the rockband – about 27,000 feet – to put two men on the summit via the

Working together in the Ice Fall, Harsh Bahuguna, the Indian climber (standing), and Wolfgang Axt, the Austrian, made a powerful team

Band. This won't be easy, it's a hell of a load to move that high! Meanwhile the West Ridge team is in debate. Some hysteria seems evident and by a narrow majority they decide to abandon their climb and opt for the South Col route. Seems a bad move to me and there is a lot of outspoken comment. Morale is better after a big sing-song in the mess tent after supper – everyone sings their own songs and the Sherpas manage a lot of laughing. It's good to feel all together again.'

23 April 'The morning is bright and we dig out the tents and dry damp sleeping bags and equipment; but by midday it's snowing again. As usual radio reception is bad, but we gather there has been a large collapse in the Ice Fall and Camp I is cut off too. Peter has issued me with sleeping pills but I still can't sleep.'

24 April 'An unhappy day. The weather lets up towards midday, and I go with seven of the lads and some Sherpas to film the retrieval of our friend Harsh's body. Several chaps are sick and Peter has kept them in bed. The sun at first is very hot, the job a sad one and the filming extremely strenuous. To make a usable sequence I have to film the cortège passing and then de-rig the camera and tripod and run ahead to repeat the process. There is a shortage of labour, so I've got to carry everything myself. Luckily our emotions are still pretty numb. But it's very upsetting even so. Snow starts falling again and the final struggle into Camp II is bitterly cold. Norman comes out to help me back with the equipment; I'm very tired indeed. The evening meal is virtually starvation rations and I sleep badly.'

Sunday, 25 April 'At last the weather seems better; it's brighter with swirling mists. There is work to do. Several of the West Ridge team start out towards the Lhotse Face to find a site for Camp III on their new South Col route, while Naomi and Ito set off up the Face to reach our Camp III. But the food and fuel situation is very grave and Norman, Don, John Evans, Bill and myself – the only fit ones left – set off down the Cwm in an attempt to link up with a supply party pushing up from Camp I. Six Sherpas haul Harsh's body wrapped in an orange flysheet in our tracks. The snow is always knee-deep, often thigh-deep and sometimes waist-deep. It's a very macabre procession. We are unloaded and moving downhill, but the going is terrible. At first the weather is fair, but it soon blows up cold and windy. In four-and-a-quarter hours we're only down near the snow bowl – not quite three-quarters of a mile – and there's no sign of the Camp I team. We leave Harsh, marking the place with flags, and struggle back to Camp II against a high wind. Thank God our tracks are still there. I cough very badly all the way and it takes three-and-a-half hours to get back to shelter. Duane comes down to meet us with a thermos of hot juice. Great news, All India Radio forecast three more days of snow! There is also no more food and our evening meal is lukewarm dehydrated mixed vegetables, cooked with our high altitude gas: a terrible waste, but the paraffin has run out and consequently there is virtually nothing to drink. Everyone has a raging thirst and is pretty depressed.

231

On the evening radio call Camp I say they pushed a team towards us but they were turned back by impossible drifts. Pin, Gary and Wolfgang are very sick and Peter thinks that Michel has phlebitis. I feel terrible and cough all night.'

Monday, 26 April 'An awful night – my throat's very painful. The morning's worse: no hot tea and no breakfast – in fact no drink at all. Peter comes to examine me. I'm coughing up disgusting phlegm and he says I have bronchial pneumonia and must go down at once: I'm torn between not wanting to retreat and relief at being ordered to go. At least the decision isn't mine to make, but can we go down? It's all hands to try and break out this morning. Things have been so unhappy here recently that everybody is keen to try. Let's face it, there's no alternative. Yesterday's tracks have still not been obliterated; a fantastic wind is blowing across the Cwm, the whole valley a gigantic tunnel of spindrift. The loose snow is being blown up the Face of Everest and back across the Cwm 5000 feet above us and down the Nuptse slopes; I've never seen anything so incredible. At least it leaves the snow shallower than yesterday. Sometimes it blows us over, but eventually we meet the team led by Dave Peterson and Dave Isles pushing up from Camp I with supplies: the meeting is rather hysterical, lots of embracing and backslapping. We feel as if we've been released

A party sets off down the Cwm to try to bring up supplies to beleaguered Camp II. In 4¼ hours we managed almost ¾ mile!

Top: Everest Base Camp, among the moraines of the Khumbu Glacier just below the Ice Fall at 17,500 feet – a real 'home from home'

Above: Camp II – about 21,000 feet – in the Western Cwm. Behind the camp is Lhotse (27,890 feet) and the Lhotse Face

from prison, a peculiar sensation. Don, Norman and one or two others who are still fit return with fresh supplies to Camp II. Good luck! Peter is sick himself and is shepherding Michel with his phlebitis; it could be serious. Most of the sick chaps stop in Camp I for the night, but it's so miserable there that Gary and Wolfgang and myself push all the way back down to Base which we reach at dusk. What relief to sit down in a chair with a hot drink and to sleep on a thick "foamy", knowing that the Ice Fall is above you and not below. The first time for many nights I sleep like a log.'

Although we didn't realize it at the time, the storm had dealt a death blow to the expedition. Don and several of the others who were still fit stayed up at II, dug themselves out and got on with the job of climbing the Face. The route was cleared and supplies started to flow once more into the Western Cwm – but things were never quite the same again. Meanwhile the Expedition voted to put all efforts into the Face climb and to cancel attempts on any other line. Our four 'Latins' disagreed with this decision and left the expedition in high dudgeon. This was unfortunate, but it left more food for those of us who remained. Base Camp was full of sick climbers, and even sick Sherpas. It is difficult for a man to spend ten days at 21,000 feet, virtually confined to his damp and tiny tent, on poor rations with little to drink, and still remain a finely tuned climbing machine. In my own case, three sudden bouts of unusually exhausting exercise, two in emergency situations, finished me off. Several climbers had to be sent down to the treeline to recuperate: a 'cure' is impossible in the wilderness of decaying ice and rotting rock at seventeen-and-a-half thousand feet, where our Base Camp was situated.

After nine days' rest I managed to shake off my bug and went back up the mountain again to carry on with the filming. But we had all been weakened by our ordeal and when, some days later, a visiting hippy brought a virus infection into Base Camp, it swept through the expedition like wildfire, knocking out all who came into contact with it. Finally it even reached Camp III, and Don, Dougal, Ito and Naomi, high above and reaching towards the summit from Camp VI, were left virtually unsupported. From this perch, '. . . like sparras in a gooter . . .', Don poked his head round the corner and found easy ground leading to the final slopes of the South Col route – the 'easy' way. But Don is honest, and in his typical forthright way he said, '. . . we'ed coom ter climb the Face, so we went back ter try again . . .'. But that is another story.

The crucial days for the 1971 International Himalayan Expedition were those nine days from 18 April. They were miserable days and they were thoughtful days: they were days when I learnt much about human nature and much about my friends. They were days which I wouldn't have missed for anything – days I shall remember always. Mountaineering is not always fun, but it can be a very rewarding experience.

233

7 Antipodean Alps

Australian climbing comes of age

Seen from space, Australia must appear as a vast, dull grey and red expanse, with only a green fringe on the east coast to break the monotony. A closer examination of this belt would reveal an almost continuous chain of mini-mountains. Mt Kosciusko, the continent's highest point, barely tops 7000 feet. Mostly wooded (the timber line extends to 4000 feet), the Great Dividing Range is the preserve of the 'bushwalker' rather than the mountaineer. Its mountains have been well described as being '. . . so old that time has rounded them to resemble sleeping dinosaurs, with here and there a skeleton showing ribs and vertebrae . . .' Australia has no permanent snowfields and few mountains you can't walk up, or drive up.

Australian mountaineering is confined to the small but growing band of rock-climbing devotees who live in the cities of the south-east. It is a lucky coincidence that the 'mountainous' south-east is also the centre of gravity of this flat continent's sparse population. Elsewhere vast distances, searing heat and inferior potential have combined against any significant mountaineering activity.

In a few cases the crags rise to over 1000 feet; but, alas, there are no 'El Capitans'. Australian rock-climbing is usually on crags only a few hundred feet high. Local climbers have devised their own open-ended grading system, which starts at 1 and currently extends to 22. Yosemite's Moby Dick Centre Route – American 5·9 – would here be 18; while Cenotaph Corner in Wales, rated XS or 5a/b, would here rate a 17. Both of them are European VI +.

Less than a decade ago the north-eastern State, Queensland, had only one significant climbing area and very few active climbers. The Glasshouse Mountains are a group of small but spectacular volcanic plugs rising above sugar cane plantations about fifty miles north of Brisbane, the State capital; for years they were the centre of attention for local climbers. However, in recent years a small outcrop has thrust Queensland climbing into the limelight. Frog Buttress is a crack climber's paradise and has been the scene of dramatic improvements in Australian jamming techniques (Queenslanders call it jambing!). Rick White, the local publicist, led the initial rush but is now accompanied by a hard nucleus of sun-bronzed 'boy wonders'. Other areas nearby have been discovered, the most significant being Mt Maroon where sustained free and aid routes have been established on its scorching walls.

A little to the south, in New South Wales, is Australia's other main group of volcanic plugs, the best mainland climbing area: the Warrumbungles. The peaks take a variety of spectacular shapes; names like Belougeries Spire and the Breadknife tell of their character. Deep brown trachyte faces sweep up for 1000 feet. The heat is oppressive and climbers generally dismiss summer visits as a bad joke. The climbing is mostly face work on small sound mechanical holds in exhilarating situations.

Immediately west of Sydney are the Blue Mountains. This great

Steep rock in Australia. The north side of Mt Buffalo — 750 feet of coarse granite — with the wooded mountains of the Main Divide of north-east Victoria in the distance

235

dissected plateau has hundreds of miles of cliffs and was the birthplace of Australian climbing. The rock is sandstone and varies greatly in quality, but gives some of the country's best-known climbs, such as the Janicepts and Gigantor.

Out to sea, five hundred miles north-east of Sydney, is idyllic Lord Howe Island. Only a few miles away a bird-infested spire of jagged, rotten rock has been thrust up over 1800 feet straight out of the sea. Ball's Pyramid is perhaps the greatest sea stack in the world. Merely effecting a landing is an epic shared with the sharks, but it was climbed in 1965 by a strong Sydney team after eight previous attempts. Since then other routes have been climbed, it has been traversed and even made the subject of a TV spectacular!

Victoria has three major climbing areas. In the west is what is arguably Australia's best single crag, Mt Arapiles. A two-mile long face of excellent rock rising 500 feet above the fields, this climber's haven has 400 routes, many of them classics. Close by, the Grampians are a range of mountains with scores of sandstone cliffs offering steep and spectacular climbs.

Mt Buffalo Plateau is Australia's major granite area and lies in north-east Victoria. The rock is very sound but coarse-grained and rounded. The climbing is excellent if somewhat arduous and abrasive. There are a number of separate faces in the area; the 750-foot north face of the Mt Buffalo Gorge is certainly the most spectacular.

In South Australia and Western Australia, climbing is still rather undeveloped; there are only a couple of very hot climbing areas. North of Adelaide are the remote and beautiful Flinders Ranges with their distinctive sandstone faces, while on the other side of the continent, Perth's climbers have partially developed several faces in the Stirling Ranges.

Travel posters tell mainlanders that Tasmania is the 'isle of mountains', and for once the ad-men are justified in using their catch-phrase. This tiny island State is composed of sculptured mountain peaks of more recent glacial background than their rounded mainland counterparts. Vicious terrain, almost impenetrable scrub, and the continent's worst weather are the guardians of many Tasmanian peaks. Locals have developed crags around Hobart and Launceston. Now they are turning to the sea coast with its spectacular stacks like the Totem Pole; but the major sea walls are still untouched. The big inland cliffs of Federation Peak, Frenchman's Cap and Mt Geryon have been largely the preserve of mainlanders. These peaks have climbs on them which include the biggest and most important in Australia. Probably more high quality, virgin rock exists in Tasmania than *all* the rock in the British Isles! Tasmanian rock is uniformly excellent, whether it be white quartzite or the rough, columnar dolerite.

Before the last war Australian rock climbing hardly existed. Post-war migration gradually swelled the climber's ranks but even in the mid-fifties the scene was still some thirty years behind that of Britain.

Above: Balls Pyramid, 1843 feet, a bird-infested spire of jagged and rotten rock rising straight from the sea. It is perhaps the greatest sea-stack in the world. The original route in 1965 was up the right-hand skyline, the South-West Ridge. The ridge facing the camera, the North-West, has recently been climbed

Above right: On the Camel's Hump, Victoria. Chris Baxter and Keith Lockwood in action on 'Witch' (Grade 17)

Right: Perhaps Australia's best single crag. Mt Arapiles in Victoria. Chris Baxter on the crux pitch of 'Judgment Day' — a hard, modern girdle traverse, graded Australian 18

Far right: Chris Dewhirst on the first ascent of 'Agrippa' (Australian Grade 16) in the Mt Buffalo Gorge

Not until the 1960's did more than a few score climbs exist on the whole continent.

In 1961 a Victorian team of mixed ability went to Tasmania with the audacious plan of climbing the impressive 2200-foot north-west face of beautiful, isolated Federation Peak. This fine mountain is almost the 'Lands End' of Australia, and one can look south from its summit over the vast ocean towards Antarctica. Contrary to even their own expectations they succeeded, but only at the price of a bivouac where the four of them stood one above the other in the crux chimney. In the morning the leader's trousers had to be removed so he would fit through the following tight chockstones! It can be argued that this was the first major achievement of Australian climbers: it was certainly years before its time.

In the early 1960's two Englishmen settled in Sydney. They were destined over two or three years to bring Australian rock-climbing right up to date. The older and more mature of the two, Bryden Allen, methodically set about producing climbs almost as hard as the hardest Welsh routes, many of which he had done before leaving the foggy isle. A decade later he is still pounding the Blue Mountains to submission

with 'pure' ascents of the hardest lines. (Paradoxically, however, it was Allen who perfected the Australian bolting system which was so abused in the Blue Mountains and elsewhere.) Allen is responsible for three of the most significant routes done in Australia. All of them were products of a short burst in the middle of the decade. In the Warrumbungles he climbed the impressive face of Crater Bluff with Ted Batty (in plimsolls) to produce what is still considered a sustained and serious climb – Leiben. Next, he was the driving force of the team which made the first ascent of Ball's Pyramid. Too many bolts and fixed ropes were used; but this climb, where it is difficult to tell rock from guano, ranks as a formidable achievement. Within months he was over a thousand miles to the south, in Tasmania. The intimidating 1200 foot south-east face of Frenchman's Cap, a massive quartzite peak, had been a much sought after prize and fell to Allen at his second attempt.

If Allen gave the local scene a shake-up, John Ewbank turned it upside-down. Youthful, competitive and, at times, bitter, he launched a full-scale attack on the hardest problems and most entrenched ideas. A stern critic of indiscriminate pegs and bolts he once described a climb as follows: 'An easy though spectacular climb, it has been raped countless times by boy scouts . . . and semi rock-climbers who were given drills and bolts instead of Enid Blyton books for Christmas.' He 'retired' a few years ago, barely out of his teens, leaving a hole which is unlikely to be filled for years to come. In the Blue Mountains he developed Mt Piddington with a series of crack problems which eight years later are still almost at the top limit of technical difficulty. Likewise with his crumbling aid routes on the oppressive Dogface he created climb after climb of a difficulty rarely encountered elsewhere, even today. In the Warrumbungles he pioneered a series of routes, all still unrepeated, on the 1000 foot face of Bluff Mountain. (Recently two other Sydney climbers added another route to this face in temperatures around 110°F.)

On a rare visit to Tasmania, Ewbank added two more major routes on Frenchman's Cap's south-east face and rurped and knifed his way up the Totem Pole, a unique and sensational sea-stack shaped like a matchstick and 200 feet high. At about this time Tasmanian climbers, spear-headed by the redoubtable Reg Williams, launched an assault on an adjacent 400-foot stack, the Candlestick. Eschewing traditional techniques, they finally bagged it with the aid of hydrogen balloons, a rubber dinghy, half the ropes in Tasmania and a small army of lackies. (A high-powered rifle was even used, alas – without success, to shoot away a bush on the stack in which the ropes had snagged.) A rope was eventually floated from an offshore island, across the stack, and anchored on the mainland. Williams made the epic crossing first and left his trousers on the summit cairn as witness to the event!

As the 1960's became the 1970's, Mt Buffalo was flashed into national prominence when Chris Dewhirst and Chris Baxter produced the biggest aid climb that had been done in Australia with Ozymandias,

Tasmania is an isle of mountains. The big and impressive cliffs of Federation Peak in the interior of the island

238

on the north wall of the Mt Buffalo Gorge. This thousand-foot route was a very significant breakthrough and opened the floodgates on Australia's best granite area. Dewhirst and Baxter were well in the vanguard with firsts of some of the finest of the remaining lines, including Where Angels Fear to Tread, a beautiful buttress climb fast becoming a classic, and Lord Gumtree. This Melbourne-based pair, either singly or together, have established hundreds of climbs in Victoria and Tasmania.

At the time Buffalo was in the limelight, a Sydney team bagged the remaining arête on Ball's Pyramid. It included Ray Lassman and Keith Bell, who were to become two of the most successful climbers in the Blue Mountains. Bell has done many of the major routes in the Alps and recently made a mostly free ascent of the Nose of Yosemite's El Capitan.

The 1970's have seen the rise of Queenslanders to national prominence as a climbing force. A small but energetic band led by Rick White and Ted Cais has been producing hundreds of free and aid climbs as difficult as anything yet seen in Australia. Although many of these routes are short crack problems which they 'jamb' so efficiently, White, on a recent visit to Yosemite, acquitted himself well on El Capitan where he completed two of the major multi-day routes.

The 1970's have already seen the fall of two 'last problems'. The first route on Ayres Rock (apart from the trail) only qualifies as a 'last problem' because of the Rock's remoteness, its prominence in tourist literature and its diligent rangers. The east face of Frenchman's Cap is another matter. The solution of this horrific wall by Dewhirst with fellow Victorians, Dave Neilson and Ian Ross, is possibly the most important route yet done in Australia. Certainly it was a keenly sought problem and has very serious climbing of both free and aid pitches.

Besides the limestone North Wall of Bungonia Gorge near Canberra, and the last remaining line of Frenchman's Cap, the list of 'last great problems' includes the two faces of Ball's Pyramid. Only the steeper east face has so far been attempted. The climb, led by the enigmatic John Worrall who is rivalled only by Ewbank as a controversial character, was abandoned in the upper section after several falls and lucky escapes with loose rock.

Each State now has its cadre of resident hard climbers – and their ranks are swelled almost daily as competitive schoolboys push up the hardest leads in the land. Because climbing in Australia is so new there are virtually no middle-aged or elderly climbers and the scene is dominated by youth – hot-blooded and controversial. There has been bolting and de-bolting, piton climbing and clean climbing, and ego-tripping and 'environment appreciation'-tripping. There are guide books, magazines and television programmes. Australians have done the major routes of the Alps and have climbed El Cap. They have crack destruction controversies, parochial rivalries and massive grading arguments. Australian climbing has come of age!

New Zealand
Southern Switzerland

'They are of prodigious height, the mountains and some of the valleys being wholly covered with snow . . .'; so wrote the amazed Captain Cook when he first sighted the great peaks of New Zealand in 1770. So impressive are they in fact that as late as the 1860's Samuel Butler wrote of Mt Cook: '. . . though it is hazardous to say this of any mountain, I do not think that any human will reach its top . . .' and then added responsibly '. . . but I am forgetting myself in admiring a mountain which is of no use to sheep . . .'! In contrast to the barren, scorched and almost flat expanse of hot Australia, the two small islands of New Zealand which lie 1200 miles westward have been likened to a British Isles ennobled by an alpine mountain range.

Both the main islands, the North Island and the South Island, are mountainous. The mountains of the North Island are volcanic cones, some of which are still active in what is, geologically speaking, a relatively immature landscape. The island's highest peak is Ruapehu (9175 feet) but better known is the classically beautiful Mt Egmont (8260 feet). The gentle volcanic slopes of these mountains mean that little serious climbing is done in the North Island. But every year their toll of victims rises as more and more ill-equipped parties venture on to their icy slopes. It is skiing, rather than climbing, for which the North Island's mountains are famous.

The South Island has a major mountain chain running for much of its length. This is the Southern Alps, crowned by Mt Cook (12,349 feet) and Mt Tasman (11,475 feet). Great glaciers pour down east and west from the mountain flanks, nurtured by the high rainfall of the prevailing damp westerly winds of the Southern Ocean, the 'Roaring Forties'. So great is the ice mass that on the seaward side of the range the eight-mile long Franz Josef and Fox Glaciers cascade from 10,000 feet almost into the sea, their lower reaches actually surrounded by rain forest. The spectacular Mt Cook National Park is unquestionably the mountaineering hub of New Zealand. It contains the nineteen-mile long Tasman Glacier, the local equivalent of the Mer de Glace, and Mt Cook and her satellites provide innumerable impressive ice and mixed routes and are readily accessible by road and light aircraft. There are many mountain huts strategically placed for climbing on the major peaks, and the Hermitage Hotel below Mt Cook has seen the downfall of many a good alpine resolution!

One hundred miles to the south is the Haast Range, famous to mountaineers for its beautiful 'Matterhorn of the South', Mt Aspiring (9959 feet). This peak has two classic ridge routes of only moderate difficulty and is much sought after by the near-novices who pour into the area every summer.

There must be few climbers who have not seen photos of Mitre Peak in New Zealand's Fjord-land. But this photogenic rock peak above Milford Sound is but a signpost to the plums of New Zealand's 'Bregaglia' in the Darran Mountains just beyond. Mt Tutoko (9042 feet) is the major peak of the area but is surrounded by scores of scarcely

Opposite above: Mt Cook (12,349 feet), the highest point in the Southern Alps

Opposite below: There is ice as well as rock in the Darran Mountains. High (on the right) and Low peaks of Madeline (8380 feet)

lesser peaks with hundreds of still virgin faces of sound, clean granite. Close to the west coast, however, the Darrans are notorious for their torrential rains, their intricate approaches through dense forest with wild rivers and the high-angle snowgrass scrambles which guard the major problems of the faces. As the rock climbing centre of New Zealand, the Darrans are enjoying a dramatic new popularity: local climbers are finally realizing the potential of this area and for the first time show confidence and proficiency on rock.

Perhaps because of the unfair reputation of New Zealand's mountain weather, with its ferocious storms, and the comparative size of its mountains, coupled with the often long and difficult weekend approach marches through dense forest, New Zealand climbers have earned a reputation elsewhere of toughness. They are said to possess great load-carrying ability and to be deft at handling long and heavy ice-axes. This reputation is justified perhaps when one remembers hard New Zealand explorer-mountaineers of the calibre of Ed Hillary and George Lowe; the record of the last ninety years goes far to support this reputation.

The history of New Zealand mountaineering is traditionally dated from the Rev. W. S. Green's near success in his attempt to be the first man to climb Mt Cook in 1882; he turned back when only twenty minutes from the summit. The attempt stirred considerable local and foreign interest and in 1894 Edward Fitzgerald and Matthias Zurbriggen arrived from Europe intent on the first ascent of Mt Cook. They had to settle for Mt Tasman when they were narrowly beaten by three young locals, G. Graham, J. Clark and T. Fyle. To this day New Zealand alpinism has felt the distinct influence of foreign climbers, particularly Europeans.

With the twentieth century came organized guiding, dominated by J. Clark and the Graham brothers, Alec and Peter. This latter pair climbed many significant new routes and traverses until the 1920's, Peter proud that he never used crampons but with a legendary ability at step-cutting with his huge ice-axe. Amateurs like H. E. L. Porter followed; Porter climbed virtually every peak over 10,000 feet. However, between them the three Mt Cook guides managed to steal the plums in even the distant ranges: Clark and Alec Graham climbed Mt Aspiring with Major Head in 1909. Ten years later Peter Graham climbed Mt Tukoto with Samuel Turner, after a series of fruitless attempts over 20 years.

Not surprisingly the Second World War saw a lull in alpine activity. When it was over, New Zealand's climbing, like that of Australia, was a third of a century behind Europe; New Zealand climbers were still preoccupied with summits and ridges. But when, in 1953, a New Zealander found himself on the summit of Mt Everest, there were repercussions at home. Old prejudices were pushed aside and New Zealand climbers enjoyed a new found confidence, influenced in no small measure by the influx of 'modern' equipment. But in the past writers have tended to exaggerate the advances of the post-Everest era. It certainly wasn't a revolution; New Zealand climbers were really only struggling out of the Dark Ages. Their achievements were still decades behind those of their European contemporaries. This is underlined when one considers that the major north faces of the European Alps had been climbed in the 1930's and that the Cornuau/Davaille Direct route on the North Face of Les Droites, long considered the greatest ice route in the Alps, was a product of the mid-1950s. Until the end of the 1960's New Zealand alpinism continued to be plagued by relatively primitive ideas and techniques, coupled with a stultifying awe of mountain problems. This was accentuated by its acute isolation from the mainstream of world mountaineering. Climbs like the steep East Face Direct of Mt Cook stand out as minor exceptions in an otherwise unexceptional period when 'snow plods' and rock scrambles enjoyed reputations far in excess of their worth.

New Zealand climbing has always borne the stamp of the leading foreign exponents. The fifties and sixties were no exception. Scotsmen John Cunningham and Hamish MacInnes both paid visits. The latter, in particular, left a small legacy of new climbs; but otherwise they broke little new ground. Over a decade later a visit by Chouinard at the peak of his ice climbing 'revolution' paradoxically bore even fewer results. It was left to an almost continuous trickle of Continental guides to make the major contribution. Even so, their results bore little resemblance to the classics most of them had repeated in Europe. Foreigners, it seems, couldn't adapt to the idea of the relatively tedious approaches, low technical difficulty and high objective danger. Having to shade your ice pegs to stop them melting out was going too far! It was up to the locals, then, to forge their own 'revolution'. It came at the end of the 1960's.

The spectacular acceleration in local climbing prowess was due to a growth in confidence resulting from several factors of which two stand out as dominant. First, at the end of the 1960's New Zealanders proved themselves for the first time on outstanding *technical* routes in the European Alps and the Andes. Perhaps the most spectacular example is that of Murray Jones and Graeme Dingle. In 1969 they climbed the six great North Faces of the Alps. Their successes also included that classic rock climb, the Bonatti Pillar of the Dru. New Zealanders suddenly realized they were capable of some of the world's most revered alpine-style climbs. The second important factor in the spectacular development of New Zealand climbing was the availability at about the same time of Chouinard ice climbing equipment. Using this equipment, New Zealanders' concepts of what constituted 'hard ice' changed overnight.

The last two seasons of the 1960's, whilst not of great significance in themselves, gave hints as to what was to follow. George Harris and Murray Jones made the first ascent of the South Face of Douglas Peak, a maze of ice-plastered ribs and couloirs of which Colin Monteath wrote later in the Alpine Journal: 'This is one of the most serious ice climbs in the country and involves extended bouts of 70°–80° ice, with many hanging belays!' Jones was also active in the Darrans where he bagged important rock faces on Sabre and Marion Peaks. The sudden upsurge of interest in this area also produced several important traverses of major peaks.

The floodgates opened in the fantastic summer of 1970–71. For almost a decade New Zealand climbing had been overshadowed by the 7000-foot Caroline Face of Mt Cook. There had been several attempts and deaths. Whilst obviously its difficulties were not too technical, its extreme length and reputedly high level of objective danger gave it a status in New Zealand not unlike that of the Eiger Norwand in Europe in the 1930's. It was finally climbed in November 1970 by two 'unknowns', Peter Gough and John Glasgow. They bivouacked only once and reported technical difficulties only at the ice cliffs at half height. The state of these cliffs varies from year to year; one recent party found them to be 180 feet of vertical and overhanging ice requiring continuous artificial techniques and a hanging belay from screws! A couple of days later Dingle and Harris repeated the route. Very shortly 'everyman-and-his-dog' was wandering up the climb which has been compared to the Route Major on Mont Blanc.

This was just the forerunner to the greatest spate of difficult climbing yet seen in the Mt Cook area. George Harris and Keith Nannery (an Englishman) scored a significant success in their first ascent of the massive Whymper Face of Mt Elie de Beaumont. The same season Jones and Dingle bagged one of the most sought-after faces in the Mt Cook National Park, the South Face of Mt Hicks. A 2000-foot mixed route, this climb has been compared with a scaled-down Walker Spur. Jones also teamed up with John Stanton and Ross Gooder (later to be killed in the Dolomites), to pull off another 'last problem', the East Face Direct of Mt Sefton. Some mighty traverses were completed, notably when Max Doerflinger, a Swiss who had made the second ascent of the Japanese Direct route on the Eigerwand, joined with Tony Lewis for a fantastic seven-day traverse from Mt Turner, over Cook, Tasman, Douglas Peak and other summits to Glacier Peak. As well as being a season of major new routes, it was also one of numerous repeats in very fast times. And now for the first time, New Zealanders were turning seriously to solo and winter ascents, the former including a remarkable fifteen hour solo of the Caroline Face by Doerflinger and the latter a winter ascent of the South Face of Douglas by Bill Denz and Chris Timms.

The '71–'72 season continued the trend, although the weather was erratic. Its highlight was the ascent of the almost inaccessible Balfour face of Mt Tasman, an 1800-foot tangle of steep ice and dangerous seracs rising above a wide verglassed rock band. There had been two earlier attempts, resulting in epic retreats. This effort by Bill Denz and Brian Pooley was as much a technical breakthrough as the ascent

One of the most sought-after faces in the Mt Cook National Park, the South Face of Mt Hicks (10,443 feet) has been compared to a 2000-foot scaled-down Walker Spur. The original route on the Face, by Jones and Dingle, takes the obvious buttress on the left of the picture. There are at least four other lines and variations to the right

Right: A world of ice – on the Silberhorn Ridge

of the Caroline Face had been a psychological one. Doerflinger considered the route appeared harder than anything of its kind in Europe. It was one of the most coveted prizes in the Southern Alps!

At the other end of the scale, severe doubts as to the authenticity of a claim to the beautiful 1300-foot South Face of Mt Aspiring provoked much controversy. Might this be a first manifestation of the unpleasant results of competition and publicity that climbers have noticed elsewhere?

But it was a season of consolidation, and as the Editor of the *Canterbury Mountaineer* summed it up: 'The '71–'72 season marks the end of a phase – ascents of the Balfour Face of Tasman and the South Face of Elie have spelt the end of major virgin face climbing at Mt Cook National Park. . . . New Zealand is beginning then on a very advanced phase of climbing – one that enables comparisons, not just contrasts, to be drawn with Europe.'

The following season was a good one for Bill Denz. After two new solo routes on Mt Cook, one of them on the Caroline Face, and first ascents on both the North and South Faces of Mt Douglas, he completed what is probably the hardest climb in New Zealand. This is the central couloir on the 2000-foot South Face of Mt Hicks, a mixed route with hard ice climbing which he made with Pete Gough and another visiting Swiss climber, Étienne Kummer. They were caught in a storm; lost and broke their equipment, and survived a difficult bivouac. They finally reached the summit after one and a half days with only one complete set of gear! Denz had emerged as possibly the most formidable mountaineer in New Zealand.

Visiting Australians too were making their mark. Ian Ross had joined with Denz for one of his Douglas climbs, and the *enfants terribles* of Australian rock climbing, the Gledhill twins, put up a sustained 3000 foot rock route on the West Face of Unicorn Peak. But they were on the wrong mountain – they thought they were on Dilemma! And even in Britain Scottish climbers have been heard mumbling about New Zealand ice.

Progress in recent years has been rapid. Routes considered to be last great problems two years ago are now rapidly becoming trade routes; climbs like the Caroline Face and the South Face of Douglas get regular ascents. In the Mt Cook area at least, the time has come for filling in and minor variations, and New Zealanders are turning their eyes to the great potential of their own more distant ranges. In fact the importance of this geographically isolated island at the end of the world, served as it is by good modern communications, is now well established in world mountaineering. Its crop of great ice and mixed routes compares favourably with many elsewhere; a few of its climbers are emerging as potentially of world class. New Zealand is certainly a place worth watching.

New Guinea
Mysterious El Dorado

Hovering above Australia on the map like a giant bird is the island of New Guinea. The bird is feathered with the green of endless swamps and jungles, but its spine is a range of mountains running east-west for 1100 miles, almost the whole length of the island. To the east, in the lately Australian-administered territory of Papua, the peaks rise to over 15,000 feet; but the highest peaks lie westward in the Indonesian territory of West Irian, and the highest of these is the Carstenz Pyramid – just 16,500 feet.

New Guinea contains the third of the world's great equatorial ice-fields, for Carstenz is a mere 250 miles south of latitude 0°. The mountains were first sighted by Europeans in 1623 when the Dutch navigator Jan Carstenz remarked in his log at the presence of snow so near the equator; but he was branded as a liar and fool in Holland and it was to be centuries before explorers even approached the high peaks. The mysterious mountains are well guarded by thick jungles and all that live in them, by wide rivers, contorted foothills, heavy rains and swirling mists.

The first serious attempts to reach the mountains were made by Dr. A. F. Wollaston, later to be a member of the 1921 Everest Expedition. In 1911 he spent a year struggling towards the range but was defeated after catching just a glimpse of the mountains. In 1913 he returned and actually reached the ice at the base of formidable crags, just a mile from his goal; but he was able to penetrate no further.

Aerial reconnaissance proved to be the key to the approach. Aircraft discovered a breach through the great southern ramparts, and a Dutch expedition led by Dr. A. H. Colijn with air support eventually reached the glaciers in 1936. They discovered a ring of high peaks they called the Nassau Range, clustered round a huge ice-filled cirque. Under the impression that it was the highest point they climbed Ngga Poloe, a castellated snow peak of 16,400 feet; but they failed three times on Carstenz.

Reports filtered through of the 'miles of 10,000 foot cliffs' guarding Carstenz, and several expeditions tried to do what Colijn had failed to do, or to explore elsewhere in the hundreds of miles of virgin mountains. In 1959 a Dutch expedition, again with air support, climbed Juliana (15,420 feet) in the remote Oranje Range. But some expeditions never escaped the clammy confines of the jungle. It was work for pith-helmets rather than perlon.

Eventually, after a New Zealand team's failure in 1961, Heinrich Harrer (of Eigerwand fame) and Phillip Temple, a veteran of the previous year, succeeded in making the first ascent of Carstenz in '62 by a rather indirect route on its North Face, giving pitches of Grade IV. They also climbed all the major surrounding peaks and many minor ones. It is said that Harrer was badly hurt on the way out from the mountains and had to be carried many rough miles back to civilization, but there is reason to believe that this might be a rather garbled story.

The Japanese climbed in the area in '64, but Carstenz was not climbed again until Reinhold Messner visited the area in 1971 with an Italian client. In 1972 Dick Isherwood, Leo Murray and Jack Baines, all Britons working in Hong Kong, made the third ascent of the peak. Their Direct Route on the North Face of Carstenz gave three thousand feet of interesting climbing on good rock, the crux was two pitches of Grade V requiring pegs for aid, and there were many excellent pitches of Grades III and IV. After spending eleven hours on the ascent they completed the traverse by descending the East Ridge.

The miles of 10,000 foot cliffs do seem to exist, and photographs show impressive ice-capped limestone walls looking like a cross between the north faces of the Wetterhorn and the Civetta; but so far there is no evidence to raise rock climbers' hopes of another El Capitan. Isherwood's party reported that a copper mine had recently been opened in the Meren Valley close under the southern ramparts of Carstenz, with bulldozers, hot showers and other refinements of 'civilization'! One wonders at the future of its mystery; but so little is known of the mountaineering potential of the rest of New Guinea that it must still remain an El Dorado dream of the Australian 'hard-man'.

8 And the

This book would be incomplete without any reference to South America. The narrow spine of the Andes stretches for 5000 miles, from Pico Bolivar (16,410 feet), Venezuela's highest mountain, rising from the warm Caribbean waters of Lake Maracaibo, all the way south to storm-lashed Monte Darwin (8700 feet), the summit of Tierra del Fuego and a mere 2400 miles from the South Pole. The Andes embrace a very great variety of mountain form, style and climate. They contain the highest mountain in all the Americas (Aconcagua, 22,835 feet), the world's largest area of equatorial ice, and three areas of active volcanoes.

North of Capricorn, the Andes consist of several parallel chains, or Cordillera, and the capital cities of Bogota, Quito and La Paz are situated in high valleys between such Cordillera. Eastward, the mountains fall steeply into the huge equatorial rain forests of the Amazon Basin, while the western flanks ease gently towards the nearby Pacific; the climate of the Range is governed by its proximity to these vastly different environments.

While Venezuela, Colombia and Equador do contain interesting mountains, among them the 20,563-foot volcano, Chimborazo, which

Left: The western flank of the Cerro Torre group from Heilo Sur ice cap. Cerro Torre itself is on the far right, with the virgin Torre Egger and Cerro Stanhardt to its left

Below: '. . . splendid ice peaks, their ridges tortured with fantastic ice formations . . .' Milpocraju in the Peruvian Andes

Bottom: The South-West Face of Alpamayo (19,600 feet) in the Cordillera Blanca. Alpamayo has been called the most perfect mountain in the world

rest...

was thought to be the world's highest mountain until as recently as 1818 and was climbed by Whymper in 1880, the most important mountains are in Peru. Not only do they cradle the ruins of the great Inca civilization, but many people consider the Peruvian Andes the most beautiful mountains in the world. Typically they are splendid ice peaks, their ridges tortured with fantastic ice formations and their fluted faces rising above tangled glaciers. Because of their location – close to, but just south of, the Equator – a usual Peruvian problem is poor damp snow on northern flanks and hard ice on southern flanks. But, thanks to settled weather, easy access and short approaches, the Peruvian Cordilleras are popular among climbers from all over the world, particularly Americans and a growing band of local mountaineers. All summits of any size have been climbed, but there is considerable scope for new and difficult routes.

Peru's highest peak, Huascaran (22,205 feet) in the Cordillera Blanca, has two summits, the lower probably first climbed by Annie Peck and the Taugwalders in 1908 and the highest by a 1932 German expedition. Recent developments include several extremely difficult ice climbs on the faces of the mountain. Other 20,000-foot peaks in the Cordillera Blanca include Huandoy and Chacraraju (20,056 feet), climbed by Lionel Terray in 1956, a climb he considered the most difficult he had done on ice.

Elsewhere in Peru are the Cordillera Huayhuash, which contains Yerupaja (21,759 feet) and Jirishhanca – the 'Matterhorn of Peru', known to the Indians as the 'Icy Beak of the Humming Bird', and the Cordillera Vilcabamba, with Salcantay (19,951 feet) and Pumasillo – the Puma's Claw (19,915 feet). The Cordillera Occidental, however, is of little interest to climbers. It is an arid volcanic range rising to over 21,000 feet, on whose summits the Incas buried their dead! Mountaineering started early in Peru.

Bolivia too has several Cordillera, and the highest point, Illimani, probably 21,277 feet, and first climbed by Sir Martin Conway in 1898, rises from the largest chain, the Cordillera Real. Snow and ice conditions are similar to those of Peru, but the climate is dryer and the snowline higher. Possibly there are still a few virgin summits in Bolivia; there are certainly many new routes to be made.

The Andes form the two-and-a-half-thousand-mile eastern border of Chile. In the north, the arid mountains rise all of 22,000 feet, but their only interest is the Indian remains found on many summits. Mountaineering is popular in Chile, and in the Central region is well developed on peaks such as Cerro Plomo (17,815 feet) and Tupungato (21,490 feet) close to the cities of Valparaiso and Santiago. There is also excellent skiing, and the facilities are first class. Further south, modern technical rock routes have been made on lower mountains of about 15,000 feet.

In Argentina the mountaineering interest matches that of the Chilean areas over the frontier. Aconcagua (22,835 feet), the highest mountain outside Central Asia, dominates the Central Andes close to the alpine resort of Mendoza. This huge mountain was attempted by climbers of the calibre of Gussfeldt and FitzGerald and finally climbed solo by Mattias Zurbriggen, FitzGerald's guide, after several attempts early in 1898. The standard route, now regularly climbed, is of no technical difficulty and there are bivouac huts as high as 22,000 feet, but the terrain is rough and loose and the weather fierce and unpredictable. Because of past tragedies, the Argentinian authorities exercise strict control over would-be climbers. On the East Flank the 1934 Polish route involves serious mountaineering, though not of a particularly high standard, but *the* route of the mountain is the famous South Face. Its first ascent, by a powerful French team in 1954, was a milestone in Andean mountaineering and involved difficult mixed climbing on steep ice and poor rock. The 10,000-foot face was climbed alpine style, with eight bivouacs, but the six climbers were badly frostbitten. The route has been repeated on several occasions and in considerably shorter times. In 1974 it was soloed by Reinhold Messner.

Patagonia is the final thousand miles of the continent – a wild area of lakes, fjords and forests with dramatic rock spires rising along the

Chilean–Argentinian march. To the north, massive volcanoes rise to 11,000 feet, while 200 miles south, on latitude 47°, a large ice cap, the Hielo del Norte, sits astride the continent's spine (but not its watershed, for the mountains are cut by rivers flowing from the east). Patagonia's highest mountain, San Valentin (13,204 feet) rises from the ice cap which was first traversed by Eric Shipton's party in '63/'64. The surrounding peaks have tremendous potential, but access is difficult and the weather atrocious.

South again stretches a far greater area of continental ice cap. The Hielo del Sur is 250 miles long and was first traversed north to south in an epic journey of 52 days by Eric Shipton in '60/'61. Among the mountains ranged along its east flank are two extremely important groups, the FitzRoy Massif and, a hundred miles south, the Cordon del Paine. Both groups have attracted many expeditions in recent years because of their extreme technical challenges, their fantastic appearance and their relatively easy access from the east or south. But climbers must brave the terribly savage weather, which limits climbing to a few days in any season.

The massive rock tower of FitzRoy itself, 11,073 feet high, was first climbed in 1952 by Lionel Terray and Guido Magnone and has since been graced by several new routes of high standard. Close by, but suffering even worse weather, is Cerro Torre (10,280 feet), a slender verglas-plastered rock-needle – perhaps the ultimate in form for a rock peak. The Cerro has always aroused interest: a claimed first ascent from the north-east by Cesare Maestri and Toni Egger was considered controversial. Egger was killed during the storm-bound descent and Maestri could recall little detail of the climb. A subsequent attempt by a powerful British team from the south-east failed and Maestri claimed a second ascent via the British route, but using a bolt ladder which he placed using a compressor-driven drill. The following season Leo Dickinson's party climbed high on the route and discovered easy free pitches by-passed by closely placed bolts. There was a storm of protest! Finally in 1974 a classic ascent was made from the west by an Italian party. In the Paine area most of the plums among these fine, but lower, rock fangs have been picked by British and Italian parties.

Across the Magellan Straits, the last land of South America, Tierra del Fuego, contains mysterious ice-plastered and mist-shrouded mountains and glaciers flowing into the sea. It is an area of terrible westerly gales; but despite this, teams led by Carlo Mauri and Eric Shipton have climbed the highest peaks and started the exploration of the region.

But the climbing is not confined to the Andes. There are dramatic rock needles in the suburbs of Rio de Janeiro, while from the jungle fastness of the north-east, on the borders of Guyana, Venezuela and Brazil, rise a series of high and mysterious plateaux and towers guarded by huge vertical cliffs. The highest is Roraima (9219 feet) first climbed in 1889 by its jungly slopes, but in 1973 the scene of a dramatic and technically extreme climb by Joe Brown, Don Whillans, Mo Anthoine and Hamish MacInnes up its 1500-foot northern prow. In Southern Venezuela Walter Bonatti has attempted the 8461-foot Marahuaca.

The Antarctic continent, half as big again as Australia, is a high, cold desert, most of its land surface and the surrounding sea covered by a domed sheath of ice. So thick is the ice – at its maximum some 14,000 feet – that the mountains which rise above it are often smaller than their altitude might suggest; in coastal areas, they may display opposite flanks of disproportionate size. The Patagonian Andes reappear as the chain of rugged mountains that form Graham Land, the Antarctic Peninsula and the adjacent islands. Although Mount Andrew Jackson (11,316 feet) – the Peninsula's highest peak – has been climbed, mountaineering in Antarctica for its own sake has had to take a second place to scientific exploration. Consequently even though many easy summits have been reached for survey purposes, there is tremendous scope for difficult ascents amongst all the Antarctic ranges.

The largest mountain chain is the Horst Range, with its spectacular block mountains, which rise to 14,860 feet at Mount Kirkpatrick, and stretch some 2500 miles across the continent's narrow neck to flank the huge ice-covered gulfs of the Ross and Weddell Seas.

The highest mountains, however, are the isolated Sentinel Range, grouped between the base of the Antarctic Peninsula and the Filchner Ice Shelf at the head of the Weddell Sea. The Vinson Massif (16,860 feet), climbed by Nick Clinch's 1966 American expedition, is the continent's summit, and the same party also climbed several other more interesting peaks, including Mount Tyree (16,290 feet). The range is an impressive one, characterized by knife-edge ridges and huge snow-dusted rock faces, strangely reminiscent of the Swiss Mischabel Peaks, yet rising little more than 6000 feet above the surrounding ice plateau. But, without full-scale aerial support, the Sentinels – like most Antarctic mountains – are inaccessible, and it is unlikely that their prizes will attract mountaineers in the near future.

The mountains of the Arctic are, comparatively, of far easier access and also hold many prizes. Greenland and Baffinland are the most interesting areas outside Alaska – which, although not strictly a 'polar' region, but a full-fledged American State, has become a domestic happy hunting ground for American climbers. The State is dominated by huge Mount McKinley (20,320 feet) and the myriad handsome peaks of the Alaska Range, but there are other no less impressive ranges, including the St. Elias, Coast, Fairweather, Chugach, Wrangell and Brooks Ranges. Each season sees frenzied activity in these mountains, almost invariably requiring readily available air support, and so great is the potential that the ambitious American mountaineer need look no further than his own semi-arctic backyard!

Baffinland, where access during the short summer season is by air,

has provided rich takings for recent Swiss, British and North American climbers. The spectacular flat-topped rock towers of the Cumberland Peninsula, such as Mount Asgard (6598 feet), have yielded difficult rock climbs on excellent granite. The highest peak, Tête Blanche, is 7074 feet.

Edward Whymper, in 1867, was the first mountaineer to visit the most important of the Arctic's mountains – those of Greenland. Since the Second War these have become also the most frequented, and each season several expeditions are active among the tangled ranges that fringe the huge Greenland ice cap along the south-eastern and south-western coasts. Other pioneers in the thirties were Tom Longstaff and Gino Watkins, while the highest peak, Gunnbjorns Fjeld (12,139 feet) in the Watkins Range of the south-east was reached in 1935 by Lawrence Wager, the Everest climber. Usually the peaks rise above large glaciers which flow into long fjords, providing ready access by boat to the scattered coastal settlements. The mountains have yielded fine routes of alpine style and scale and, recently, difficult technical rock and ice climbs. More remote mountains further north have been visited by stronger expeditions. Typical perhaps was the 1969 British Joint Services Expedition to the Roosevelt Range of Pearyland, Greenland's northern tip which contains mountains up to 6300 feet. As might be expected, there is still much to be done in the world's largest island.

We have touched now on some mountains in each continent – all different, and in their own ways, unique. But in most instances we have not been able to travel very widely, notably in Europe and Asia. Europe, where it all started, has a wealth of mountains outside the Alps – the 11,000-foot chain of the Pyrénées for instance, the granite island of Corsica, the spiky granite crests of the Czech and Polish Tatra and the huge and spectacular walls of Norway. We have not touched on Ireland, and only barely on those important microcosms – Wales and Cumbria.

The Caucasus could just as well be in Europe as in Asia, for their highest summit, Elbruz (18,481 feet), is surrounded by a chain of superb and difficult rock and ice peaks very similar in appearance to those of the Mont Blanc Range. Further east the mountains stretch through the near-East into Central Asia, to the hub of the world's mountains, the great ranges of the Hindu Kush, the Pamir, the Karakorum and the Himalaya. They all embrace mountains higher than any elsewhere in the world, and the Karakorum contains the world's second highest – K2, at 28,250 feet.

From the roof of the world the ranges fan out: they run up via the Tyan Shan and Siberia to disappear three thousand miles later above the Sea of Okhotsk and the Bering Straits; they arc down into China, and they outcrop in Formosa, Korea and Japan. Even in these days of jet travel and extremely severe' climbing grades, there are more than enough mountains to last a dozen life-times.

Glossary

Abseil see **Rappell**

A Cheval Method of climbing a narrow ridge or arête with one leg either side – astride as on horse-back

Aid Climbing Artificial climbing: progress using gadgets such as pitons, expansion bolts, bat-hooks, or nuts for direct-aid on ground where free climbing is not possible. In theory, given the effort and rock of any quality, no climb is impossible using aid tactics

Aiguille French for 'needle': used in the Alps, particularly the Mont Blanc Range, and now elsewhere to describe a sharp-pointed mountain – usually a rock peak

Arête A narrow or knife-edged ridge or rock feature; may be vertical or horizontal

Belay An attachment, or point of attachment, to the rock or ice for security purposes

Bergschrund 'schrund or rimaye: the crevasse between an ice or névé slope and the glacier or further slope beneath, which is moving in a different direction or angle. Often a serious obstacle at the bottom of a rock-wall or ice slope

Bolt Expansion bolt: a nail-like fitting used as a piton but requiring a hole to be drilled in the rock in which it is inserted. There are various methods of expanding the end or locking the bolt into the hole. Used with discretion by a first-class climber to overcome a blank section of rock or to provide essential belays or protection, bolts can make possible routes where otherwise there would be none – but their use is considered by many to be unethical

Bong A large piton made of metal folded at an angle and originating in California

Bridging A climbing move where the body, usually the legs in a wide stride, acts as a bridge between holds which may only be usable by the opposition pressure of the 'bridge'

Cagoule A long hooded smock-like weather garment with no front opening

Chockstone A stone, boulder or pebble, jammed in a crack or chimney

Cornice An overhanging curl of snow or snow-ice usually along one side of a ridge crest or plateau edge and formed by wind action. May overhang for many feet

Couloir A gulley, usually a snow or ice gully, on a big mountain

Crampon A steel frame closely fitting the sole of the climbing boot with – nowadays – 10 downward-pointing spikes and 2 forward-pointing spikes (lobster points) about 2′ long. Used for ice climbing or moving over verglassed rock

Crux The most difficult or crucial move, pitch or section of a climb

Cwm A cirque or corrie: Welsh word describing a small hanging valley, holding – or once holding – a glacier. Sometimes the blind head of a valley

Descendeur A metal (usually alloy) friction device, used for rappelling – the best is shaped like a figure 8; much favoured by British climbers

Dièdre A dihedral: a vertical rock feature, two walls set at an angle like an open book, often with some form of crack up the angle

Exposure That psychological factor, to which height above the ground, distance from safety and steepness of the rock all contribute, which makes a given move on rock or ice more difficult than the same move would be at ground level

Free Climbing Climbing without artificial aids using only the natural holds on the rock for progress. On ice, using only the accepted techniques of crampons and ice axe or hammers, but not pitons, for progress

Friction Climbing On smooth rock, which is not too steep, progress may be made even if there are no holds by using only the friction of the boot soles, friction of the palms of the hands and cunning distribution of weight. At its greatest development in Yosemite Valley a highly skilled and 'hairy' technique

Girdle A traverse, particularly the horizontal traverse from side to side of a cliff

Glissade A technique of sliding down steep slopes of hardish snow on the boot-soles, a sort of 'poor man's skiing'

Grades There are several different grading systems used to describe the difficulty of a climb, and these are often confusing and conflicting. On big mountains the best system is the French 'Vallot' system, used also by the British. A big mountaineering route is given an adjectival overall grade such as 'Assez Difficile' (AD) through 'Difficile' (D), 'Très Difficile' (TD) to 'Extrêmement Difficile' (ED) which takes into account the length, seriousness and objective dangers of the climb. The hardest individual pitches are then given a numerical classification, I to VI, which describes their technical difficulty in normal conditions. Thus the Eigerwand is graded ED with several pitches of V, while the easy way, the West Flank, is graded 'Peu Difficile' (PD). Artificial (Aid) pitches are graded A1 to A4
The British use three domestic systems: the traditional adjectival one of Moderate (M), Difficult (D), Very Difficult (VD), Severe (S), Very Severe (VS) and Extremely Severe (ES) with subdivisions of 'Easy', 'Mild' and 'Hard', and a numerical system I to VI (with usually a, b and c subdivisions) reserved for outcrops, in which V approximates to VS (Very Severe) and to continental VI. Very confusing! The Aid grades are similar, A1 to A4. On Scottish ice a further numerical system is used which bears no relationship to any other system. For instance Grade I is an uncomplicated snow climb with no ice pitches but maybe cornice difficulties at the top, while Grade V, although no harder technically than Grade IV, covers a long sustained route of the greatest difficulty, a really serious undertaking requiring not only a powerful party but also favourable conditions
In the U.S.A. there are further systems, perhaps the best known being the Californian Decimal System. For an Englishman this is fairly complex, but once mastered is at least logical if often superfluous. Thus Class 3 is easy ground, 'scrambling' not requiring a rope, Class 4 might need a rope while Class 5 requires a rope and protection. Class 5 is subdivided into 5.1 to 5.10 and further, 5.8 being approximately British VS. If therefore one solos a pitch of a technical difficulty of 5.7, it reverts to 3rd Class! A further 'grade' of I–VI covers the length and seriousness of a climb; Grade I could be a single pitch 'problem' of 5.10 difficulty and Grade V an extremely hard route requiring two days. Grade VI is reserved for very serious multi-day climbs only. The Australians have a logical and sensible system using cardinal numbers – their hardest climbs are currently running at grade 21!

Grass Piton Extra long piton or stake which can be driven into grass tufts or earth to provide some sort of security

Hand-Jam A hold formed by jamming the hand or fist in a crack, often by just tensing the muscles. Usually feels reassuringly safe if used properly. Other parts of the body may also be jammed – finger, arm, foot etc

Hexentric A form of nut shaped like an eccentric hexagon, developed by Yvon Chouinard in the U.S.

Ice Screw A modern form of ice piton threaded for easy retrieval – may be corkscrew form or tubular

Inselberg A peculiar rock formation: an isolated rock spire or fang rising steeply from the surrounding flat country

Iron Ironmongery, hardware: American slang term describing pitons, karabiners and other metal gadgets used by climbers

Jug handle (Jug hold, jug): a perfect hand-hold

Jumar A Swiss metal clamp which, when clipped onto a rope, will slide up it but not downwards. Two are used for climbing a hanging rope

Karabiner 'Krab' – a snap-link with a spring-loaded gate usually made of light alloy and used for a wide variety of attachment purposes

Karabiner Brake Several karabiners linked in such a way as to provide considerable friction to a rope running through them and used, particularly in the U.S., as a rappel device

Kloof South African term: a gulley or steeply descending river gorge

Névé The upper snow or snow-ice slopes from which a glacier is born

Nut A small artificial chockstone, originally an engineer's nut, but nowadays a specially designed metal or plastic chock or wedge, which is cunningly inserted into a crack in such a way that it cannot be pulled out in the direction of any likely loading. Used now instead of pitons. The use of nuts for protection has revolutionized free climbing

P.A. Originally a highly specialized lightweight canvas and rubber climbing bootee with a smooth hard rubber sole designed by French guide and equipment manufacture, Pierre Allain. Nowadays used to describe any of the many similar 'magic boots' on the market

Peel A peel-off, a fall

Pendule A horizontal move made by swinging on the rope like a pendulum

Pin Piton, peg, nail. A steel blade, in various forms, shapes and sizes, which is hammered into a crack either for security or as an aid to progress. Nowadays considered unethical if nuts can be used instead

Pitch Section of a climb, usually of 60–150 feet, between ledges or belay points. A 'lead' – the distance a leader will climb before stopping to bring up his second man

Rappell Abseil. Roping-down, a means of descent by sliding down a rope under the control of the friction of the rope passing either round the body or through a friction device of some kind. See Descendeur, Karabiner Brake

Rimaye (Fr) a bergschrund

Rognon Literally a 'kidney' – a rock island in a glacier or ice-field

Roof A horizontal overhang

Running belay Protection: a point of attachment to the rock or ice, usually using a rock-spike, a nut or a piton, on which the climbing rope runs freely through a karabiner. There may be several 'runners' at convenient places between the bottom and top of a pitch

Serac An ice-cliff

Sky-hook A simple gadget shaped like a picture-rail hook and originating in California; used in aid climbing. Hooked onto a rock crystal or slight flaw in the rock surface it will support the weight of a climber

Sling A loop of rope or nylon tape: it has a multitude of uses, but particularly for running belays

Stack An isolated pinnacle, usually rising from the sea or foreshore

Stance A belay ledge on which a climber can adopt the best position to hold a fall by the leader above him or the second man below him – or the position itself

Swami Belt A length of nylon tape wound round and round the waist to which the climbing rope is knotted

Tension Using tension from the rope to remain in balance, particularly when moving in a horizontally trending direction

Terrordactyl A form of advanced ice-climbing tool; described in 'The Ice Revolution'

Three-point contact moving only one hand or foot at a time so that the climber is on three holds at any one moment

Traverse A series of side-ways moves – a horizontal section of climbing

Tyrolean Traverse A traverse made by climbing along a rope fixed at either end. Originally used in the Tyrol where an otherwise inaccessible pinnacle was lassooed from the summit of an adjacent pinnacle

Verglas Thin film of ice covering rock: it makes climbing difficult and dangerous and often necessitates rock-climbing in crampons

Zardsky Sack A lightweight bag or small pole-less tent used for bivouacs on small ledges or elsewhere during long and difficult climbs

Zawn An old Cornish word adopted by sea-cliff climbers, and describing a sea-filled gully or chimney, a common feature peculiar to sea cliffs

Further reading

Bell, J.H.B. *A Progress in Mountaineering*, Oliver & Boyd 1950

Benuzzi, Felice *No Picnic on Mt. Kenya*, William Kimber 1952

Blackshaw, Alan *Mountaineering*, Penguin 1965 (the definitive how-to-do-it book)

Bonington, Chris *I Chose to Climb*, Gollancz 1966

Bonington, Chris *The Next Horizon*, Camelot Press 1973

Brown, Joe *The Hard Years*, Gollancz 1967

Clark, Ronald *A Picture History of Mountaineering*, Hulton Press 1956

Clark and Pyatt *Mountaineering in Britain*, Phoenix House 1957

Cleare, John and Smythe, Tony *Rock Climbers in Action in Snowdonia*, Secker & Warburg 1966

Cleare, John and Collomb, Robin *Sea-Cliff Climbing in Britain*, Constable 1966

Diemberger, Kurt *Summits and Secrets*, George Allen & Unwin 1971

Gray, Dennis *Rope Boy*, Gollancz 1970

Haston, Dougal *In High Places*, Cassell 1972

Longstaff, Tom *This My Voyage*, John Murray 1950

Mason, Kenneth *Abode of Snow*, Rupert Hart-Davis 1955 (Definitive history of mountaineering in the Himalaya)

Noyce and McMorrin *World Atlas of Mountaineering*, Nelson 1969

Patey, Tom *One Man's Mountains*, Gollancz 1971

Rebuffat, Gaston *Starlight and Storm*, Kaye Ward 1956

Shipton, Eric *That Untravelled World*, Hodder & Stoughton 1969

Steele, Peter *Doctor on Everest*, Hodder & Stoughton 1972

Ward, Mike *The Mountaineer's Companion – An Anthology*, Eyre & Spottiswoode 1966

Whillans, Don *Portrait of a Mountaineer*, Heinemann 1971

The particularly important thing about the following books is their pictures.

Hagan, Toni *Nepal*, Kummerly & Fry 1961

Garris & Hasler *A Land Apart*, Reed 1972 (New Zealand Alps)

Hornbein, Tom *Everest – The West Ridge*, Sierra Club 1966

Kazami, Takehide *The Himalayas*, Oxford & IBH Publishing 1968

Maeder, Herbert *The Mountains of Switzerland*, George Allen & Unwin

Rebuffat, Gaston *Mont Blanc to Everest*, Thames & Hudson

Roch, Andre *On Rock and Ice*, Adam & Charles 1947

Roch, Andre *Belles Ascensions Alpines*, Editions Jean Marguerat

Schulthess, Emil *Antartica*, Collins 1961

Sella, Vittorio *The Splendid Hills*, Phoenix House 1948 (The first great mountain photographer)

Index